The Theatre of Jean-Louis Barrault

Also by
Jean-Louis Barrault

Reflections on the Theatre

The Theatre of Jean-Louis Barrault

by Jean-Louis Barrault

Translated by Joseph Chiari

with a preface by
Armand Salacrou

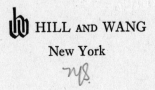

HILL AND WANG

New York

ng

First published 1959 by Flammarion, Paris
under the title *Nouvelles Réflexions sur le Théâtre*
English translation first published and © 1961 by
Barrie and Rockliff (Barrie Books Ltd)
2 Clement's Inn, London WC2

Library of Congress catalog card number 61–9965

Printed in Great Britain by
W. & J. Mackay & Co Ltd, Chatham

Contents

Contents

TRANSLATOR'S NOTE

Jean-Louis Barrault's style cannot be imitated or, as far as I can see, transposed without transformations which I deem unwarranted, for the final product would be far too different from the original, and certainly unworthy of the author. Whether on the boards or with a pen in his hand, Jean-Louis Barrault is always an actor who aims at communicating his experiences, enthusiasms and knowledge through his whole being. He does not lecture or talk to his audience, he offers them a performance, and much as I admire him and should love to don mask and buskin and step in the wake of the master, I'd fain look pedestrian and gauche and yet reach the end of this performance, rather than attempt what cannot be done and lie sprawled out in the middle of the stage during the five acts which the public has paid to see or to read about. That is why I have decided to give a literal translation of Barrault's experiences of the theatre and not an attempt to relive them in a style of my own.

Barrault is the actor-manager *par excellence*, a rare mixture of irrepressible enthusiasm and histrionic gifts, with mastery in choreography and business acumen. His Hamlet was a remarkable contribution to the numerous interpretations of this great part and some of his productions bear the hall-mark of an inventiveness and dynamism unsurpassed in our time. All in all, he can reasonably be described as one of the most vital forces of the contemporary theatre.

Preface

Jean-Louis Barrault had intended to write this preface himself, but he is short of time; he is fully engaged in preparing the inauguration of the first season of the Théâtre de France, he has therefore asked me to write this brief foreword in his place. In truth the texts you are going to read need neither commentary nor explanation. Jean-Louis Barrault thinks and expounds his thoughts with clarity. All I need to do is to make it clear that this book is made up of hitherto unpublished texts, and also of articles and lectures which have already been published.

The lecture on Shakespeare was first delivered in Edinburgh. 'How drama is born within us' is an unpublished text. 'The Rules of Acting', 'Concerning Gestures' and the pages on Claudel have already been published in the 'Cahier' of the Renaud-Barrault Company, but Barrault's farewell to Paul Claudel delivered at his graveside at Brangues has never been published.

Why does Jean-Louis Barrault publish this book at this moment of his life? Could it be that he wishes to cast a backward glance over the ground which he has covered, before a new move forward? One could perhaps hear the voice of a traveller who stands up after a rest and says: 'That's where I was, and now let's start on a new journey.'

By a strange coincidence I seem to have found myself on Jean-Louis Barrault's way at every one of his new moves in a new direction. First his departure from the school of Charles Dullin where he was a pupil full of questions; then his flight from the Atelier in order to continue his researches. He was then twenty-five years old, and it was at that moment that I asked him to play the leading rôle in my play *Un homme comme les autres*.[1] He hesitated, probably wondering whether his appearance in a show of which he was not in full control might not mislead his friends and cause a confusion in his plan of action which was clear and without ambiguities. Later on, Jean-Louis wrote: 'It was Armand Salacrou who compelled me to act in *Un homme comme les autres*. I had been

[1] A man like any other.

ix

away from the Atelier for a year, and I lacked simplicity; he helped me to understand that first and foremost I had to embrace a profession wholeheartedly and cease behaving like a semi-amateur.' If Jean-Louis accepted running the risk of obscuring the direction of his first steps in the theatre and also of confusing his friends by scoring a success as an actor, something which might lead him away from the direction he wished to follow, he did so out of friendship. Jean-Louis only lives for the theatre, and he is immersed in it to an extent which he himself is not aware of. After all we are not conscious of living surrounded by oxygen, yet we do. As the saying goes, he is in the theatre like a fish in water. He has found in it his love and his friendships, and one cannot understand him if one ignores the great importance that friendship plays in his make-up. To love friends and to be loved by them are for him two such important things that love and friendship are like twin islands bathed and surrounded by the warm and pure waters of his whole being.

After the wonderful productions of *Numantia, Hunger* and after *La Terre est Ronde*[1] which he was going to produce but which was produced by his master Dullin at the Atelier, Jean-Louis entered the Comédie Française. I still remember his enthusiasm at his discovery of the great French classical works which were given at the Comédie. There he worked with Charles Granval, and listening to this great man of the theatre, he listened to a voice which came from afar and carried with it echoes dating from the very foundation of this illustrious institution and which mingled with the perennial topicality of great plays. There, this 'young passionate of the theatre', who not only wished to be a writer but also dreamt already of total drama, fed upon traditions which helped him better to understand and better to present what he wished to present.

It is extremely difficult to know which memories to select when one talks about a friend whose life is intimately connected with one's own. What should one reveal or hide? Where does indiscretion begin? Yet there are anecdotes which would, I am sure, be revealing of the man and would help one to understand some of his works, some of his productions and some of his attachment to certain dramatic characters and climates. It is often said that Jean-Louis Barrault is served by an exceptional physique, but I don't think that that is true. He is served by an exceptional love of the

---

[1] The earth is round.

theatre, and it is this love which fills his soul which has given him the physique which he has and the kind of aura which he carries about him. I remember that one winter evening, during the black years of German occupation and of boiled turnips, I was dining with a friend who is now an Ambassador, in a small restaurant in Lyons. I was seated with my back to the door, and suddenly my friend, who was not in the habit of making such remarks, said: 'Turn round and look at this extraordinary character who has just walked in; he's the living image of Rimbaud.' I turned round and I recognized Jean-Louis standing there with his rucksack and actually looking for me. He had come from Paris, passed the demarcation line and, badly shaven and travel worn, he was making for Brangues where he was due to meet Paul Claudel the following day. The name of Rimbaud struck me; Jean-Louis was already possessed by the prospects of his impending meeting with Claudel from whom he wanted to obtain final permission to produce Le Soulier de Satin.[1] Besides that he needed to persuade him to make large cuts in his play so as to reduce its performance to five hours. Who could resist this young man who had managed to persuade Claudel and his fellow-actors of the Théâtre Français and to win the heart of the public! Nobody could resist such an extraordinary faith; and it is faith which matters. Sometimes a certain physique can produce the illusion of a certain soul, but in the case of Jean-Louis Barrault, it is the soul which gives the illusion of a certain physique.

In 1946, a new venture began, that of the Renaud-Barrault theatrical company based on the Théâtre Marigny. Jean-Louis has already narrated this story, which is not only that of a company but also that of a partnership or an association so unique that it is neither Jean-Louis nor Madeleine who in turn directs, decides, hesitates, refuses, takes risks or rejoices, but a composite being known as Renaud-Barrault, created by love and which resembles neither and is not a mixture or a compound of both, but a true entity which has its individual life and behaviour. Under the guidance of this couple, the company whose ten years of work and peregrinations are described in this volume, has produced fifty-four plays, ancient and modern, and embracing Aeschylus and Shakespeare as well as Claudel and Jean Vauthier.

[1] The satin slipper.

After the Liberation, the French Government had appointed me director of the Théâtre de l'Odéon. I immediately called Jean-Louis Barrault to my side. He wanted to turn this 'second' theatre into a theatre for students, workers and young writers. For reasons which it is not necessary to state here, I soon resigned my post. Now, fifteen years later, Jean-Louis Barrault, Madeleine Renaud and their company have come to this theatre and they bring with them a very varied experience and a repertory which they have shown on practically every stage of the world. What will they do, what will be the new face of the Théâtre de France at the Odéon? These are fascinating questions for anybody who loves great theatrical ventures.

Gozzi used to say: 'I don't know whether or not men have a soul, but I feel sure that theatres have one.' The history of the Odéon seems to show that through its vicissitudes and ups and downs, this theatre has a soul. Its first director, Poupart-Dorfeuille, stated in 1795 that his aims were: 'to make of this dramatic institution a centre for the growth of a new generation of artists pertaining to all levels of dramatic art, . . . to stimulate the genius of poets . . . in short to give a new life to all talents which could enhance dramatic art in France.' One of his successors wanted to make of the Odéon: 'the theatre of youth, of all new ventures and efforts for new initiatives.' Another wanted to make of it 'the house of youth'. Lireux, who was its director between 1842 and 1845, installed the proscenium, took away the drop-curtain and replaced it by another device. Théophile Gautier wrote: 'The Odéon is a necessary theatre: the young poets, the writers who have not yet made a reputation, all the elements which have vitality and a future in front of them, need a kind of progressive stage or gymnasium where they can attempt experiments which would frighten the cautious habits of the first theatre of France which is only used to dealing with already well established reputations. . . .'

I was going to continue but I have heard the three famous knocks . . . a new curtain is about to rise upon a silence pregnant with expectation, and the pages which you are about to read are an integral part of the theatre of our time. . . .

Ever renewed, eternal youth of the theatre!

ARMAND SALACROU

11 October 1959   of the 'Académie Goncourt'

How Drama is Born Within Us

Drama is as old as man; it is as closely linked to him as his double, for the theatrical game is inherent in the existence of any living being. Man has invented fire, together with Dionysian and Apollonian arts and that is what makes him different from the animal, but man and animals have one thing in common, they both love playing. Animals, like men, know how to play, and as soon as they begin to do so they display a kind of imagination which one would not credit them with. A dog does not know how to draw, a horse cannot sculpt, a cat does not show any sign of deep delight when the radio plays Bach, and a beaver will not think of adding decorations to the house which it builds, but when it comes to dancing, singing, or to mimicking fright or enjoyment, all the animals can do that.

Observe a dog playing with a ball or a cat playing with a piece of paper held by a thread, and see how it enjoys the merry-go-round of faked fears, feints, pseudo panics and wild excitements. Suddenly in the middle of all that, an abrupt stop! An imaginary enemy has been seen, and one has to crawl, hold one's breath, and approach it with precaution. This is a tense moment! The climax is near, the price of it may be life itself! Ready: the enemy is now within reach! One, two, three, and the dog makes a sudden pounce on the deadly enemy represented by the ball with which he was playing. He catches it, holds it prisoner, he bites but without killing it, he throws it in the air, barks with joy and performs a swift victory dance around it. Five minutes later, this very same dog will come to you pretending to be in agony because of an imaginary thorn in his paw, or adopt an attitude of perfect indifference if he sees you with a suitcase in your hand. To superimpose an imaginary reality upon actual reality is a tendency shared by all living beings—whether men or animals. What's the cause of it?

Does the reason for it lie in the desire to live imaginatively a story which could not be lived if this story were true? One has all kinds of courage in imaginary situations. It is pleasant to play with the notion of fear when there is no real cause for fear. This desire for 'acting' comes perhaps from the urge to get a full grasp of real life and its problems through an artificial re-creation of life, something which is really 'filtered' life, or life at one remove. This is something in which attitudes and behaviour are more clearly outlined and lucidity is not blinded by the urgency of decision. It is therefore a training ground for virtual actions which can be beneficial in cases of incapacity to act; it is a school of energy, a place where one recharges one's batteries.

All men are double, that is a well-known fact, and one would not be surprised to hear that men are multiple: 'there are many men in one man'. Yet if each of us is a compound of many personalities, the fact that another self seems to be always present in us, makes us say that we are double. Our double has its own individual life; it is he who at night lives our dreams. Life on the stage is a dream dreamt when one is awake. There has been in recent years a good deal of talk about the lie of the theatre. It is frequently said that the actor when acting deludes himself and lies, and the spectator does the same and lies when he believes what he sees. Diderot's famous paradox of the comedian or of the spectator is supposed to be the result of a connivance between two liars. That is very possible; but what of it? Dreams also are supposed to be lies but in fact nobody knows anything about it. Let us content ourselves with saying that the theatre, like life, is a dream, without caring too much about the question of lie.

The whole history of the theatre shows us that it has its source in imitation, which of course is not the lifeless copying of nature, but the re-creating of life through artificial means. The artist gives life to a kind of magic object which has more life than any ordinary object. A picture, a bust, a symphony, ought in fact to belong to the living world. 'Creation' is for the artist a kind of sexual action at the end of which he gives life to something. If life is a symphony of colours it is normal to invent the painter; if it is a dance of forms then a sculptor must be born; and if it is a pattern of sounds then it is clear that music exists as well as man. What appearances will life take in order to justify the invention of an 'imitator'? Painting, sculpture, architecture, music, poetry, are historically valid; can we also say that the art of the 'imitator' deserves a history? Our friend Fluchère in a fascinating study of Shakespeare and the Elizabethan theatre said two things which deeply impressed me: 'The theatre which interests us', he said, 'is the spoken theatre, the theatre which belongs to literature,' and he added: 'the theatre is above all an experimental art of language whose primary mission of entertaining and instructing rests on the success of the ceaseless verbal experiments and on the actor who endeavours to convey these experiments to the public.' From these two sentences, I retain two points:

1. The 'spoken' theatre, considered as 'an experimental art of language', deserves its history which will be a branch of the history of literature.
2. The author, bent upon his primary task of entertaining and instructing, will adopt as a means of expression, that is to say of creation or procreation—speech, that is to say language with which he will experiment ceaselessly.

These two points imply that the history of the theatre does not date from the origins of man. Man in his struggle for life began with dances, shouts, songs, incantations and warlike mimes meant to bring to him the strength of his ancestors and power over his enemies. These manifestations do not belong to art, which implies gratuitousness, but to the world of magic; they were part of a profound, mysterious and metaphysical reality which was at one with life. When men began to trace graffiti of animals on walls, it was in order to protect themselves from animals, to master them in order to eat them or to make use of them. It was therefore a form of magic. When men sculpted their first masks, they aimed at giving form to their inner face or to the traits of their assumed role; they were trying to bring to light the appearances of their most mysterious instincts. The primary aim of these attempts was not art but efficacy. Whatever art there was lay in the technical perfection of these magic acts; (the drawings made with powders, upon the earth, during voodoo ceremonies in Haiti have a kind of perfection which is due not to their beauty, but to their efficacy; yet it just happens that one serves the other).

Human behaviour is made of gestures, songs, dances, drawings, masks, sculptures, choices of perfumes, incantations accompanied with drum and bells, or simply of human bodies clashing one against the other in frenzies, of trances or possessions, which have nothing to do with literature but have everything to do with man. The origin of the theatre lies in the attempt to imitate and to re-create these forms of human behaviour. If we ask ourselves how the theatre is born in us and what it endeavours to re-create, I should be inclined to answer instinctively—a certain silence. Let us see what this means. When the arts reach our senses, they satisfy them one by one. For instance, we might be deaf and appreciate painting, we might be blind and appreciate music, and sometimes we even shut our eyes in order to hear better. Life, when re-created by the artist, reaches us in a kind of 'specialized' form, and only through one sense at a time. In normal life, on the contrary, we absorb the outside world simultaneously through all the senses and pores of our body; there is not a single nerve in us which does not record some kind of contact. While the outside world is thus impinging on us, we perceive at the same time all the various aspects of an internal life—memories from our past, the industrious agitation of our blood, the noise of saliva in our mouths, the crackings of our joints, the bellows of our breathing, etc. etc. . . . If we concentrate our attention on any one of these moments in the present when the outside world continuously impinges on our internal world, we soon perceive beyond that medley of noises and distant sights and sounds a kind of faint murmur which is caused by the slight and surreptitious breeze of the present-on-the-move upon silence. Claudel used to say that the stars make a noise, and he used to call the sky the celestial kettle. The present causes silence to vibrate. Time flows, the present moves on, life passes, silence trembles, and we do the same, we tremble with anguish at the continuous movement, flow and vibration, which is irrevocable and which terminates in death. Consciousness of the tragic rolling carpet condemned to end in the dark abyss, tightens up the throat, and sends the blood buzzing to our head; one has at once a feeling of claustrophobia and of being stifled under blankets, yet the machine has been set in motion and cannot be stopped. Silence, the present, and all the perceptions which reach us, plunge us into a panic; anxiety nearly chokes us, and there is only one way of getting out of this terrifying state, it is by breaking this silence and making the present inaudible, so we plunge into talk, noise, whirls of ideas and discussions of all kinds. We try to become conscious of life in order to do away with the consciousness of death. Action is not enough, we plunge into agitation, we think of the future, and of the past, but we no more mention the word present than we would mention the word rope in the house of a man who has been hanged. We prefer to live in a world drowned in noise than in the real world where a kind of silence unavoidably leads to Nothingness . . . or to God . . . two notions equally terrifying. To become conscious of the present is to become conscious of death, for the present is continuous death. The only real and concrete thing in life is the present, yet as if to torment us, the present is impossible to grasp and to hold. The present ever lies between something which is not yet, and something which has already been, and it changes ceaselessly. Nothing can hold this march towards death, and what is more, everything truly real in life takes place at that very moment which, so to speak, is nothing, and outside such a moment nothing is real. This is a terrifying enough statement and it is not surprising that we whistle with bravado in order to hide our fear. To re-create life, seen from this angle, is to go back to the source of the theatre.

Theatre is basically the art which takes place in the present and appeals simultaneously to all the senses, all the nerves, all the instincts, all at the same time. It is essentially the art of sensation, the art of the present, therefore of reality in all its aspects, from hell to heaven, as they would have said in the Middle Ages. It is also the art of putting to death, that is why there is a bull's head on our emblem. Recently Montherlant told me, 'I have understood at last the deep meaning of bull fights! They represent the history of man, the bull plays the part of man, and it is the very art of Life.' The actor receives life through the present, which is simultaneity and a 'kind of silence', from that he decomposes life and re-creates it. How does he decompose it? The present is the ephemeral spark of which we are the image; through its continuous births and deaths it is ceaseless movement of exchanges, rejections and absorptions according to an implacable pattern which cannot alter its rhythm. The actor who observes life is struck by whatever is movement and exchanges and by whatever transports itself into a rhythm. He is so close to real and complete life and to the life of sensations that he cannot use for his creations media so remote as abstract writing, two-dimensional painting or the massiveness of stone. Music is what is closest to him, but even music cannot convey the impression of physical reality which he obtains from the contact of the present.

If man could truly become an instrument worthy of art, he would be the ideal artificial means of re-creating the life of the present. That should be possible, for man has in his body the seat of movement (which is his spine, pliable as a whip), the centre of exchange (which is his respiratory apparatus and the continuous comings and goings of appetites and refusals) and the seat of rhythm (his heart which is also his magician). In order to translate the intoxicating sensation of man caught in the life of the universe, one has only to plunge man into space, the individual into the world, the one into the infinite and the being into the whole. That is why drama is essentially the conflict between the individual and the collective, between inner and external forces. Whenever the 'chosen' man or the ideal actor becomes conscious of the silent murmurs of his space-present, he will, as we suggested, first feel anguish, then, according to his temperament or his humour, he will either turn his anguish into metaphysical or divine drama attuned to esoteric liturgy, or in order to reassure himself he will take to whistling, telling stories or dancing 'in order to forget his fright'. Then his theatre adopts the free forms which one finds in farce, satyric drama and Bacchic ceremonies. Confronted with the type of life which strikes us as if it were an apparition, we adopt two lines of behaviour, both dictated by our emotions. We either transform it into something divine which we can face and which is tragedy, or we pretend to ignore it, and we can then indulge in all types of merriment, and that is comedy. In the first case we trust life, and in the second case we rather fly away from it. That is why tragedy is exalting while comedy is not so gay after all.

Honorius said: 'The priest is a tragic actor who re-enacts in front of his Christian audience in the theatre of the church, the struggles of Christ and the victory of Redemption.' This is all the more striking in that it was said in the twelfth century. Mass can be divided into three acts which are:

1. The proclamation of the Faith;
2. The tragedy of the order of the Mass;
3. Communion and joy.

The order of the Mass follows the pattern of a symphony: there is the first movement which is rapid, there is the anguish-laden and opaque andante and there is the joy of the third movement. Bearing in mind Menander's sayings in one of his comedies: 'Joy prevents me from knowing where I am', one could conclude that tragedy and comedy are the two faces of this very same thing which is precisely the 'kind of silence' which only appears in the present. Tragedy and comedy are the two opposite faces of terror or sterile anguish: 'Gods, free me from my sterile anguish,' says Aeschylus in the *Oresteia*. In fact, until Aeschylus, every poet ended his tragic trilogies with a satyric drama which dealt with the same subject. We therefore had the face and the obverse of the same medal. *Proteus* was a kind of farce which went with the *Oresteia*, and it described Menelaus's return with Helen, it was a burlesque song accompanying the funeral of a whole race. When, after Sophocles, poets began writing satyrical dramas which were unrelated to the tragic themes of their trilogies, comedy and tragedy ceased to be connected one with the other, and they were uprooted. The single cell which they formed originally was divided into two which assumed independent lives from then on. When they were one, they were connected by a religious attitude to life; their separation meant the end of a religious attitude. If art blossoms as soon as the profane is separated from the sacred, its decadence is not very far. This is true of all ages and of all countries. When the religious spirit disintegrates, art for art's sake appears and flourishes. A whole heritage, a golden age, is squandered and replaced by a slow period of decadence. 'We have kissed away kingdoms and provinces', says Shakespeare in *Antony and Cleopatra*. Like life the theatre evolves in cycles. A new religion born from a period of dark depression revives existence and gives rise to a new civilization. For a while, the theatre which had decayed during the period of decadence, is rejected and condemned to go through its 'purgatory'.

But the theatre does not die easily, and it leaves its prison for a clandestine existence: peripatetic comedians, minstrels and tumblers keep the flame alive in inns and pub courtyards. Once the new religion is well established it feels the need to re-create the theatre which finds its place again in liturgical ceremonies. It begins with a voice and a chorus, then 'imitation' progresses, the acting is perfected, and one day dialogue is invented. The theatrical ceremony moves away from the altar, passes into the nave, comes out in front of the church, and in no time it is again in the public square. The theatre becomes a social art; it is the acme of collective art; all the various corporations take part in it. The gods and the city enter the dance, and politics bring a new life to it. The priests are overtaken by events and satyrical farce and carnivals are an excellent means of letting out human exuberance. Tragedy becomes more and more refined and comedy more and more teeming with life. Meanwhile religion keeps growing and getting old, and people become more educated and tend towards emancipation. One day, comedy goes off to live its own life, leaving tragedy on its own. Civilization becomes more refined, and people tire of holy wars. Politics corrupt everything and sow confusion everywhere. The more taste develops, the more the revolt towards the collective and the social element increases. Then the theatre concentrates on domestic dramas. Psychology makes its appearance, drama loses its violence and becomes 'bourgeois'. The people try to react but unfortunately they, too, have lost their religious feelings, so drama decays. In the early religious phase, while drama was still connected with magic, the Dionysian element was called eroticism, and phallic art was part of religious life; they were in fact two aspects of the same physical rite.

Now that religion is no longer part of life, and the profane is independent of the sacred which has become an abstraction, eroticism becomes obscurity and corruption spreads like a disease. The day is not far off when a new religion will appear and the theatre will be again banned, excommunicated and condemned to take to clandestine living. Whether religion is called Christianity, Buddhism, or otherwise, the cycles and the fate of the theatre are the same and they belong to the phases of life. One might sum up by saying that the theatre is the first serum that man invented in order to protect himself against anxiety. In order to combat solitude, men come together and sometimes form the magnetic gathering called the public; they gather in order to live together dramas of life which have been rendered 'harmless' through imagination. In the course of the performance everyone is injected with the serum of the disease which is anguish. Art consists in transforming the disease into a serum, otherwise the injection communicates the disease. Naturalism is the disease which propagates itself by contagion. The poetic theatre is on the contrary the beneficent serum which brings health to man. The art of the theatre has therefore since the beginning been a means of defence and not a gratuitous or debased form of entertainment. Since man has existed the theatre has always been something of public utility. In order to preserve life, man sleeps, eats, procreates (so as to maintain the race alive) and plays. To play is to struggle against anguish and to invent happiness which suppresses it. In order to play, man has since the beginning, relied upon himself.

II

Our Company

ITS CREATION

Madeleine Renaud and I had pledged ourselves 'for life' to the Comédie Française. In 1946, this institution was provided with new decrees which were far from satisfying to all its members. Those who were not satisfied were given a fortnight during which they could leave. Madeleine Renaud and I decided to do so, and on 1 September 1946, the Comédie Française gave us our freedom. Six weeks later the Madeleine Renaud-Jean-Louis Barrault Company was formed and it started playing at the Théâtre Marigny under the management of Madame Simonne Volterra. Our dream —to have an independent company—had come true. Friends from the Comédie Française had followed us—André Brunot, Georges le Roy, Pierre Bertin, Catherine Fontenay, Desailly, Dacqmine; some friends like Marie-Hélène Dasté, Edmond Beauchamp and Outin joined us. Young actors and actresses who had faith in us formed the company. They were: Simone Valère, Jean-Pierre Granval, Jean Guillard, Jean-François Calvé, Jacques Galland, Pierre Sonnier. Léonard, who for seventeen years had been the right-hand man of the great Georges Pitoëff, joined us to become the administrative and technical director of our company. On 17 October 1946, we gave our first play which was *Hamlet*, and a week later we gave *Les Fausses Confidences*.[1] We had chosen to place ourselves under the protection of Shakespeare and Marivaux, and they did not fail us. Since then our ship has continuously kept afloat. What was our aim? To create a theatre and to run it prosperously in the same way as one creates and tries to run 'a model farm'—the elders supplying the grafts, the adults the bulk of the crops, the younger ones the seeds for new crops. A company can

[1] The false confessions.

only be good if it has three generations of actors and actresses, and
we all loved good acting, professional efficiency and the cult of
beauty. We wanted our theatre to be alive, and a theatre can only
be so if it is run on a repertory basis; that in turn can only be done
by producing new plays. In order to do that one has to be able to
present many plays at the same time, on a rotation basis. With the
exception of the attempts made in 1913 and 1920 by Jacques
Copeau at Le Vieux Colombier, no private company had ever been
able to keep the repertory system alive for long. A short subsidy
was the only way to carry it out. Nevertheless we have succeeded
in maintaining this scheme alive since 1946, and its advantages are
extremely important. The alternation rhythm maintains vitality.
The good actor who knows that he might play a great part one day,
and a small one the next day, consents to play any part, and does
well whatever he does. Playing many and very different parts at
short intervals enables the actors to widen their range and to
discipline their talent. They don't become bogged down and rusty
in routine work. Knowing all the aspects of an actor's possibilities
facilitates better casting, and good casting is half the battle of
production. The continuous change of plays requires a large group
of technicians; this of course increases running costs; but it is
beneficial to the profession. The stage-hands, the electricians, the
upholsterers, and all the tradesmen who participate in the collective work benefit from this alternation system, and perfect their
skill.

The regular production of new plays attracts a public which
follows our efforts, supports us steadily and saves us from being at
the mercy of those who are only attracted by successes. In order
to be daring, and to contribute to the life of the theatre, one
must have the right to make mistakes. The repertory system,
together with a public which follows closely the efforts of a
theatre, makes that possible and takes them in its stride. There are
quite a few plays which we could not possibly have dared to produce except as part of a repertory system. The alternation rhythm
makes it possible to serve the classics without neglecting the living
dramatists. The study of the classics enables us to go back to the
sources, to elaborate a style and to become conscious of the
density and the harmony which emanate from exceptional blends
of taste and genius. Strengthened by the sustenance derived from
the classics we can explore other aspects of dramatic art: in other

words we can indulge in experiments. Most of our new authors do not know the full resources of the stage and the possibilities of actors. We must note that the greater dramatists like Shakespeare and Molière were actors. We therefore try to help young authors with the creation of their work. We have also contributed some personal works such as adaptations from the novels which seem to us interesting—As I lay Dying by William Faulkner, in 1935; Numantia by Cervantes, in 1937, and Hunger by Knut Hamsun in 1939; but our essential task is to serve modern authors. If our personal aspirations and adaptations are guided by the absolute standards in which we believe, we try on the other hand to be most liberal and catholic in our approach to modern authors, and we produce whatever we choose, with humility. Finally, if the study of form and diction constantly attracts our efforts, we also devote a great deal of attention to the art of gesture and to the profoundly helpful and very poetic use of pantomime. The theatre, like life, is complex and varied. Every approach is good as long as it starts from an authentic sensation which, above the mind and the senses, is aimed at the heart which rises above flesh and spirit. That is why we feel truly rewarded when we become aware that our productions overflow the framework of the theatre and reach the human plane. Drama, like the other arts, is above all a means of exchange and communication with other men; it plunges its roots in the greater love of men, it is a kind of primitive communion, it is the art of human communion. That is why we took as a motto: 'About man, by man, for man!'

THIRTEEN YEARS LATER

Un bonheur tout uni nous devient ennuyeux; il faut du haut et du bas dans la vie, et les difficultés qui se mêlent aux choses réveillent les ardeurs, augmentent les plaisirs.[1]
—SCAPIN.

After we had started with Hamlet, Les Fausses Confidences and Baptiste, we planned to produce Les Nuits de la Colère [2] by our

---

[1] Unbroken happiness becomes boring; life must be made up of ups and downs, and the difficulties which we encounter stimulate our enthusiasm and increase our pleasure.

[2] Nights of wrath.

great and faithful friend, Salacrou, and *The Trial* by Kafka so as
to keep alive the line which had been inaugurated with *As I lay
Dying*, *Numantia* and *Hunger*. This programme shows the various
ways in which we wanted to serve the theatre; we wished to serve
the classics, the living authors, experiment with original plays,
continue to cultivate the art of pantomime, do whatever we did
with the constant care of rising as high as possible. We still have
the same aims today and we are more convinced than ever that we
should have as wide a range as possible. We were right to try
vaudeville and melodrama, and we should like to add to these
diverse styles that of the operetta which seems now to be lost [1]
and even that of 'revue' or the variety show. (The *Impromptu* of
the Marigny is a kind of variety show.) Some people have chided us
for what they called eclecticism; they said they could not distinguish the kind of line that we were following. This is one of the
few points we are prepared to defend by saying that our line is a
maze of lines, or a plait.

It is not easy to launch and to keep alive a new theatrical company. The first serious handicap was the lack of funds. We never
had the good luck to discover a patron, whether interested or
disinterested. I know that my 'associate' Madeleine Renaud
detests the discussion of these material problems, and I fully
agree with her that there is a certain lack of tact in dealing with
such details; on the other hand, there is so much gossip, there are
so many false rumours, that it is sometimes useful to reveal the
exact truth. Here are the crude facts of our financial situation: We
had saved 500,000 francs, and a film had brought us 1,000,000
francs; that is all we had. *Hamlet*'s production cost 1,200,000
francs, and *Les Fausses Confidences* and *Baptiste* about 800,000
francs. To these sums we must add 500,000 francs for rehearsals,
settings and other preparations. Our capital had therefore been
far outstripped by our expenses. The public saved us, and we can
only express our deep gratitude. Since then our enterprise has
had its ups and downs, but we have never needed any new basic
investments; that is the story of 1,000,000 francs thrown on a
gambling table, and it still continues to produce results, but we
owe it all to the attention, support and goodwill of the public.
Paris made us, and we shall never forget it. I give these details for
no other reason than that they might be of some use to younger

[1] *La Vie Parisienne* enabled us to try the operatic style.

colleagues in need of encouragement and to whom I say that one must always try to achieve, whatever the cost, what one wishes to do.

The other difficulty was to find a theatre. For a long time we had been attracted by the Théâtre Marigny which was well situated in the middle of Paris, and standing on its own, among trees. We love trees; besides that, this theatre had no particular style or face, therefore it was likely to conform to our idea of independence. The direction of the theatre had passed from Léon Volterra to Simonne Volterra who had the lease. Léon Volterra was also in favour, but which of the two was going to sign the contract? There were rumours that an operetta called *Plume au Vent* had some rights over the theatre; on the other hand we had engaged our actors and actresses from July. I remember with emotion the signing of the first two contracts—that of Jean Desailly and then that of Brunot. We had arranged to meet in the first days of September, and Madeleine and I were rather surprised as well as pleased to see that they had all turned up punctually. We rehearsed for a month without having a theatre; none of the actors knew this, and the contract was only signed on 10 October, seven days before our opening night, which goes to show that one can be stubborn without being pugnacious. Jouvet, who was always slightly raw with worries and used to find relief in teasing others, had said to me: 'Marigny? Bad theatre; too big, badly situated, too many trees, what are you opening with? *Hamlet*—All right, you will hold out for a week, after that?—*Les Fausses Confidences*—Three days; a damned boring play! After that? Salacrou's play—What subject? Resistance—Poor man! Three days! After that?—*The Trial* based on Kafka. . . .' I can no longer remember his answer, but I can still see his blue eyes fixed on me suddenly clouding over with compassion. But he said other things which I thought important and never forgot. 'You will have flops, and your theatre will be empty, you will have successes and your theatre will be always full up, but you will also know a third phenomenon: when the public will not back you up even though you have a successful play, and when the public will come in spite of the rather poor quality of a play. This is a kind of tidal phenomenon, and it is a most painful thing, for it is something which cannot be rationalized.' This was a profound remark. There are moments indeed when the public does not come in spite of the success of a play.

Then one gets into a panic, and one wonders whether the public has suddenly become indifferent, then without reason the public returns; it simply wanted to do something else for a little while.

In the course of thirteen seasons in Paris we have presented fifty-four plays, comprising thirteen classical works, thirty-seven modern plays, three pantomimes, and one variety show. The thirty-seven modern plays included twenty new plays. The authors produced were ten historic authors: Aeschylus, Shakespeare, Lope de Vega, Ben Jonson, Molière, Marivaux, Musset, Paul Féval, Feydeau and Chekhov; and twenty-one modern authors: Marcel Achard, Jean Anouilh, Ferdinand Brückner, Albert Camus, Paul Claudel, Maurice Clavel, Jean Cocteau, André Gide, Henry de Montherlant, André Obey, Jacques Prévert, Armand Salacrou, Jean Giraudoux, Jules Romains, Georges Neveux, Crommelynck, Ugo Betti, Georges Schéhadé, Jacques Vauthier, Jules Supervielle, Christopher Fry.

Out of these fifty-four plays, fourteen were a great success; they had more than 100 performances and we made money on them; 100 performances at the Marigny means more than 100,000 spectators. Twenty-six were successful plays; they either approached the hundred mark, had an exceptionally good press, or covered their expenses. Six were half-successes. They were discussed and they earned a reasonable amount of money. Finally, five were flops, they were harshly treated by the press and they obtained little support from the public, so they had very short runs. What lesson can one draw from such results? First of all it is normal that a classical play which has been tested by time should be more readily accepted by the public than a new play. The public knows what to expect and if the new production succeeds in reconciling tradition with freshness there is every chance that the public will find in it pleasure and profit. All in all, 50 per cent success is a good average if one bears in mind the risks incurred when one creates a play, which is something amounting to giving birth in public. I believe that a producer ought to produce what he likes, and that reminds me of Stanislavski who was very sad that he had never had the chance of producing a variety show. New productions of modern works are excellent things and we feel that there ought to be some kind of subsidy so as to make it possible for a theatre to stage every now and then the best plays of the last fifty years. One could establish a repertory which ought to be the basis of a Modern National Theatre. It is regrettable that one cannot see regularly the masterpieces of modern writers, beginning with *Le Bossu*, right up to *Huis-Clos*[1] and taking in *Ubu-Roi*, *Tête d'Or*, *Le Cocu magnifique*, *Volpone*, *Jean de la Lune*, *Je vivrai un grand amour*, *Le Grand Poucet*, *Histoire de rire*, *Les Mouches*,[1] *Plainte contre inconnu*, *La Machine infernale*,[1] in fact all the plays of Claudel, all those of Giraudoux, etc.

As for the flops, they are part of the task of producing new plays. I am not ashamed of any of them and I hope to return to two of them. I should be ashamed to have a flop with a classic! I am not very proud of the way in which I produced *On ne badine pas avec l'amour*[2] which remains one of my most disquieting memories. I wish to make it clear that it was my fault, and I hope it will be a lesson to me. One last point: out of the fifty-four plays which were produced there were only two foreign plays. This does not mean that we wish to neglect foreign plays. It is entirely due to the kind of activities we have; our company plays for six months in Paris and six months abroad, and our foreign friends when we visit them want French plays. That is the only reason we don't produce more foreign plays. We admire many of them, but our international activities tend to limit us to the French theatre which we export. Our ambition, at the start, was to become an international company of French language, and making our country appreciated by our foreign friends was our best reward. It is always a great honour to be sent by our government to represent our theatre in foreign lands, and we are frequently very moved to see how much French culture is appreciated and welcomed the world over. It is a real joy to become acquainted with these countries, to make new friends under the banner of art, and to share in international fraternity. I can't help remarking on one visit to New York in 1952 when, thanks to Molière, Shakespeare, Marivaux, Claudel, Gide, Kafka and the enthusiasm of the public and the critics, Franco-American relations reached a kind of harmony which was slightly different from the atmosphere of UNO. Above all, the most exciting thing is to discover everywhere in the world people who belong to the same kind as we do. We come into the world as parts of a family, to which we are connected by the ties of blood;

---

[1] Plays translated into English under the following titles: *In Camera*, *The Flies*, *The Infernal Machine*.
[2] One does not trifle with love.

beyond those ties there is the motherland to which we belong and the place where we live. Besides our family we have friends with whom we share affinities, and going farther afield, we find that wherever we go we sometimes meet people to whom we feel mysteriously attuned, who belong to 'our own kind' and to whom we might become more attached than to our relatives or normal friends. These people can be found anywhere in the world, and now I know that in Brazil, Argentine, Chile, in Montreal, New York, Mexico, London, Copenhagen, Berlin, Rome, Venice and Edinburgh, there are human beings with whom I feel at one, and who feel at one with me. This means that beyond the community of the blood or of the mind, there is that of the heart and it is the kind of community which renders our international journeys so pleasant and does away with the word 'foreigner'.

Having said these things I must point out that it is nevertheless not easy to compose a repertory of French plays to produce abroad. Quite a few French writers exhibit traits which are specifically French, such as the love of satire and the love of sharp criticism and derision. These writers spend their time attacking institutions, laughing at justice and at the Church, burying God, or concentrating on homosexuality and abortions. By so doing they show an independence of spirit and love of truth for which France is famous, but the fact remains that their works are not the best things for export to countries where these things are not generally discussed in public. As one does not visit countries to start controversies or to be provocative, one cannot but regret that our authors should devote so much energy to social problems and failings which do not produce a very exciting or ennobling theatre. One must also note that any given spectator never has the same attitude twice. A spectator visiting our country might like a certain play which he would probably dislike if we brought that same play to his country, and vice versa. The point is that the spectator prepares himself in advance for the performance which he is going to watch, and success takes place or does not take place in so far as the performance which he watches does or does not meet his expectations. Chameleons adapt themselves to the colours of the place where they are; for the spectator it is the other way round; the spectator enters the theatre with his given colour, and the show will achieve success if it is attuned to this colour, and this is one of the reasons why it is impossible to decide in advance whether a play will be a success or a failure. Recently I heard a very intelligent lady express surprise that one could not anticipate a flop. The flop, which in French is called 'un four' or oven, is a term which comes from the time when theatres were lit with candles; when there were no spectators, no candles were lit and the theatre remained as dark as an oven. This same lady said: 'When one sees the play it all seems so clear, and that without being professionals of the theatre! One often wonders how a director who has experience, could consent to risk so much money on such an obvious flop!' The choice of a play rests more on instinct than on intelligence. As far as I am concerned I only produce a play when I like it, and I am sure that the actor follows the same rule. The actor may or may not feel attuned to certain characters and that determines whether or not he likes to play the part; the producer may or may not be attuned to certain plays and that determines his style or the way in which he produces it. In order that the play which the producer likes may be a success, the producer's taste must coincide with that of a given collectivity. A producer must therefore produce the plays which he really likes and have a 'collective' heart, and the success of plays is just as mysterious as the success of a love affair.

A theatrical performance is fundamentally a spiritual *rendez-vous* which spectators and actors have made with the author. If everybody is in tune, and if there is understanding, there is success; if the spectator is a bit late or slow, and the author a bit early, it is an *avant-garde* performance; the successful *rendez-vous* has to be postponed. If the two partners are waiting at different places the whole thing is a flop. Where is the genius or the prophet who can anticipate the result of a first *rendez-vous*? If in the theatre one does not act out of love and if one begins to calculate and to choose plays for all sorts of reasons, such as political topicality, social value, ideology, or because one thinks that the public like such and such a type of play, or perhaps to please an actor or a literary clique, one gets completely lost. Deciding on plays becomes then a gambler's game and not an artist's work. The favourite device of the gambler is the martingale, that of the artist is love. This is not a gratuitous image; anybody who lives in the world of directors and theatrical producers knows that there are many gamblers among them. In fact those who have just come into the theatre do nothing else but gamble; they put down 15 per cent for the production of a given play, 30 per cent for the production of another, etc. They do not practise any art, they simply put down their money with the hope of a win, and of course they make as many mistakes in their gambles as the others in their loves. We make probably as many mistakes, but we can at least claim that these mistakes correspond to the ideal which guides our work.

That is why, for instance, I still retain a very definite predilection for two of my flops: *L'État de Siège*, [1] by Camus, and *Lazare* by André Obey. I have often compared the production of a play to the delicate work of making a mayonnaise. A production catches or does not catch on in exactly the same way as does a mayonnaise. For six or seven weeks one beats the play until one feels that it begins to rise; at long last the mayonnaise has caught. But it often happens that if the weather is stormy and the oil has been poured in too quickly it cannot catch on. It is exactly the same in the theatre; certain imponderables prevent the mayonnaise from succeeding. The eggs, the oil and all the other ingredients were good! Yet the play did not succeed; it is exactly the same term for both. That's just what happened with Camus's *L'État de Siège*, yet I still continue to think that this play is based on one of the best subjects one can think of and contains some exceptional moments. *L'État de Siège* was my first theatrical disappointment. I had placed great hopes on collaboration with Camus; I admired him and I got on well with him. I was very enthusiastic about our relations, and as I believe that a theatrical enterprise requires authors, I was hoping that Camus would become our author; I had the feeling that he and I could provide a team similar to the Jouvet-Giraudoux team. *L'État de Siège* was meant to be a beginning, and in my little head I formed plans for the Camus-Barrault tandem—a couple of keen, hard-working cyclists. On the first night, there were people who could barely hide their joy at our discomfiture; I felt a kind of physical pain; and the wound is still there. It was the opening of our third season, it was our first flop, and it was the one I should have liked most to avoid. I knew that Camus in spite of his sensitiveness, would bear up, although I knew that he would feel it and I feared that he might be lost to us, for I felt that we might lose one of our dearest hopes. Where was the mistake? For we must have made one. Which one was it? I thought that 'The Plague', because of the accumulation of dark forces reaching a paroxysm, had a redemptory effect. I saw in it a

[1] The state of siege.

kind of initiatory, magic concept inspired by Artaud, and I felt that this ought to communicate a kind of Aeschylean lyricism to the play. Camus equated the plague or the dictator with evil, social evil which only fear kept in being, and which ought to fade away with the end of fear. The style was therefore more modern than the one I conceived and could easily become Aristophanesque. The meeting-point of our two conceptions was the suppression of fear since it had reached the confines of despair. One is afraid as long as one believes in life, but the moment one accepts fully the idea of death, fear disappears and one begins to live again, and this time in freedom. We respected each other's point of view. I should have liked to give full rein to an Aristophanesque style; Camus on the other hand wanted to cling to a kind of tragic mystery. I believe that sincere people could not quite make out whether the plague was a means of salvation through the maximum of evil, or an evil which one ought to avoid. There were marvellous, exciting evenings, and the few people who came enjoyed the show. If critics had not assailed it so violently at the beginning, this is the type of play which could very well have been a success. I know that it is very much appreciated abroad, and I often meet people of every nationality who come and talk to me about it. We should have liked to keep the play on much longer than we did, but we could not stand the financial strain. As a skipper responsible for the well-being of about 100 people, I was compelled to lay aside my love for the play, swallow my sorrows and hope that Camus would give us other works.

Lazare also had some very exciting evenings; yet the thrashing we got was far worse than the previous one—a real flagellation. In spite of that I still think that the first half of *Lazare* is one of the most deeply felt dramatic creations of the past few years. If Obey decides one day to compress his *Lazare* into one single act comparable in length to Sartre's masterpiece *Huis-clos*, [1] I am ready to put the play on again. There is the fact that in *Lazare* Obey has made Christ speak, and the public does not like Christ in the theatre. One must confess that the character of Christ on the stage is rather intimidating and the dialogue between Lazare and Christ, meant to be the apex of the play, is also its flaw. These kinds of works have the Icarus complex, but they are perhaps destined to posthumous glory.

[1] *In Camera.*

While, because of the character of Christ, I expected far less from *Lazare* than from *L'État de Siège*, I hardly expected anything from *Maguelone*. Clavel wanted to experiment, and I had put myself at his disposal for whatever he wanted to do. On the first night I was very much like the infantry lieutenant who is waiting for the zero hour of the assault, knowing full well that he will not come back. But that did not matter; I was doing my duty by the young authors. People were clamouring for help for young authors, I was doing my bit, and this one had authentic talent. With *Maguelone* I really learnt about the cruelty of the public and of those who talk too much about the theatre. When I produced *La Répétition*[1] by Jean Anouilh I was congratulated by everybody, but when it came to *Maguelone* hardly anyone encouraged me and supported me. Moral: only the result matters, and not the intention; it is the same with love! 'You must not only be able to talk about music; you must be able to play,' said Chekhov in *The Cherry Orchard*. That is exactly what the public wants; it wants to love, and it wants those who deal with it to know how to love it. That is the theatre! But just as one differentiates between pleasure and love, in the same way there are many dramas which give pleasure, and very few in which one finds love. This is the difference which exists between the theatre of entertainment or digestion, and artistic theatre. The theatre of entertainment has a very easy passage when contrasted with a so-called serious theatre which is simply boring. Of course we all prefer pleasure to boredom, but I am sure that if we can find love we are quite prepared to forsake a little bit of pleasure for a little more love, when it is the love which leads to true knowledge, to harmony and to fusion with the great whole. This is the kind of feeling one has when one watches *Hamlet*, *Les Fausses Confidences*, *Partage de Midi*,[2] *Amphitryon*, *The Trial*, *Christophe Colomb*, the *Oresteia*, or *Occupe-toi d'Amélie*.[3] After these plays we feel freer, we breathe better and we feel that our blood runs faster in our veins; our eyes see more clearly, we are freed from anxiety, and we feel in much better health because we have loved. Good plays produce a kind of liberating euphoria which cleanses and fortifies spectators and actors. The virtue of a good play often reminds me of the virtue of acupuncture. A good play hits at the very point

[1] The rehearsal.
[2] The division of noon.
[3] *Look After Lulu.*

T.J.B.—C

where there is a maximum resonance. One millimetre away from the right spot and the resonance completely fades away. Two perfect illustrations of this point are *The Cherry Orchard* by Chekhov and *Les Fausses Confidences* by Marivaux. This master-piece of Marivaux always reminds me of true French cooking prepared on a slow fire. Wherever we have given this play, the public always begins to warm up at the same points, then prepares to boil and to sing like a kettle which whistles out vapour at the end of the second act. The reactions caused by this play always fill me with wonder, and I look upon *Les Fausses Confidences* and *Baptiste* as our good luck shows.

I made my first attempt on *Hamlet*, this Anapurna of the theatre, twenty years ago; it was in 1937, I tackled it from the 'Laforgue' side or translation which is a variation on *Hamlet* written by another Hamlet. Laforgue's Hamlet is a young man full of humour and philosophy, an odd student of Wittenberg.

> Ma rare faculté d'assimilation
> contrariera le cours de ma vocation [1]

In 1941, thanks to Charles Granval to whom I owe so much, I came at last in contact with the real Shakespeare in a translation by Pourtalès which, although prosy, was very faithful. In 1942 while Madeleine Renaud and I were attempting to produce a radio extract from *Le Soulier de Satin* [2] in Marseilles, we met André Gide. We knew that Gide had already translated the first act of *Hamlet* and we encouraged him to complete his task. Gide was then on the way to Sidi-Bou-Saïd, where he spent eight months, and from there he sent me his translation, act by act. We launched our company with *Hamlet*, and it is through Gide's language that I have produced *Hamlet* in all sorts of climates. Hamlet has be-come for me the criterion of the superior being; he is a kind of superman who has such a pure and scrupulous sensibility that he reaches beyond action into the realm of hesitation. I consider *Hamlet* the greatest play of all time, or at any rate the greatest play of modern times since there is also the *Oresteia*. I have just read a very interesting book on *Hamlet* by Jean Paris; it deals with the main character at the level which it deserves. I mentioned before

---

[1] The ease with which I assimilate things will interfere with my vocation.

[2] The satin slipper.

the word acupuncture; Hamlet is the very centre of man's sensibility, the apex of ambiguity, the meeting-point of man and woman, sanity and madness. He is every one of these things in turn and he goes beyond, he is the hero of superior hesitation. Playing Hamlet makes one ill; first of all one loses two pounds in weight every evening, secondly, one begins to be stricken with Hamlet's disease from 5 p.m. onwards, then the performance itself is exhausting because of its length; it is indeed a long-distance race and if one starts too fast one runs the risk of collapsing at the end. Melancholy heir of a patriarchal civilization, and witness of a disintegrating and corrupt age, Hamlet has suffered so much that he has no tears left. He carries within him the seeds of a new civilization, and also the means to choke them to death, he unites in himself the worst and the best and he is conscious of this contrast, for he has the most penetrating human consciousness that can exist, and he is beyond the human. He is my dream and my torment; the more I frequent him the more I am frightened by him, and I feel that in order to penetrate him one must have suffered a great deal. When in 1942 I produced *Hamlet* at the Ziegfeld Theatre in New York, I began by informing the members of my company of the serious risks that we were facing in performing *Hamlet* in French for the American public. I knew that everyone would do his or her best, but I pointed out once more to them the fact that our greatest drawback was that we were a happy company, and that one cannot play *Hamlet* if one is happy. If there is happiness there is no anguish, and everybody in *Hamlet*, except Fortinbras and the common people like the sailor and the gravediggers, is swamped in anguish.

Le froid est vif, et j'ai le coeur transi. [1]

Yet, however frightened I might be by Hamlet, I love him as an elder brother; he is somebody who is alive and who exists, and if I don't know him well enough, it is because I am the one who is ill-defined, not he; it is I who cannot see him as he is. There are other characters which gravitate around myself; there is Joseph K. of *The Trial* by Kafka, there is Baptiste of the pantomime *Les enfants du Paradis*, and there is Mésa of Claudel's *Partage de Midi*. I have the impression of sharing the life of these characters. Hamlet existed before I did, but in the strange world of the theatre

[1] And I am sick at heart . . . 'tis bitter cold.

I have the feeling that Joseph K., Baptiste and Mésa are satellites of my being. I consider them as mine; they people my solitude. I had that feeling towards Rodrigue in *Le Soulier de Satin* and I remember the sorrow and the feeling of betrayal I experienced when my good friend Jean Chevrier played Rodrigue. It was the same with *Partage de Midi*. Edwige Feuillère, who is a wonderful Ysé, and to whom one cannot refuse anything, had asked me to lend her *Partage de Midi*, and I had therefore to surrender the part of Mésa, which I played, to somebody else. When I accepted, I had no idea of the kind of sorrow this would cause me; it was as if I had lost someone whom I loved. It is stupid and childish, but it ought to be something understandable.

I don't think that spectators realize how much we belong to certain characters. We have to make such an effort in order to interpret them and to try to believe what they are, that once we separate from them and return to our own selves, we cannot help carrying with us some odd bits of their skins which remain attached to ours. In fact our love for them is in proportion to the suffering that they have caused us in order to become them. Just as we cannot fail to love those with whom we act and share our worries, anxieties, lapses of memory, tiredness and tears, in the same way we cannot avoid, up to a point, turning illusion into reality and believing in the life of the character whom we incarnate. This problem is far more complicated in the case of characters who belong to the same author. Take the case of myself who has played Rodrigue, Mésa, Louis Laine and Christophe Colomb, all born of the same author—Claudel. In twenty years I have absorbed Claudel and tried to live him through what was most himself—his dramatic creations. What is the result of such a prolonged contact with the same poet? Well, a few instances will clarify this point. If Claudel was kind to me I was full of joy, if he did some stupid thing to me, I 'cursed' him. When he refused me *Tête d'Or* [1] it was sorrow and deep disappointment, etc., but as soon as we met and looked at each other, I was overwhelmed with affection towards him. The conclusion is that in the theatre, those who give themselves fully without holding anything back become the prey of the monster which torments lovers, they are continuously harassed by disappointments and betrayals and they end in being as ridiculous as Alceste. That reminds me of the indignation of Copeau,

[1] *Golden Head.*

the disgusts of Dullin, and the raw sensibility of Jouvet. The best
way to avoid all that would be to be able to sublimate oneself as
Hamlet did: 'That is the question', and that is in fact what I am
trying to do with the best will in the world. But the theatre has its
compensations, its profound joys. To bring about the production
of *The Trial* by Kafka proved as complicated as a polar expedition.
When I read the first sketch of the text to Gide in order to win
him over, it all seemed quite hopeless. He could not see how one
could stage the scenes when three characters, each one in a different
place, are made to converse; I can still see his amused smile. We
were working in his small room heated by a gas fire, and I had no
sooner uttered the last words 'comme un chien', which end the
play, than the chandelier fell from the ceiling and remained suspended from the electric wire of the lamp. 'Kafka approves,' said
Gide, laughing, 'we shall work on under this chandelier.' In fact
the chandelier remained menacingly brooding over our heads like
the absurd atmosphere of Joseph K. right throughout the work.
After the first night I received three letters of congratulations.
The first was from Henry Bernstein, the second from Paul
Claudel, the third from Jean de Létroz. The battle of *The Trial*
had been won. Since then we have given the play everywhere and
it has been a great success. The play broke all records in Buenos
Aires, and it had the same great success in North America. I love
to act *The Trial* in spite of the anxiety it causes me, for the show is
as complicated as the most precise clockwork mechanism, so that
I can never afford not to keep an eye on the production which has
about twenty different sets and at leasty sixty changes of lighting.
The Japanese, who are the most sincere actors in the world, and
who have been known in some cases to bring about their own
death when they are miming hara-kiri, say that the actor must
always have a third eye watching the audience. The actor-producer
requires a fourth eye to watch backstage.

This reminds me that Dullin sometimes found his inspiration
backstage. I remember that one day when he was playing Richard
III he was waiting in the wing to make his entry; he had to enter
the stage in anger, and every evening he somehow managed to find
a pretext or an excuse to work himself into a temper, but that night
he had found nothing, and the moment of his entry was very close.
He suddenly noted a hole in the curtain (a most common sight at
the Théâtre de l'Atelier) and staring at the hole he exploded in

anger, saying: 'Oh! to wear away one's life for such results!' He stamped his foot in a rage and he was then ready for his entry on the stage which was due at that moment. Every show which requires great precision in staging is a kind of trapeze act without a net; the accident is always possible. The most amusing scene in *Occupe-toi d'Amélie*[1] is the one with the blanket. The art of making the blanket slide along is described with the greatest accuracy by that master craftsman, Feydeau. So while the audience roars with laughter and actors do the same, if one is backstage one can see two men kneeling down, their bottoms up and hauling carefully two pieces of string, just like fishermen hauling a net from a river. Don't try to distract them; they seem to perform the most important task of their lives, and so the blanket slides on amid laughter. On the other side of the stage, the chief electrician, locked up in his cabin as if he were a train driver, waits for the signal for full light on the stage. At the end of this operation the actors are very relieved, the two men backstage stretch themselves up, light comes full on, the public applauds while Amélie, dear Amélie, exclaims: 'We had a good laugh.' It is this mixture of joys, fears and loving anxieties which encloses as in a net every member of the theatrical company from the prompter to the leading lady.

The atmosphere of a first night is something special. Practice probably develops in actors a kind of antenna which enables them to feel and to guess the likely reactions of an audience before the curtain rises. Actors can guess from the very start of a performance whether the audience is warm or is, as we say, 'painted'. I remember the first night of *Malatesta*; the first is always the worst. *Malatesta* opens up with an empty stage, and after a few seconds, while one hears voices coming from off-stage, Malatesta and his opponent come on the stage fighting with daggers. I remember being backstage with Beauchamp waiting to come on the stage, and we were both very tense through excitement and fatigue. When the curtain rose we both felt as if we had been hit by a cold wave and I could not refrain from saying, 'Ah, the swine, they are hostile!' We went on the stage but we could not warm them up. In both cases, in the case of the public and in ours, the subconscious had taken up positions—and that is why *Malatesta* and *Bacchus* are two very nasty surprises. I still continue to believe that these two plays are amongst the best works of Montherlant and Cocteau.

[1] *Look After Lulu.*

They are masterpieces of style, of honesty, and they bear the
imprint of splendid intellects. *Malatesta* was not a flop but it
never reached the level of steady success. Perhaps I lacked the
stature required to play the part of a Renaissance condottiere, the
convention being in this case stronger than, and in contradiction
with, historical truth. It is also possible that Montherlant's hero,
who was highly individualized, lacked the universal element which
ensures success. Sigismond's situation was quite interesting but
it was not moving, and when he died nobody was moved except the
'individualists' like Malatesta or Montherlant who are used to
fighting their own battles alone. Madam Simone, in a lecture
about Rostand, explained that the reason for the failure of *Chan-
tecler*, one of the best plays by the author of *Cyrano*, was because
it did not connect with the average person's subconscious preoccupations. Malatesta's character was probably alien to the
preoccupations of the majority of spectators, yet this play contains
beautiful scenes of great resonance. The case of *Bacchus* is different,
for here we move out of the theatre, the play attacks the Church
as a political institution and I learnt that it was better to attack
God than the Church. Yet *Bacchus* remains one of Cocteau's best
plays. I am proud that both Montherlant and Cocteau entrusted
me with their plays and I am sure that time will bring to them
the success that ought to be theirs, for they are two great works
of the modern theatre. I also consider Salacrou's *Les Nuits de la
Colère* one of his best plays and I am glad to say that Salacrou has
rarely had a better press reception than with this play. I am waiting
for his next. I am also very grateful to Salacrou who in 1936
compelled me to act in *Un homme comme les autres*; I had just left
the Atelier and I lacked simplicity. Salacrou convinced me then
that I had to embrace a profession and practise it and not remain
a semi-amateur and a purist.

I have twice invited producers to direct plays with my company.
The first one I asked was Jouvet. He used to say to me, 'Come and
play Scapin with my company. If you were with me I would have
you play Scapin.' So one day I said to him, 'Why don't you come
and produce Scapin with our company?' He readily accepted
with goodwill and modesty, and I thank Providence for this wonderful experience. First of all it enabled me to go back to school
and with a master like Jouvet; then it enabled me to know Jouvet
better and the more one knew him, the more one liked him. I have

in fact the greatest admiration for these men who led for twenty-five
years the life of theatrical directors. After twenty years of struggle,
Jouvet had become something like a solitary leader, surrounded
by a crowd but very much alone. To watch him work was fascinating; he had reached such a mastery that he did not seem
to prepare his production. What mattered to him was not the
question how to walk on or off the stage, but the characters which
were the object of his sustained studies. He had been thinking
about this comedy of Molière for a long time. He had first played
the part with Copeau who played Géronte, and now in his turn
he was handing the part to us, and this gives an idea of the traditions which linked us together. Jouvet, who was a great man
of the theatre, made extraordinary discoveries in staging, as for
instance when he produced *Don Juan*. The scene with Silvestre
and the famous scene with Zerbinette and Géronte were most
impressive. On the other hand, he wilfully neglected certain
details; I say wilfully, for it is only when one has reached a certain
degree of perfection that one leaves some stains or flaws in one's
work. A well-placed stain or flaw is important, for too much perfection and polish dehumanize; but one can only do such things
through absolute mastery of one's medium. After Jouvet we asked
Charles Dullin to direct *Georges Dandin* with Madeleine Renaud
and Pierre Brasseur, but it was unfortunately too late. My good
master was already ill and he died on 11 December 1949. It was
a Sunday and at that time we were giving *Hamlet*; Madeleine
Renaud had gone to the Hôpital St Antoine to see him. At the end
of the first act, I asked if there was any news from the hospital,
and I was told that Madeleine had just telephoned to say that he
had died. I went back on the stage, and I shall never forget what
I felt when I uttered the words, 'And my father died only two
hours ago.' What a strange profession, in which sometimes one
does not quite know who one is! Since then I have kept up the
tradition of inviting producers to come and direct our company.

The next one was Jean Vilar. Gide had given me *Oedipus*. Meanwhile Vilar had asked Gide to give him *Oedipus* for his season at
Avignon which came before mine; he had asked for five performances, I did not have the heart to refuse to let Vilar have
Oedipus; I saw on the contrary an opportunity to offer him the
hospitality of our theatre. We decided that he should direct
Oedipus with our company. It was a great success, and I am very

glad that *Oedipus* took its flight upwards with our company. The summer after, Jouvet died, the very day when Vilar was appointed director of the Théâtre National Populaire. I can still see Vilar in the Place St Sulpice on the day of Jouvet's funeral. While generations of men and women were paying tribute to a man who for twenty years had given them dreams and joys, there was a young man already in full possession of his gifts and ready to offer his generation new joys and dreams. Strange fate! While Jouvet was entering the world of legend, 'young' Vilar was beginning his history.

Now a few words about pantomime. Out of fifty-four works given in ten years I have produced only three pantomimes: *Baptiste*, in 1946, *La Fontaine de Jouvence*, in 1947, and *Suites d'une Course* in 1956. Why so few pantomimes? First because it is difficult to find good subjects, and second because pantomime is still an ill-defined genre. Pantomime is an action which takes place exclusively in the present; it contains neither narrative nor explanation. A ballet may take its start from a simple idea which develops like a Japanese flower in water, into numerous variations. If one single idea can supply enough material for a ballet, a pantomime which lasts half an hour requires the same amount of material as a five-act play. *Macbeth* could be reduced to a pantomime of forty minutes. This is a point which is not always understood by the authors of pantomime. I should have loved to continue the life of the character of Baptiste which seems so close to my own nature. For years, I have asked Prévert to send me some more Baptistes in the same way as there are many types of Charlie Chaplin—there is for instance Charlie Chaplin the soldier, Charlie Chaplin the fireman, etc. My calls have remained unanswered. What a pity, for so many important things could have been expressed through Baptiste who is surely related to Kafka and to Hamlet. What a splendid satire of our age could take place through him! I am very disappointed that no dramatist has taken Baptiste in hand and made him say something every month. One could not confine oneself to old pantomime, which is greatly in need of being modernized. *Baptiste* was something exceptional. I believe that *La Fontaine de Jouvence* was a mistake. Auric's music was good, but the whole thing was nevertheless a hybrid mixture of amateur ballet and pantomime by insufficiently trained actors. There is nothing more to do in that direction. Modern pantomime must be different from the ancient in the sense that it is a silent action and not a mimed language. The language of gestures which gives charm to ancient pantomime aims at replacing words by gestures. One draws words in the air: 'Your eyes, like stars,' 'My heart,' . . . etc. If miming only consists in expressing silent speech, its only value lies in the comical and the effete aspect of the incapacity to express oneself silently. If the details of the expression are excessive, the style of pantomime falls into comic puerility. Yet pantomime is an art which can become as noble and majestic as all the other arts. There can be a tragic pantomime. This kind of thing is well known to oriental artists. In the Nõ theatre, the art of the gesture is majestic and it is so because the mimic is not only mute, he is silent. Since 1933, Decroux and I have tried to reach this kind of modern mime built on silence. Decroux taught me all he had learnt from the Vieux-Colombier; he has kept up his work and created a kind of mime which he called statue-like mime, and recently I have seen it described as animated statue-like mime. This is indeed the most interesting type of mime we have just now, but I don't feel completely satisfied with it; I find that it distorts the bodily expression instead of making it 'truer than truth'. As far as I am concerned I am determined to take up my researches again, and they will lie between statuesque miming, which is poetic art rather than dramatic art, and pantomime which confines itself to a kind of comedy which is touching because it is obsolete. The art of the gesture of which I dream is nothing but essential theatre, that is to say finding its source in silence. But I think that a good mimic must not be the caricature of an actor, on the contrary he must be more able than anybody else to act in a realistic play with gestures which ought to be simple and true.

CONCLUSION

Never cast your net too low.
—A. GIDE

My aim is to continue my activities in the fields which I have mentioned—classical authors, modern playwrights, personal research and the art of the gesture. I want to do my utmost so that young authors may envisage their task not only on the plane of dialogue, but on the plane of the whole human being; it is only by so doing that they will reach a form of expression which will have style. Expression in the theatre is not confined to conversation, it is a kind of plastic with all the explosiveness that this notion carries with it. Since 1946 I have believed that the rarest and noblest thing is to be able to last, and to last without selling oneself. In 1956 we celebrated our company's ten years of life. On this occasion a little gold medal was struck and presented to all those who had been with us for ten years. We required seventeen medals. Thus seventeen people had of their own free will shared with me ten precious years of their lives! That was a very encouraging number and it is still the same today, in 1959. What kind of feelings guided these seventeen human beings, who for so many years felt the need to unite and to work together? It is said that during childhood every child wishes to resemble those with whom he lives. How is such a desire born in him?

III

About the Actor

RULES OF ACTING

What follows is not a lesson in dramatic art but simply a personal recapitulation of a few rules which are necessary to the actor. Being continually engrossed in the same work leads one not only to grant an excessive importance to secondary details but also to neglect the fundamental laws which govern true acting. Let us therefore try to recall a few of these obvious rules which one tends all too easily to forget.

The first rule which an actor must observe is that of making himself heard and understood. In fact this is not a rule, it is a matter of elementary politeness, and failure to conform to it is an insult to the spectator. Making oneself heard is within everybody's capacity and has nothing to do with special gifts or talents; it is purely a matter of training, barring of course cases of physiological incapacity.

The second rule rests on observation and imitation, and here natural gifts play a part; nevertheless one must bear in mind the fact that the faculty of observation can be developed by practice and training. There are at least two methods of observation: the objective and the subjective method. For instance, take a box of matches and observe it analytically; concentrate your attention on the content, the quality of the wood, the writing, the marks, etc. After a few minutes of this kind of observation, hide the box of matches and describe it objectively. Practise this method of observation on any object which may come under your gaze, and you will soon note that your sight becomes quicker and sharper. After this apply the same method to the observation of your fellow beings; scrutinize them, take them to pieces in the same way and you will find that this kind of observation will supply you with precious data for future characterizations.

Let us now pass to the subjective method of observation. This time you only take one match but you not only look at it, you feel it, and you say to yourself: 'I become wood or a memory of wood from a Swedish forest. What remains of this body? I am thin, very thin, and elongated, and the slightest pressure could crush me, break me into pieces; I should crack up, crinkle, but those who use me do not crush me but strike me on the box and my head becomes alight, for all my fire is in my head. I live in a congested state, my forehead burns, my ears are red. I am living under the shadow of cerebral haemorrhage, my fate is to die at the moment when I myself generate life, heat and light. My existence consumes me; I am a symbol of life and of death at the same time. That's perhaps why I am laid out in advance in a grave, side by side with my sisters and without the slightest room to stretch my feet. There is no room in our box, but perhaps those who make them are right, for I have been told that in serious cases of heart illness one must remain motionless, if not the result is a cerebral haemorrhage. That is what lies in store for us, etc. etc.' This kind of subjective observation develops the art of imitation. In order to be able to observe and to imitate one must have certain gifts, but in spite of those gifts one might not know how to observe and how to imitate, and that is where practice comes in. To know how to observe and how to imitate is the second rule of the actor; it is the rule of authenticity. The question of producing effects only comes later. Any attempt at producing an effect in the theatre unfailingly reminds one of the shopkeeper's last words, 'And now, Sir or Madam, shall I wrap it up for you?' But one must remember that these are not the words with which he greets you, they are his final words, meant to produce the effect he is aiming at, if he is a good salesman.

Once an actor can make himself heard and understood, and once he has so thoroughly observed a chosen character that he is full of him, and can easily imitate him, impersonate him or give him life, he comes up against the rule which can be summed up by the three vital questions 'Whence do I come, where am I going and in what state am I?'

There are various opinions as to the way one should answer these questions, but the actor must have a clear-cut opinion about them at any moment of the performance, even when he is in the wings or backstage. Let us take Scapin as an example. We are in Naples; Naples is a hot place; we are in the Mediterranean world, a world where one practises siesta. Scapin must surely practise siesta, he may even be the king of siesta. Scapin, like every other animal, eats, sleeps, makes love and plays. He is either relaxed or he is active. He is a master at relaxing. Where does he come from? The answer is easy; he has just been shaken out of his moist sleep by the lamentation of Octave and Silvester. Where is he going? Nowhere, of course. Why should he go anywhere? He has renounced all things, he says these things come to him by themselves. In what state is he? Sleepy, he will awaken progressively. His first tirade flows forth from the fumes of sleep and wine and is garlic flavoured. He who is generally so talkative lets the others do the talking. No useless efforts (he knows that he will need all his energy later; but this point will be discussed in connexion with another subject). When the others have ceased chattering, he yawns, stretches himself and says, 'Here you are, quite as big as your father and mother and you couldn't discover in your brains or contrive with your wits . . . etc.' And he stretches himself again, and once he has done so he has a clearer mind. Hiacinthe awakens him completely. Scapin has a heart and he is not insensitive to young women, so he thinks to himself, 'she is not bad at all,' then he turns a bit of charm on her, and with that he is off. 'All right, I want to help you both,' he says, so Scapin gets started and will only stop at the end of the famous scene with the 'sac'.

The third rule, which we have just discovered, is vital, it is called the rule of verisimilitude. The fourth rule could be summed up with the words, 'What am I doing here?' It is a rule about environment. The plot is unfolding, the characters play their respective parts. Agrippine nags Nero who listens, gets bored, thinks of Julia, ends by being angry and completely shuts himself off from his mother's presence. The more one progresses in the rules the more complicated they become. The question 'What am I doing here?' implies at least two alternatives. One, what am I determined to allow the other to see, and what am I determined to hide? This rule is very complex for a character because although he thinks he knows himself, he may know himself badly and may sometimes confuse good faith with bad faith. He attaches importance to things that have none, and he is suddenly caught up by things from which he felt protected. A character may think that he is walking in the light and be in darkness, and then the passion against which he is struggling may unsettle his equilibrium, distort his reactions and plunge him into errors. He may think he is walking with a steady step and he stumbles; he may think he sees clearly and he is blind. Now blind people find help in walking-sticks. A character who is at a loss as to what to do, might be greatly helped if he could find an object to which he could cling. During Agrippine's sermon, Nero plays with his coat which becomes his help, his refuge and also his means of expression. An actor who finds the object which connects him with the scene he is playing imparts concrete efficiency to his behaviour. To find the right object was the golden rule of Stanislavski; it is a most precious rule which has countless effects and it is one of the most important rules of realistic art.

The fifth rule is the rule of control, and it is also very important; it deals with sincerity and exactness. There is a prevailing belief that sincerity is automatically right; that is not always true. The actor might be sincere while at the same time the character he is portraying is not quite right within the performance. The reason is that the actor never identifies himself absolutely with the character he is playing, and that is normal since we are in the theatre, a place where life is re-created through art. The point is that it is the character who must be sincere, irrespective of the fact that the actor may or may not be so. The acting will be right if the character is constantly sincere. The closer the identification between actor and character the more sincere they will be. But there are situations in which total identification of the two would bring about disasters. The death of a character compels the actor who plays the part to disconnect himself from it and merely to project the picture of death out of himself, with as much sincerity as he can command. Death is an extreme case, yet there never is complete identification between actor and character. The actor must work within the play's setting, keep on remembering his relationship with the other characters of the play, remain aware that he is in a theatre, and that he must be heard, and that he must stick to the plot, keep an eye on the lighting, etc. The superimposition of the actor's person on that of a given character resembles those cheap coloured prints in which the colours overflow the contours of the drawing. Exactitude of performance depends on

the sincerity of the character and on the power of control of the
actor who must constantly ask himself the question: 'In spite of
my sincerity is my character truly sincere?'

Such are the five main rules for the basic training of an actor.
They are the foundations of his studies and art, and his talent can
only blossom thanks to them. Just as in the course of primary,
secondary and university studies we spend a great deal of time
going through the same cycle or unlearning what we learnt with
so much difficulty, we seem at this point to run the risk of coming
up against rules which might seem to contradict the preceding
ones. Yet, in fact they don't. In our young days we might have
learnt that two and two make four, and later we might have been
compelled to realize that it is not quite so; yet this rule does not
lose its virtue or its efficiency. In fact, superior rules do not abolish
efficient rules, they only refine them. In the same way poetic
theatre does not nullify realistic theatre; on the contrary, it raises
it to a higher level.

After these five elementary rules which are the basis of normal
drama which is realistic, there exist more practical preconceptions.
First, the rule of transposition. Once one has carefully laid down the
foundations of one's work on truth (whether one is an actor, a
producer or a stage designer) one can take the liberty of forgetting
everything and begin anew. And so it happens that sometimes,
guided by inspiration, one discovers a way of doing things which,
although it does not at first sight rest on truth, contains nevertheless aspects which are the very essence of truth. That is truly poetic
interpretation.

Let us now return to Scapin. We have previously described the
way in which, according to logic, he ought to make his first
appearance on the stage. The conception outlined previously was
also that of Jouvet who produced *Scapin*, yet that is not the way
in which he produced me when I played Scapin under his direction.
Jouvet was a great producer and he knew how to invent and to
transpose, while starting from reality. He thus invented how to
make me appear as if from nowhere right in the middle of the
reality of the stage. It was something like the appearance of the
Prince of Valets. Truth was respected since the internal rhythm
of Scapin remained slow, but the fact of turning his entrance into
a kind of sudden emergence produced at the very beginning of the
play a poetic tone which echoed from scene to scene. Even if *Les*

Fourberies de Scapin[1] was a farce Jouvet was entitled to produce
it as a poetic farce, yet in fact Molière did not call it a farce but
a comedy and it is a comedy which contains a kind of poetry to
which Jouvet was particularly sensitive. His invention about
Scapin's first appearance on the stage follows the rule of transposition. In a transposition there is no apparent logic, there is a
metamorphosis. Happy those who possess this sixth sense which
transposes truth through poetry. There we have all the art and
all the difficulty of Giraudoux's theatre!

Let us pass to another rule. I love horse racing but know nothing
about it. Yet I feel that it is with the terminology of horse racing
that I should discover my next rule. This new rule which concerns
those who play big parts deals with the art of running a race. The
actor who plays Hamlet, for instance, loses approximately two
pounds in weight at each performance. If he starts too fast he will
be short of breath in the second half of the third act; in order to
avoid that he will increase his efforts, and will probably be flat out
for the fifth. One of the great difficulties of Hamlet is its length.
Right up to the beginning of the fourth act (the departure for
England) the actor is carried forth by his own impetus without any
time for cooling off; during the greater part of the fourth act,
Hamlet is no longer very active and he cools off during the scene
of Ophelia's madness. His head tired by a three hours' performance
is bubbling with all the words, curses and sighs which he has just
uttered and his will is liable to flag. The last effort of the fifth
act, notably the Graveyard scene, is particularly painful. It sometimes takes him a few minutes before he is again in full control of
his reflexes. If *Hamlet* is a long-distance race, *Scapin* is the 800
metres, and everybody knows that 800 metres is a very difficult
race to run. Once when I was in Buenos Aires I was curious
enough to take my blood pressure before the start of the play
and immediately after the scene of the 'sac'. From 7.11 it had
gone up to 9.165. Every race must be run in its own particular
way. The actor is like a jockey, he rules his character, or, like one
of Goya's witches, he gets on his horse and plunges into the night
for his infernal race. There are parts which require a fast start,
a sustained tempo with some spurts here and there and then a
slight slackening off as if one were travelling on one's acquired
speed, in order to gather strength for the final speed burst of the

[1] Scapin's tricks, or ploys.

T.J.B.—D

end. Other parts require that the actor should keep his strength in reserve as long as possible until a given bend of the race. The actress who plays Phèdre[1] must rein in her mount during the first act; she must in fact hold her back, and she must continue to control her during the second act (Hyppolyte's declaration). She lets her go in the third act—long strides, deep breathing, fluent diction, avoiding tensing up. Like that she will be prepared to give everything in the fourth act—muscular strength, heart, nerves, senses and intellect. In the first two acts the fire is smouldering; it begins to crackle up with Hyppolyte's declaration, but it only catches on under the wind of the third, and it only spreads and brings down the building in the fourth. In the fifth, we have the smouldering ashes. This way of running the race sets out the worth of the part. Just as small unfinished patches in Despiau's busts enhance the beauty of his work, in the same way it is useful to slacken off for certain brief moments during which actor and public gather strength for the best moment when they will get drunk together. The problem of timing belongs to the rule of control. There are very many rules of control for the actor, and there comes to mind one which I find extremely difficult to apply: it is the rule of relaxation. There are so many exercises to bring about relaxation, but they are not easy to carry out and good results are few.

It seems to me that one of the most important causes of tension is timidity. It is possible to crave to get into somebody else's skin, and to have the gift of changing personality in order to become a character, but only when one is by oneself, and not before spectators. Timidity renders such an operation impossible. In the presence of the public certain actors become nervous and tense and lose the best part of their means. As they cannot relax, they are likely to be unable to infuse the character that they are playing with the sincerity, the authenticity and spontaneity which it requires. In order to avoid these pitfalls, one must concentrate on the most important rule of all, that of concentration and control of the will. This is the foundation of the whole discipline of acting. There are many excellent exercises for the development of the art of concentration and control of the will which are the basic principles of acting. The rest is silence, and that is, I think, true for theatrical

---

[1] Phaedra.

performances as well as for musical performances, which only exist in order to cause silence to vibrate.

ABOUT DICTION
(Concerning *Phèdre*)

THE LANGUAGE
Il n'y a pas encore des mots, il n'y a que des syllabes et des rythmes. [1]

—PAUL VALÉRY:
De la diction des vers.

THE ALEXANDRINE (IAMBIC HEXAMETER)

The verse used in *Phèdre* is the alexandrine. The alexandrine is a line of twelve syllables, some unstressed, some stressed, either according to the normal rule of linguistics or to the requirements of sense. The rhythm of the alexandrine depends on the subtle blends or contrasts established between the stressed and the unstressed syllables. Besides the fact that it has twelve syllables, the alexandrine is divided into 'rhythmical elements' which are groups of words, each expressing one simple and single notion. The accent, whether linguistic or rhetorical, is generally placed on the last syllable of any rhythmic group. The alexandrine is generally divided into hemistichs by a pause which comes after the sixth syllable.

Que toujours dans vos vers le sens coupant des mots
Suspende l'hémistiche et marque le repos.
—BOILEAU, *Art poétique.*

The pause can never be in the middle of a rhythmic group; therefore, since the rhythmic group must end with an accented syllable, and since the sixth syllable of the alexandrine necessarily terminates a rhythmic group, this sixth syllable must necessarily carry a stress. In the seventeenth century the alexandrine was not allowed to overflow; the meaning had to coincide with the line, therefore the twelfth and last syllable could not but be stressed. In spite of this strict rule, there are two overflowing lines in *Phèdre*; the first is in line 423, when Aricie says—

[1] There are no words yet, there are only syllables and rhythms.

> J'ai perdu dans la fleur de leur jeune saison,
> Six frères . . .

The second is at line 1,445, Aricie again—

> Mais tout n'est pas détruit, et vous en laissez vivre
> Un . . .

Besides the two main pauses, one after the sixth and the other after the twelfth syllable, the hemistich can be subdivided into the various rhythmic groups, of which the most important are:

(1) Division in three groups of two syllables each:
2/2/2, each of them comprising either:
2 stressed
1 stressed and 1 unstressed
1 unstressed and 1 stressed
2 unstressed

(2) Division in two groups of three syllables each:
3/3, each group comprising either:
3 stressed
2 stressed and 1 unstressed
1 stressed and 2 unstressed
1 unstressed and 2 stressed
2 unstressed and 1 stressed
3 unstressed
1 stressed, 1 unstressed and 1 stressed
1 unstressed, 1 stressed and 1 unstressed

(3) Division in two groups, one of two syllables, the other of four syllables, disposed as 2/4 or 4/2. The group of two syllables can have all the permutations of accents of the first division. The group of four syllables generally comprises:
3 unstressed and 1 stressed
3 stressed and 1 unstressed
or
2 stressed and 2 unstressed
etc.
with possibilities of other patterns.

(4) Division in three groups comprising:
the first—1 syllable
the second—2 syllables
the third—3 syllables

so that one may have 1/2/3, 1/3/2, 3/1/2
or 3/2/1 . . . etc., each group having the same possibility
of permutation as outlined in the preceding divisions.

Exception: the alexandrine can be divided into three groups of
four syllables each; in this case of course the sixth syllable could
not be stressed, but alexandrines of such a type are very rare.
There are some in Boileau and apparently none in *Phèdre*.

Analogy with Classical Prosody:
These divisions based on the qualitative value of the syllable
present certain analogies with Greek and Latin prosody. If one
accepted the principle that all unstressed syllables correspond to a
short one and a stressed to a long one, one would find in the preceding divisions: spondees, trochees, iambs, pyrrhics, anapests,
etc., with a marked predominance of iambs and anapests. We shall
not attempt to decompose each alexandrine into the feet of classical
prosody, yet although it is preferable to discover intuitively the
individual rhythm of the alexandrine, it is quite useful to be able
to check it according to the laws of prosody. In French, the only
thing that seems to matter is whether any given syllable is stressed
or unstressed. Nevertheless there are some poets, and some among
the greatest, who insist that there could be a real prosody of French
verse, at least for the spoken verse. Claudel was one of these poets
('Réflexions sur la vie française', in *Positions et Prépositions*, Vol. 3);
Gide also discussed this problem in his *Journal* and in the course
of some imaginary interviews. This is, one must admit, a very
delicate problem, and we must confess that the more we explore
it, the more we realize that besides the question of stressed and
unstressed syllables there is also the problem of long and short
syllables. One might remark at this juncture that a long syllable
is not worth two short.

THE HIATUS AND LIAISONS
There are people who say that to make or not to make liaisons is
purely a matter of taste. In the seventeenth century they observed
the liaisons. The conclusion seems to be that liaisons must be
used with taste and discrimination. In the seventeenth century,
the word *Achéron* was pronounced as if the *ch* were soft. Lulli
insisted that it should be pronounced in the Italian way, therefore
hard; Racine was against it, so there was the 'operatic' diction

which used *A-kéron*, and the 'theatre' diction which insisted on
Achéron with a soft *ch*. In the seventeenth century the *r* of the
infinitive was pronounced. They said 'chantai*r*', and that of course
did away with the liaison. Molière was supposed to have had a
serious discussion about the liaison in the expression: *l'un et
l'autre*. Molière did not make the liaison; somebody else insisted
that the liaison should be made; the conclusion was that *l'un et
l'autre* with the liaison was the Norman pronunciation (cf. Corneille)
while *l'un et l'autre* without liaison was the French way. These
examples show clearly that there was no general agreement about
the liaison.

Inconvenience of Liaison:

(1) Abuse of liaisons can falsify the meaning and the musicality
of the line.
(2) In connecting together the various rhythmic elements as
if they were a long garland one renders the meaning more
difficult to grasp.
(3) The vowels lacking the support which they need in order to
have shape, lose their character and tend to fall into the
pronunciation of a soft *e*. Diction becomes soft and grey,
and loses its individual flavour and colour.
(4) The stressed syllables are slurred and there is a tendency
to have all syllables made to sound as if they were unstressed.
(5) The meaning of the sentence might change; speeches are
all the more laden with meaning when the liaisons are
used sparingly.

There are practically no rules for the use of liaisons in poetry, but
there are rules for their use in prose. These rules could be applied
for the speaking of the alexandrine according to the wishes of each
individual speaker. Most of these rules are taken from the *Traité
de prononciation française* by Maurice Grammont. The most
important rule is that liaisons can be made within a rhythmic
group, but not between one group and the following. One can
have a liaison between an unstressed syllable and the next, but
one cannot have a liaison based on a stressed syllable. For instance:
ces peti(ts) z'enfants/ont perdu leur chemin. Such a rhythmic
group generally ends with an accented syllable; it is therefore

normal that this syllable should not be connected with the one which follows; according to this rule one can say that the sixth syllable of the alexandrine, which is always stressed, practically never takes the liaison: ex: 'Le(s) z'ombres par trois fois/on(t) t'obscurci les cieux.' In certain cases (particularly at the caesura), Ronsard used strongly to advocate the clash of two vowels in order to produce a marvellous effect of harshness, but we know that between Ronsard and Racine there was not only Malherbe but also Boileau.

> Ronsard . . .
> Réglant tout, brouilla tout, fit un art à sa mode.
>   —BOILEAU, *Art poétique.*

Other rules:

(1) Monosyllabic words, such as pronouns, articles, prepositions and conjunctions, which are used as accessories, always take the liaison when they come first, and do not, when they come second. For instance:

le(s) z'hommes, but: avons-nou(s) eu tort?

One says: Allez-vou(s) z'en, because 'vous' comes before *en* which is an integral part of the 's'en aller'.

(2) The same rule applies to the adjective. There is a liaison between adjective-substantive and no liaison between sub-stantive-adjective. For instance:

un lon(g) k'hiver
des travau(x) admirables.

There are cases in which the liaison completely alters the meaning of a sentence. For instance:

Un savan(t) t'aveugle, means a blind man who is learned, and un savan(t) aveugle, means a learned man who is blind.

(3) There is a liaison in ready-made expressions, such as *mot-à-mot,* but one must carefully note the difference between, for instance: avoir un pie(d) t-à-terre, which means to have a small lodging or a shooting box, and: avoir un pie(d) à terre, which means to have one foot on the ground.

(4) A very important rule concerns the words ending in *rs*; there is no liaison with the final *s* unless it indicates the plural. For instance:

Je vais ver(s) elle, and not ver(s) z'elle,
toujour(s) aimer, and not toujour(s) z'aimer.

Many actors make an excessive use of these liaisons with
s, when it is much more euphonious not to do so. The
liaison with the s should only be used to indicate the plural,
such as:

Dans quel(s) z'heureux climats.

(5) There is no liaison with words beginning with h when h has
the value of a consonant, with numbers, or with 'oui'; for
instance:

un/héros
les/onze
les/oui.

The hiatus is tolerated here, and today it is also tolerated
for nasals. Molière won the battle over l'un et l'autre, one
says: Néron/est amoureux.

(6) The word 'sang' does not make the liaison with a 'k'. With
the nasal sound 'an', the hiatus is tolerated. What weakens
considerably the rule of the hiatus is the tolerance granted to
it in the case of e mute and nasals. For instance:

Aricie/a son coeur

The Hiatus: Opinions about the hiatus have varied throughout the
centuries; some writers advocated it, others were against it;
Ronsard, Valéry, Claudel, have all discussed this problem. This
is what Charpentier said in his book: *De l'excellence de la langue
française*, published in 1683, six years after the creation of *Phèdre*:
'On the contrary, the French language, by sounding two vowels
which meet, has retained the sweetness of Greek pronunciation.
Thus:

on louera éternellement la bonté ineffable de Dieu et la
charité ardente et infatigable des premiers chrétiens qui a
été admirée de leurs ennemis mêmes.

The meeting of all these vowels introduces a kind of harmony of
speech, which could not possibly exist if every vowel was always
followed by a consonant. Thus, it is far more harmonious to say:
Ce Roy a qui . . . rather than: Ce Roy de qui . . . because as
the diphthong is followed by a vowel, one cannot drop the voice
after *Roy*, one must on the contrary make a slight pause which adds
to the majesty of speech.' Such is the opinion of a good Greek

scholar of the seventeenth century. Racine also was a Greek scholar, and he was unlikely to protest against these views. The hiatus has the advantage of compelling the actor to articulate properly. It might produce a slightly harder but also a more tripping diction, and it certainly is more individual and more laden with meaning. If, thanks to the *e* mute and to the nasals, the hiatus does not exist in the written language in phrases like '*Néron est amoureux*' or '*le joug que Thésée a subi tant de fois*', it exists in the spoken language. We can find many examples of it in *Phèdre*.

Consonant Vowels: When two vowels meet in spoken language, there is a practical way of avoiding the harsh effect of the liaison; it consists in transforming the second vowel into a consonant by a swift movement of the glottis. For instance:

Mais sa haine sur vous/autrefois(s) z'attachée.

These vowels which we shall call consonant vowels are sometimes used at the beginning of certain rhythmic groups. For example in: 'Aricie a sa foi', we have two hiatuses. All in all the point to bear in mind is that liaisons should be used very sparingly.

PLASTIC VALUE OF VOWELS AND CONSONANTS
Sometimes a vowel, a consonant or an interplay of vowels and consonants can have such a physical and direct impact that the listener feels the deep meaning of those words before he has time to grasp such meaning by rational processes. Thanks to the sound value of vowels and consonants, speech has an incantatory and magic power which is of the greatest importance in the theatre. Vowels and consonants have on the whole a mimetic origin. One has only to observe the facial gymnastics of any speaker to realize the truth of this suggestion. Nine times out of ten the mouth imitates physically the action represented by the words. One can quote as instances: pout, disgust, superb, tailor, to grind, to blast, to spin, to fire, to pull, exchange, sale, etc. . . . It was only in the nineteenth century that particular attention was paid to the sound value of words; in the seventeenth century this was not an important point, nevertheless one cannot neglect this aspect in the case of such a precise writer as Racine. Without trying to make too much of the whistling effects of the famous line: 'Pour qui sont ces serpents qui sifflent sur vos têtes', there are plenty of

instances in *Phèdre* where the musical blend of vowels and consonants adds to the meaning, for instance:

'J'ai pris la vie en haine' is like a lash of the whip.

> L'essieu crie et se rompt. L'intrépide Hippolyte
> Voit voler en éclats tout son char fracassé.

or

> . . . les campagnes de Crète
> Offrent au fils de Phèdre . . .

or: 'le peuple pour le voir court et se précipite', in which we have two long syllables—*voir* and *court* framed by the tripping syllables of the beginning and the end of the line which show the rhythm and the physical movement of the crowd.

> Athènes me montra mon superbe ennemi
> Je le vis, je rougis, je pâlis à sa vue, etc. etc. . . .

Here one can see again the admirable use of long and short syllables; the longer one lingers over the *thè* of Athènes, the *er* of su*per*be, the *i*'s, and the *u* of *vue*, of the following line, the more resplendent Hippolytus is, and naturally, the more Phèdre admires him. If we scan these two lines we have: an iamb/a paeon/an anapest/a cretic, and an anapestic line.

DIFFERENT ASPECTS OF THE ALEXANDRINE

The alexandrines do not always have the same aspect; their quality varies with the part which they play, and their very varied aspects fill up the intervals between prose and song. First, we have what might be called the *action alexandrine*, which is muscular, clear and precise, and which paws the ground like a restless horse. In such moments the actors move at speed, the outlines of the character are clear, everybody is awake and active. Act II, Scene 3, comprises a typical group of these action alexandrines (561–70); in the same act, Scene 6, we have a new charge of these alexandrines which rush to the end of the act at lightning speed. These alexandrines seem to be slightly uncouth, their main quality is 'speed' and they are the most clear, not to say the most prosaic and 'earthy' of all the alexandrines.

Then we have what could be called the *basic alexandrine* which is the very framework of tragedy; it stands like a mast and it is the hinge round which gravitate desires, answers, prayers and imprecations, that is to say the 'period' and 'recitative' parts of the play.

If one extracted these alexandrines and placed them one behind the other, one would have a summary of the whole action of the play. Let us take an example:

Act I, Scene 1, from line 75:

> Tu sais combien mon âme, attentive à ta voix
> S'échauffait au récit de ses nobles exploits [referring to Thésée]

> Mais quand tu récitais des faits moins glorieux,
> Sa foi partout offerte et reçue en cent lieux

> Tu sais comme à regret écoutant ce discours
> Je te pressais souvent d'en abréger le cours,

> Et moi-même, à mon tour, je me verrais lié?

Here are seven basic alexandrines, part of a group of twenty-two alexandrines which carry the woof of the action and connect it with Hippolyte's great monologue of Scene 1.

Side by side with these two types of alexandrines there is another type of writing which prepares the reader or listener for entrance into a dream-world, and which culminates in the period. The period is an impressionistic type of writing and its effect is incantatory; its aim is to use the music of the words to transform the atmosphere and to prepare the dawning of a reality which is more real than perceptual reality. A period comprises a certain number of alexandrines which act upon the spectator not indirectly, but collectively and cumulatively. It is not what it says that is important but the music of it which expresses the ideas that it contains. Thus the group of lines going from 9 to 14 forms a period in which the music of the proper nouns conveys to us a physical sensation of Théramène's journey in search of Thésée. The period therefore warms up the temperature of a scene and brings it to a point where delirium, vision, dream or hallucination takes over. Let us consider for instance Act III, Scene 3, from line 869 to line 909 and let us pick out the basic alexandrines:

Oenone
Il n'en faut point douter, je les plains l'un et l'autre;
Jamais crainte ne fut plus juste que la vôtre.
Mais ne me trompez point, vous est-il cher encore?
De quel oeil voyez-vous ce prince audacieux?

Phèdre
Je le vois comme un monstre effroyable à mes yeux.

Oenone
Pourquoi donc lui céder une victoire entière?
Vous le craignez? Osez l'attaquer la première,
Du crime dont il peut vous charger aujourd'hui.

Phèdre
Moi, que j'ose opprimer et noircir l'innocence?

Oenone
Mon zèle n'a besoin que de votre silence
Je parlerai.
On vient, je vois Thésée.

The other thirty-eight alexandrines form a period which with its swift movement, its stops, counterpointed rhythms and its murmurs and muffled sounds of Oenone's contralto voice (like wood knocking on wood) conveys to us a physical impression of two people caught in a trap and forms an impressionistic picture of all the ideas which criss-cross their minds. Thésée, the straightforward growing threat (something which could be represented musically by a continuous note which would rise through buzzing to stridency), is coming back. The two women, particularly Oenone, since Phèdre is unable to do anything coherent, hurriedly try to restore some order in and about themselves. Having sought refuge in a dark corner of the stage which has the semi-darkness of an alcove, they emit sounds which show the distraught disorderly state of their minds. To conclude, one can say that the period is a group of alexandrines, the main effect of which rests on rhythm and music; it is a means of removing us from reality and of exercising an hypnotic effect which is the prelude to feverish excitement.

ABOUT DICTION

THE RECITATIVE

On ne peut prendre trop de précautions pour ne rien mettre sur le théâtre qui ne soit très nécessaire. [1]
—RACINE (Préface de *Mithridate*)

The recitative is the most difficult obstacle which confronts the actor. The difficulty rests in the fact that the actor can only grasp all the implications and the full meaning of the recitative if he

[1] One can never take enough precautions so as to avoid putting in drama anything which is not absolutely necessary.—Racine.

himself has reached the state of awakened dream called the lyrical state, which is a state of 'extra lucidity' not far from ecstasy. There is a tendency to believe that the recitative is a separate piece which the author has inserted as a kind of poetic digression which should be delivered in a style different from the rest of the play. In *Phèdre*, for instance, the passage which is unfailingly cast for this kind of misinterpretation is Théramène's famous narrative which if it is considered out of context is of course rather long. In fact there is in the recitative a sudden change of rhythm, or a change in the speed of speech, something similar to going into a higher gear in order to attain a greater speed, although the engine goes more slowly. The lyrical state is a general broadening out of thought and sensations, and this change cannot take place without the intermittence of a quite normal passage. Just as it is necessary to declutch in order to change gear, so in the same way, in order that the recitative might be, as Racine says, 'necessary', it can only come into play through a kind of mental declutching comparable with delirium. The best image of the recitative is in fact that of a plane about to take off. Before taking off, the plane taxies along the runway, its engine generating greater and greater thrust so as to reach the maximum power; the plane runs along the ground bumping, tossing about and vibrating as if it were going through a real 'crisis' of vitality and movement. Then suddenly while the roar of the engine continues, the plane seems to become motionless, as if it had reached a kind of neutral flat level and given up its attempts to leave the ground; but the earth and the trees fleeing by show that the plane is airborne and steadily climbing up. The recitative has begun. At the end of its flight when the plane returns to earth, there is again the same bumpy movement and agitation as at the moment of taking off. A recitative is always situated between two periods of agitation or movement, and the graph of its development could be described as follows:

(1) Crisis of agitation or movement.
(2) A strange brief moment when the rhythm changes and a new rhythm is established.
(3) The flight of the recitative, its rise and fall.
(4) A sudden return to agitation and movement.

A singer of a Wagnerian opera gives an excellent picture of the pattern of the recitative. He starts with two or three quick steps, plants himself solidly on his splay legs and gathers up all his energy; after that, he seems to have lost all trace of agitation and suddenly the song rises, follows its parabola and finally dies down. After that the singer, after a few vague movements and shudders, seems to return to earth. The recitative seems to be a natural way of expressing human feelings in certain situations. Imagine for one moment somebody sitting drowned in tears by the dead body of a dear being; his grief is such that his nerves are at breaking point and he feels as if he were about to choke. Suddenly he stops, gets up and he who was so upset before, now finds the strength to extol the virtues of the dead person. Why does he torment himself like that? He describes all his good points and his most admirable actions; that description takes him to the illness and death of the person whose loss he mourns. Then he comes down to earth, becomes again conscious of reality and sinks again into despair and a painful agitation which seems to be about to break his nerves. *Phèdre* is strewn with recitatives and each one of them is more beautiful and more moving than the other. Let us examine for instance the recitative of Phèdre's declaration (Act I, Scene 3).

(1) The agitation begins with line 247, 'Ciel! que lui vais-je dire, etc.'[1] and it fades away by line 258: 'Je péris la dernière et la plus misérable.'[2]

(2) Level stretch before 'take off': from line 260 to 265: Phèdre has stopped tossing about on her chair as if she were so weak and depressed that she could not entertain the slightest hope; she stiffens up; she has a glazed, far-away look, her face sags and she looks a broken-down puppet. She can hardly hear Oenone who is pressing her with questions; she seems to be completely unmindful of the ways which Oenone uses in order to extract the truth from her; she smiles, sweetly and with relief, when she says: 'c'est toi qui l'as nommé', in fact she no longer is quite the same and she can hardly hear the cries uttered by Oenone who is like an ancient mourner. She cannot hear them because she no longer is present in mind as she is in body.

(3) Suddenly she begins to lift up:

A peine au fils d'Egée
Par les lois de l'hymen je m'étais engagée . . .[3]

[1] Heavens! What shall I say to him.
[2] I am the last to die, and am the most wretched.
[3] I had no sooner become the wife of Aegeus's son than . . .

the recitative has begun, it rises to its zenith:

C'est Vénus tout entière à sa proie attachée [1]

then falls with lines 307 and 308.

(4) With line 309 agitation reappears. Phèdre has returned to bumpy earth, and she laments and turns towards Oenone for help; she looks exhausted; her rhythm of speech slackens and at the end the last alexandrine (316) is no more than a whisper.

Common Chords: Some alexandrines seem to be like common chords in music; they are used as starting points for a recitative, but more often they are used as its crown; for instance:

Mon arc, mes javelots, mon char, tout m'importune [2]

we have six iambs, or:

Le jour n'est pas plus pur que le fond de mon coeur [3]

one iamb, one paeon, and two anapests.

Des princes de ma race, antiques sépultures [4]

one iamb, one paeon, one iamb, one paeon.

The relationships between the long (or stressed) syllables are comparable to all common chords in music.

The great advantage of these remarks is that they cannot be transformed into rules.[5] They are above all a schematic set of reflections placed at the disposal of the good taste of any actor. The most striking aspect of spoken French is its pliability, it is truly the language of free men, and it is because the French language is the language of free men that we think it fitting to submit to certain disciplines. May these reflections be regarded as a mark of politeness towards our language.

CONCERNING EMOTION

Emotion is a state which the actor must never be conscious of. One can only become conscious of an emotion which has already passed, for the act of consciousness dissipates the actual emotion.

[1] It's undivided Venus concentrating upon her prey.
[2] My bow, my spears, my chariot, everything bores me.
[3] The day is not purer than the bottom of my heart.
[4] Ancient tombs of the princes of my race.
[5] We are nevertheless convinced that they could become the basis of a solfeggio of diction which would be very useful.

The actor only lives in the present and he continually jumps from one present to another, carrying out actions which are bathed in a kind of vapour which is the appropriate emotion. This vapour is as much a part of his acting as juice is a part of fruit; but if he becomes conscious of it, the vapour fades away and the acting dries up.

No actor could act his own genuine emotion. Actors who wish to make use of emotions are therefore compelled to fake them, but their tears, their trembling voices and shaking hands do not delude the discriminating public, which is the very one they try to please. 'I know that I please those whom I must please' says the Antigone of Sophocles.

One cannot say to oneself: 'I am moved', without ceasing to be so; one can say 'I was moved', or better still, 'I was probably moved'. In the present one can only say: 'He or she is moved', for one can only be aware of another person's emotion. It is therefore the public which has the strange joy of perceiving and enjoying the emotion lived by the actor. If the actor, whether he is moved or not, is himself moving, the public has nothing to say or think, it has only to enjoy the emotion. To sum up, one can say that emotions are very elusive phenomena little discussed in the theatre, where spectators and actors, although they move under their impact, are only concerned with actions. Whether the actor cries or not, does not matter; the essential thing is that he should make the audience cry. In the case of tragedy, which requires a great physical effort, too much emotion could be harmful. The more the tragic actor manages to convey emotions through rhythm, the less he will have to use his nerves to transmit it, and therefore the more, of course, he will remain in possession of his strength so as to use it in the difficult and tense moments of the play. When collective emotion in a theatre reaches an unbearable pitch, the spectators have a reaction which reveals their extreme tension and at the same time slackens it and renders it more bearable— they applaud. In such cases, the emotion is so strong and the illusion so perfect that the spectators are no longer quite sure as to where they are; they may have thought that Nero himself was on the stage, and in order to regain their equilibrium they applaud the actor who is playing that part. The applause is therefore a mechanism of defence against an emotion which was becoming too strong for comfort. The emotion is less a state than a reaction, and it is as such that it can interest us.

Let us see what kind of reaction it is. To act is to struggle, and to struggle implies the existence of two antagonistic forces. When at the climax of the struggle one of the two contending forces is on the point of being overwhelmed, it seeks refuge in a kind of magical reaction which we call emotion. This reaction generally assumes one of the following forms:

(1) It causes the complete disappearance of the force against which it struggles.
(2) It can artificially transform this force by diminishing its power.
(3) It causes its own disappearance.
(4) It transforms itself magically and turns itself into something more dangerous than it was previously.

Thus, through an illusory disappearance or transformation of the force which opposes us, we think that we can either escape or conquer it, or we might hope to obtain the same results by the disappearance or by the transformation of our own selves. For instance, if I have to walk across a dangerous patch of ground, I whistle and walk in a carefree manner as if I did not care about anything. In reality I suppress the danger artificially. Suddenly an armed aggressor springs on me; I faint and in reality I cause my own disappearance. When I awaken I realize that policemen are trying to bring me back to life; their behaviour shows that they have a very low opinion of my frightened state. That makes me feel ashamed; what can I do? I get angry and insult them; in truth, I make myself more fearsome than I am in reality; in their turn they too get angry and threaten to arrest me for insulting behaviour; I then rock with laughter. In reality, I metamorphose them into friends or 'chums', I magically transform the atmosphere and I turn this whole incident into a farce. Back home, I fall into a sultry mood; nobody can extract a word from me; I behave like an amnesiac; my family concludes that I am sad. In reality my whole being concentrates upon forgetfulness; I have successively gone through fear, laughter and sadness. Dramatic characters behave in just the same way, and their reactions in moments of great emotion are the best illustrations of their character. Lorenzo's fainting fit at the moment of the duel, Hamlet's shout of 'a rat, a rat!' when he kills Polonius; Phèdre superimposing Theseus's image on that of Hippolytus in the scene of the declaration, are

T.J.B.—E

facts which enable us to know the souls of these various characters.

Thus the actor need no more concern himself with emotions as such, than he concerns himself with his perspiration in the course of the performance. But he must, on the contrary, attach importance to emotions viewed as means of behaviour and actions, and that will lead him to realize that characters never pause for one moment in the middle of their actions in order to offer gratuitous displays of feeling. They are involved in continuous actions and reactions; they argue, they plead, they discuss, they fight against others or against themselves, they delude themselves and others, sometimes in good faith, sometimes in bad faith, but they never stop. The spectator might try to analyse their behaviour, feelings and emotions, but for the actor who is caught in the middle of the dramatic game, there is nothing else but action.

CONCERNING GESTURES

Until now I have loved miming too much, and I still care too much about anything connected with bodily expression, not to express myself on this topic with the utmost frankness. After the exciting performances with masks carried out at the Vieux-Colombier under the direction of Suzanne Bing, after the sometimes striking discoveries of Etienne Decroux, after our attempts —perhaps not sustained enough, and after the constant and successful efforts of Marcel Marceau and some of his disciples, I have the feeling that the art of miming is now once more at an impasse. Everything changes so quickly nowadays. The life of the theatre which in the past progressed at walking speed, has been for the past few years moving at racing speed. Today, taste in the theatre no longer walks, it gallops.

Like sportsmen who have been over-trained, one finds oneself 'sickened' by a lot of things. Today, for instance, one finds it difficult to look at water-colour sketches for stage décors or settings; although one tries to say to oneself that this water-colour will be transformed into wood or clothes, it always leaves a kind of sour taste in the mouth, and when one looks at décors made for the stage one cannot help being aware that they have been made according to a sketch, whether it was a water-colour or something else. The reason for the success of Scapin's dress lies in the fact that Bérard had not painted any preliminary models. I am perhaps overstressing the after-effect of certain impressions, but the fact nevertheless remains that one is sickened by too much 'poeticality', too great a concern with 'plasticity' and also by certain aspects of miming. Whence comes this saturation, this rather sickening feeling caused by excess? How is it that when, in the course of auditions, I ask for two or three minutes of miming in order to ascertain the actor's gift of expression, I can no longer bear to watch certain incredible contortions which try to pass for the stylization of simple gestures such as lifting a pencil from a desk or drawing a line on a sheet of paper? There is obviously something wrong in the field of the gesture at this moment, and I am the first to be concerned about it.

A mime ought to be able to move about with much greater simplicity than any other person who does not possess, as he does, the knowledge of his own body; for to be a mime is first and foremost to possess an excellent knowledge and mastery of one's body. How is it then that the young people who try to practise miming cannot make the least gesture without overlaying it with garlands of useless movements which distort the very architecture of their gestures? The result is a kind of visual mannerism which, if it were transposed into speech, would be utterly unbearable. Yet miming is a means of expression which is practically as rich as speech, but while one is taught speech in a way which enables each one of us to add, through individual inflexion and tone, the marks of one's own personality, miming seems on the contrary to be taught or passed on with the intonation already glued on to it. Therefore it is no longer possible to express oneself in a personal manner through a language which is already fixed in an unchanging form.

A language, or any other means of expression, can only be useful if it is impersonal, so that everyone has the possibility of adding to it his own manner or personality. This is the only way to keep a language alive, and one cannot think of a whole people using exactly the same compulsory inflexions and tones of speech. Confronted with such a phenomenon, one is likely to be overwhelmed by the same feeling of sickness which I mentioned before.

Let me make clear the fact that it is not the value of miming which is questioned, but the use which is now made of it. My words are addressed to those who sincerely love miming and who devote to it a good part of their time and sometimes at the cost of heavy sacrifices. I am not betraying a cause in which I believe, I remain with the friends with whom I share the love of bodily expression, and I am not trying to encourage those whose bodies are stiff, and who, as born 'sitters', despise, deny and reject the practised skill of miming which is undeniably an art. Indeed, if I choose to sound the alarm against this distorted and overmannered way of practising miming, it is because it plays into the hands of those who oppose miming and who, making use of these weaknesses, fasten upon them in order to condemn and to ridicule the very principle of miming. My strictures and warnings are therefore specifically addressed to those who have faith in the art of miming, and they are meant to contribute towards the fight against those who believe in the woodenness of the body and who seek refuge in words and words only, not out of love for them, but out of sheer mental laziness. Besides, it is good to have doubts and to look sometimes at problems, not as if they were already solved, but on the contrary as if they were insoluble, for when a solution is found, the joy is all the greater and our faith is renewed.

Can the body, axled on the spine, fed and strengthened through the respiratory bellows, contain a natural means of expression worthy of being called a language? The answer seems to be evident, for if language comprises the basic elements which are the subject, the verb and the object, the body also comprises these three fundamental elements, which are: the attitude, the gesture and the indication. 'The warrior draws his sabre.' If the spoken language is well stocked with epithets, adverbs, indirect objects, interjections, exclamations, participles, etc., mimed language is just as well supplied. For instance, 'the angry warrior throws in the air the scabbard of his broken sabre, falling to the ground, etc. . . .' Therefore the language of miming is as rich as spoken language.

Speech, whatever its kind, always requires an interlocutor. Let us imagine somebody who can speak with his body; to whom could he address himself? He will find very few people capable of understanding his language, for if it were not so, they would not walk, sit down, move around the way they do. The task therefore consists in rediscovering the art of miming and in educating a public up to it. A first step has already been taken. Thanks to the efforts of a few people there is a public ready to accept miming, and it is just because there is already such a public that one must not sicken it with certain distortions which are now imposed on miming.

What are the chief difficulties of the art of miming? As long as miming remains objective, that is to say as long as it seems to be a kind of exercise, simply destined to create the illusion that a given object exists, it is useless. It may amuse for five minutes but it soon becomes boring. One says to oneself, 'When I was a child this kind of game was called playing at being tradesmen. *Guess!* You are at the dentist's—No, I am drinking; you are sawing a piece of wood. No, I am ironing my shirt . . .', etc. Another inconvenience of miming whenever it attempts to ape or to follow too closely the spoken word, is that it looks too much like a lame kind of art or a dumb language. One is tempted to say, 'This actor is gifted, he only lacks words.' In this case, the mime makes faces and draws in the air all sorts of shapes which do not so much suggest states, but on the contrary suggest words. He may cause laughter, but in this case the mime or the pantomime only succeeds in producing an inferior art charming by its quaintness. On the other hand if the mime is a true poet who can rise above techniques or the notion of dumb theatre and transpose his gestures, he can realize the true physical poem or the motionless statue. Then he might be confronted with another difficulty, he runs the risk of not being understood. This is the aspect of miming which comes closest to true art, but it can also be a closed art, in fact all the more closed that the public is limited, and in this case the public is not sickened, but lost. What can one do? Does the concept of miming carry with it an inherent weakness which prevents it from reaching the level of the other arts? If it were so how could the silence and the solitude which exist within the noise and within society be expressed? Why is pantomime such a popular art? Because the average human being is not vocal. Could we represent the lampman better than by a figure completely dressed in white and silent—as silent as if he wore a mask and as white as solitude? Gestures often reveal the secrets which lurk behind them. Psychologists can detect the inhibitions of their patients by the gestures which they make while they talk. A doctor knows the true meaning of the gestures of a man who looks as if he were trying to reduce his tie to shreds, or of the woman who fumbles constantly with her handbag, when either of them is making a false confession. Gestures have a revealing power. I don't pretend to offer here a solution to the problem of miming. I only wish to restate the problem in general terms. As far as I am concerned, my point of view is that miming should not aim at being something simply visual, but a presence, that is to say the embodiment of a dramatic present. The visual aspect of things is only a means and not an end, in the same way as objective miming is a means and not an end. If miming is born from silence it means that it is essentially present. When I say nothing purely visual, I mean no attitudes purely for the sake of beauty or because it might simply be suggestion. The problem is not to be understood, the problem is to be evident, and of course one must not be incomprehensible on the pretence of poetry. Charlie Chaplin consented to make talking films only when he had mastered the whole technique. Miming must be used not as an object, but as part of dramatic expression. Miming is an essentially 'physical' art. Man is caught in his own special dimension and it is a death struggle; it is man himself who is put to death. It is a continuous state of siege. The five senses are on the alert, and the ninety-five other senses which, because of our ignorance, we lump all together into the vague, rich and complex sense of touch, are all ready at their receiving posts. The eyes placed in the head sweep around from their control tower; the eyes placed in the chest pierce the subterranean night. The whole body is bathed in a magnetic fluid which connects it with the outside world, before the mind comes into contact with objects. The spine sways, the abdominal muscles twitch, breathing reacts with the kind of sensitivity which one finds in snails' horns. The hundred dials of this thermo-nuclear machine have all been perfectly adjusted, and the plexus gives the order to advance. The spine displaces the body right up to the tiptoeing position, and just when the centre of the force of gravity is going to move out of the basis of equilibrium, that is to say, as Sganarelle would put it, at the precise moment when man is about to topple forward, his other leg swings forth and creates a new basis in which the law of gravity will again find its equilibrium. We need not talk of course of the countless wild adventures which may have taken place in these few seconds. It is in this state of permanent readiness to be put to death that the foundation of good miming lies. Everything in a good mime will be economical and will bear the imprint of masterly technique for he must save his strength, and everything will be pure and clean for that is the only way of progressing and surviving. Miming is the art of living and maintaining alive as long as possible what is alive, it is the art which makes full use of the 'natural radar' which has been put at our disposal; it is the art of the gesture. It is the 'anti-death' art, and it is something remote from fancy gestures, adornments and obsolescence. It is an art which starts from a tragic situation.

THE TRAGIC MIME

MAN AND HIMSELF

What is the internal world with which I have been entrusted during my existence? It is a fragile and mortal world. As soon as I find myself in possession of this internal world, I realize that my life is a continuous confrontation with death, and therefore a continuous struggle against time. One single battle-cry rises from the battle-field which is the body: to delay the moment of surrender, the 'moment of truth', and from the tips of my toes to the tip of my brain every part of my body is on the alert.

The resources of the body are very great, on condition, of course, that the different parts work with cohesion. Like well-fitted machines they could be grouped under four headings: (1) the gathering up of strength based on the visceral life; (2) the power of the body connected with sensual life; (3) the defence of the body connected with the nerves and the life of the senses; and (4) the realm of imitative controls connected with intellectual life and directing our whole behaviour. All this seems to be both evident and simple, but the mime must never forget the fact that every one of us holds under his control a perfect and complex world which is the exact replica of the ambient world. Man in his earthly journey carries with him a microcosm (his self) which is the reflection of the macrocosm (which is the universe). The life of the sky reflects itself in our hearts as the moon reflects itself in the glaucous waters of a well. The successive stages of our interior life manifest themselves in attitudes. From the moment the newly born babe lets out his first cry, he adopts an attitude. Every one of our attitudes influences the next one and is the result of our past attitudes. Each human attitude is a problem, the component parts of which have to be discovered. Why, for instance, is this man's right shoulder lower than the other? Is it because he is a conductor or because he is ill? Why is this one slightly hunch-backed? Is it because he does a lot of sowing or because he has had a great sorrow . . . what are the basic elements or component parts of this human problem? How can one grasp this attitude? This is the first problem of the mime: how to grasp the attitude or the inner man he wishes to portray.

MAN IN THE OUTSIDE WORLD

Let us close our inner eye and let us look through our windows. All around us lies the outside world which presses upon us, and makes proposals to us. From the pressures which weigh upon us we must have the power to choose and to absorb what has been chosen and to reject what has not been chosen. From the proposals proffered to us we must have the wisdom and the discrimination to accept only what is useful to us. These operations are carried out through instinct, experience and intelligence. Our relations with the outside world are pervaded with a kind of magnetism; the instinct is a kind of compass, the senses are a kind of radar set which lets us know in which direction our limbs should move in order to capture what we need, to avoid what is useless to us. The range of our senses is varied, and they also have different wave-lengths.

The sense of taste only comes if one has the external object 'on the tongue'. The sense of smell goes further; in man it is atrophied and it is much weaker than the sense of sight. With animals, on the contrary, the sense of smell is far more important than the two typically human senses, hearing and sight. But there is a magical sense which, though hardly known, leaves behind all the others, and it is the sense of touch; it is the sense which goes physically beyond us. Just as the earth is surrounded by an atmosphere, the living human being is surrounded by a magnetic aura which makes contact with the external objects without any concrete contact with the human body. This aura, or atmosphere, varies in depth according to the vitality of human beings. It could stretch into kilometres and that is why there are magicians who come to meet you without having been told of the date of your arrival. It is said that 'they have *seen* you', in fact they have been contacted in spite of the distance which separated them from you. The sense of touch is the divine sense. The expression—to have been touched by Divine Grace—has no figurative meaning. One talks about the finger of God, and the finger is the representative organ of touch. It is possible to believe that the saints who see Christ or His Holy Mother are put in a state of vision, thanks to a real contact from them. The sense of touch pierces through things and puts us in contact with the unknown or the invisible and is also the sense which reaches beyond accepted boundaries. The mime must first of all be aware of this boundless contact with things. There is no insulating layer of air between man and the outside world. Any man who moves about causes ripples in the ambient world in the same way as a fish does when it moves in water. The external and the internal world weigh upon each other in the body of man. To walk means to push something away: atmospheric pressure is not a grammar school teacher's fantasy, it is a constant weight against which man must struggle in order to ensure his very breathing. To illustrate this point here is a brief story attributed to a dunderhead, who was trying to pass the oral examinations of the 'Baccalauréat'. The examiner, bursting with indignation at the revelation of so much ignorance, shouted to the numskull who was sitting in front of him, 'What caused Philippe le Bel to ascend the throne?' and the candidate in a panic replied: 'Atmospheric pressure.' And this is not as impossible as it looks at first sight. Philippe, in his ambition, may have found it difficult to withstand atmospheric pressure, and he may well have believed that once he had ascended the throne he would breathe more easily. Atmospheric pressure is no mean force; it is the permanent symbol of our final downfall, and if we are not constantly on our guard, it might crush us at any moment; we must always oppose it with our skyward energy.

> Heureux celui qui peut d'une aile vigoureuse
> S'élancer vers les champs lumineux et sereins![1]

Thus the outside world contains both what we need and what we do not need. It is up to us to choose, through the indications supplied by our senses, our instincts and by the range of our minds. This is the second problem facing the mime, the problem concerning the point where man meets what is outside himself; after that we come to the third problem facing the mime which is that of his actions.

[1] Happy he who on strong wings
   Can rise towards serene and luminous heights.

MAN AND ACTION

Caught between two worlds, one of which is that of being in a
constant state of decay and the other offering both the means of
destruction and the means of salvation, man ceaselessly wages
a tragic struggle. The first world is the world of will, the other
is the world of power. Caught between these two forces man
must choose what is 'for himself' and what must remain 'out of
himself'. His present attitude, the result of his past attitudes,
supplies him with all the means he needs and which he uses in
accordance with the information which he has received. Every
part of his being is on the alert and goes into action. His thorax
insures both his voluntary and his instinctive breathing; his
diaphragm vibrates like a drum, his spine sways, his heart beats
the rhythm and the blood like the tide sweeps the body with
its to-and-fro movement. Man's struggle takes place on three
planes: the objective plane, the subjective plane and the imagina-
tive plane. Every form of human behaviour involves these three
planes. Firstly, behaviour exists objectively; that is to say
it is what it is, and is perceptible as such by the eyes of the on-
looker. Secondly, man may have an affective notion of his behaviour which more or less conforms to his real behaviour. For
instance, as far as the spectators are concerned, Hippolyte meets
Aricie because he cannot make up his mind to leave without seeing
her again. As for Hippolyte, he sees Aricie for the last time in order
to offer her the sovereignty of Attica; at least he thinks so, for he
has an affective apprehension of his behaviour which does not
correspond to its reality. This difference between two different
apprehensions of the same behaviour might rest upon good faith,
or upon bad faith. Thirdly, man has the imagination which
transforms and can metamorphose into something else, what is
objective or subjective. In certain critical situations a man who is in
a panic might transpose reality into an imaginary reality which
causes in him extreme reactions which we call emotions. If he
imagines that death no longer exists he is full of joy; if he imagines
that Polonius is nothing but a rat, he is trying to overcome his fear;
if he imagines that the outside world is no more varied than the grey
wall which is facing him, he can yield to his overwhelming sadness;
if he imagines that his enemy who was previously dangerous has
now become small and weak, he can give full rein to his anger,

etc. As far as the world of objects is concerned, the mime's approach is on the realistic plane; when dealing with subjective life he tries to express feelings. Through his imagination he transposes both feelings and reality into poetic reality, and from there he evolves a poetic art which in turn will become music, that is to say all in one—language, dance and song. Such a transposition is not a distortion, for poetry is not caricature. In the mysterious silence of life every aspect appears as an hallucinating and fascinating presence. The subjective reactions which are brought forth by this presence are extremely moving. Our imagination works on these elements, either in joy or in sadness, always in search of the truth from life which until death is movement rhythmed by time. Both our survival and our downfall depend upon this continuous struggle between us and the objects which surround us. One might go towards the object, reject it or avoid it; it is always 'for oneself', or 'out of oneself'; one might add to these two attitudes a third; the standstill attitude. Such are the three types of actions concerning the third problem of the mind which is that of action. Such seem to us the starting-points of the attempt to mime truth and also of tragic miming, the secret of which has nowadays been lost and which we should like to see revived.

IV

The Plays

PROBLEMS SET BY GREAT WORKS OF ART

PROBLEMS RAISED BY THE ORESTEIA

I have always had a great liking for Aeschylus. In 1941, at Roland-Garos Stadium I had produced, in daylight, the *Suppliants*, helped by the splendid music of Honegger, conducted by Charles Munch. In spite of these two masters, in spite of Obey's text, and in spite of the considerable help which I received from Paul Mazon, whom I could never praise enough, a dazzling sun had knocked us out. Paris was then occupied by the Germans, and blackout regulations made it impossible to play by night in the open air. It was a splendid June day; the firemen of Paris whose part was to simulate the capture of the ladies of the chorus, had a great time racing up and down the steps, too obviously built of cement. Great archaic statues made by the sculptor Collamarini were shining in the sun; plasters, glue and cardboard masks held no mystery in broad daylight, and every member of the audience, swept away by Honegger's music, preferred to follow the gambols of white clouds in the sky or the dance of the poplar trees rather than to follow attentively the sombre drama of the Danaids. This unsatisfactory experience nevertheless left me with happy memories, and with my admiration for Aeschylus unimpaired; I therefore promised myself to have a new try at one of his tragedies: *Hamlet*, *Le Soulier de Satin*, *Antony and Cleopatra* and *Phèdre* had whetted my appetite for great works. Claudel, who had written some remarkable pages about Aeschylus and Homer, was urging me to get to grips with Aeschylus as soon as possible. The Sorbonne's dramatic society for the production of ancient works had given an unforgettable performance of the *Persians*. I was thinking of the part of Prometheus which I had played in a radio production

64

of the *Ocean*, directed by Lugné-Poe, I was thinking about the *Seven Against Thebes* (Montherlant, when I was producing *Malatesta*, had pressed me to produce this play) and I was, of course, thinking of the *Oresteia* (Dullin's dream had always been to produce the *Agamemnon*). Last but not least, long conversations with Sartre had led me above all to see in drama a problem of justice. Aeschylus was precisely the dramatist who had dealt with the problem of justice in the theatre. But I must add that the seven tragedies of Aeschylus, fully alive for over twenty-four centuries, were not in desperate need of my help or personal services.

In the course of our visits abroad, I had had the occasion to witness occult séances, particularly in Brazil. I had been entranced with these popular ceremonies which come from Africa. I had tried, in spite of my work and social commitments, to get as much information as possible on these rites so as to grasp their meaning. The way in which someone, black or white, finds himself struggling with a spirit, the way in which a medium connects someone with that spirit, the way trances develop and the flat calm which follows the ritual of these nocturnal ceremonies, all these things had struck me and made me grow fond of these mysterious and attractive people. When we were in Rio, thanks to the introduction of a good friend, we went one night to a centre of occult séances. On that night they were celebrating the birthday of the great priest. The place where we went was situated not far from the Bank of Brazil, close to the market place and of course close to the harbour. It was an old and unimpressive building; we found ourselves at first in a dark, narrow corridor lit by an electric bulb hanging from a wire; at the end of the corridor a flight of steps led to the first floor; the whole place seemed silent; we passed through a door into a smaller corridor, and from there we heard what seemed like a normal hum of conversation, something one might hear in a sacristy before a ceremony. On the right there was a door opening on a wide hall looking like a gymnasium, or the fencing hall of a club. All along the walls there was a row of seats, separated from the rest of the hall by a thin wooden barrier. The middle of the hall was completely bare like a large arena. On one side of this rectangular hall a huge Christ was hanging on the wall; under it, there was a rectangular table fixed to the wall and jutting out from it. This table was covered with a white cloth, and on it there were all sorts of little objects pertaining to the magic and also to the Christian world; there was a St George and his dragon, a St Anthony and many other statues, together with triangles, stars, iron locks and some pearls. A man was seated by the side of the barrier; he looked as if he were in his sixties; he was dressed in ordinary clothes; his face was sunburnt and deeply furrowed with wrinkles, his hair was white and his eyes seemed huge, deep and piercing; he smiled gently and kept on chatting to one or two people in a low voice. On the other side of the table there was a kind of warming-pan from which incense rose slowly. As the audience increased, we were asked to go and sit down on the wooden seats, but without crossing our legs or arms. The audience was composed of Negro women of all ages—a good few of them were probably maids or employees of some kind, Negroes who were also workers or employees, all very clean, and many Europeans. There were as many men as there were women; they knew one another and were obviously a circle of simple and kind people. The presence of the priest who looked on and smiled, the huge Christ dominating the table with his sorrow, and the pervading scent of the incense, gave an unusual touch to this country-town cocktail party, as it were.

A company of men and women all dressed in white, short blouse and trousers, and singing a canticle, suddenly emerged from the corridor. A drum kept up the rhythm of this ancient choir whose members were walking one behind the other and beating time with their body and particularly with their legs (it's a mistake to believe that it is with one's hips that one keeps up a rhythm; on the contrary, it's above all with the feet and the knees, and the true samba is chiefly a matter of foot work). One by one they passed by the warming-pan, and in turn seemed to bathe in incense, rubbing their arms, their chest and their heads. They were led by a man in his fifties who was very thin. He wore a very intense expression and looked rather as if he were the chorus-master; in fact he was the medium; perhaps it is the same thing. As soon as they had passed by the warming-pan they bowed in front of the altar (the white-clothed table), looked at the cross and made the sign of the cross, waved their fists at Him, bowed again with fervour on the edge of the table and continued their rhythmic march, stressing every alternate step by flexing the knee, and finally ended in taking up various positions in the middle of the hall or arena.

Once the canticle was concluded, they formed a circle; after that there came a slight pause, during which cigars were lit. I have not sampled any of these cigars, but I could see that they were meant to induce hallucination. Instead of adopting the usual pose of the cigar-smoker, which consists in leaning back, cross-legged, in a comfortable armchair, and in trying to throw as far as possible light circles of smoke, the aim seemed to be to pump out the cigar as fast as possible and to smoke out one's neighbour. This smoke, added to the incense, thickened the atmosphere of the room; the high priest remained motionless with his quaint smile and deep gaze; he did not move during the whole evening; the ceremony was in his honour, so he had nothing to do. After this slight break, the medium started another canticle which was taken up by the choir, then he began to move around from one to the other, warming up, bending his head here and there to confide something to some members of the choir. Suddenly he began to shake a little, and to wheel round, then he retired, returned and continued his round of visits. The singing became more intense, the audience began to get caught up in it, and suddenly one of the choir singers was 'electrocuted' by the medium. Like a wounded man he bent forward and moved inside the circle. The spirit of the race had seized him, the tempo of the singing increased in intensity, the 'game' had started, and from then on, the audience wrapped in smoke began to sway with the rhythm of the song and with the shouting.

Let us now follow 'the wounded man'. At first, the others do not pay any attention to him. He looks surprised; something like a burning arrow has stuck in the middle of his heart: 'Ah me! What fire is this!' [1] He looks right and left, anxiously watching; then a sudden jerk, as if somebody or something had bitten him in the back of the neck; he puts his hand on it, winces with pain and, his body arched back, stands still a few seconds; then follow four or five seconds of intense physical excitement in the course of which the man looks as if he were violently sick or in the throes of spasms; his mouth is twisted, his eyes bulging out: 'Apollo, Apollo!' His two nearest neighbours who are not yet affected by the spirit keep an eye on him so as to protect him in case he is carried away too far. He then begins to whirl round like a top, while rising and crouching, bending and jumping, his face completely distorted, his mouth twisted, one eye closed, the other on the contrary with the eyebrow arched up, showing the white. His nostrils are pinched and he breathes with difficulty, every now and then

[1] Cassandra in the *Agamemnon*.

he turns round as if to see who is behind him; sometimes he seems
to be in contact with the spirit which holds him by the nape of the
neck, speaks to him, and makes him lift his eyelids and eyebrows
as if to ask: 'Apollo, god of voyages, where are you leading me?'
After that there is a brief exchange between the possessed and
the spirit which is not prepared to relinquish his prey easily; this
time the spirit bites him in the liver and the man folds up in two
and begins to whirl round. 'The prophetic trance maddens me and
makes me whirl round.' The spirit continues to assail from all
sides without respite, the poor wretch struggles desperately: he
tears out his hair, kneels down, gets up, whirls round hysterically,
wringing his hands, stamping his feet, knocking his forehead on
the table as if he wanted to kill himself; then, after a pause he
slowly starts again, whipped on all sides by the spirit who holds
him; then suddenly he stops dead, bent in two, his arms stretched
out crosswise like somebody who, having just stopped being sick,
says: 'Don't come near!' The two assistants who have constantly
followed him get hold of him, lift him with kindness, stand up
against him, speak in his ears, and surround him with the smoke
of their cigars. He is covered in sweat, stunned, yet calm, and still
far away, with his hair dishevelled as if he had been in a fight.
The trance is now over, the spirit has 'left' him, yet the medium
continues to pass on the spirit in the same way as the priest,
during communion, goes from one to another, giving them the
holy bread. Suddenly a woman, caught by the spirit, begins
to writhe like a worm, and we understand at this point why the
women wear trousers. Why do some women tense themselves up
like bows, while others bend in two like wooden old men? It is
simply because the first are visited by their Indian ancestors, and the
others by members of their own negro race, who remind them of
their slavery and their humiliation at the hands of the cruel and
barbaric white peoples. Are there many occultist centres in Argentina? There are about 470 in Rio alone. The centres which are
working in towns cannot invoke demons or ask for revenge, but
those which work in the forests can ask for revenge and there the
devil presides over their rites. In fact near the houses of the saints
where these ceremonies take place, one generally finds a small
hut no bigger than a dog kennel which is supposed to be the
devil's hide-out. There are voodoo ceremonies in the course of
which some gods are summoned 'while other gods sleep' (as

Clytaemnestra says). The little houses of the saints are like little pagan temples where from the darkness shines the effigy of the god, at whose feet lie offerings, incense and jars of lustral water. In the course of the rehearsal of a ceremony of 'candomblé' in Bahia, one of the women, probably the choir leader, seized a jar and traced a magic circle with water, then a frenetic dance began which lasted until the complete exhaustion of the 'daughters of the saints', that is to say of the vestals; this is really the Erinnyes dance.

After witnessing these ceremonies in Rio, it is easy to understand why when I reread my dear old Aeschylus three or four years later, I found in him traces of this magic world. Cassandra's trances, the grief of Electra and Orestes on their father's tomb, the Erinnyes, the black masses, etc. It seems to me that in the twenty-four-century-old shell which covered the *Oresteia* there was a breach through which life was flowing, a new type of life, not something erudite, not the famous harmony of our grammar school days, but the Greece of coloured statues, an archaic and magical Greece, which was in constant contact with the mystery of life. The *Oresteia* seemed to me the synthesis of what we know of Aeschylus's work; we found in it the archaism of the *Suppliants*, the historical and political strength of the *Persians*, the theory and speculations of *Prometheus*, and the mythical power of the *Seven Against Thebes*. If one could give the trilogy of the *Oresteia* in one single performance, one would realize that each play is a movement of a great symphony. I wondered if through this breach which is like some of the caves through which speleologists explore the secrets of the earth, we might reach the centre of a great civilization and discover its true flesh and blood and not simply its marble statues. What I had learnt from African ceremonies, together with the fresh impressions derived from my new readings of Aeschylus, were perhaps going to enable me to reach a more humane and therefore a more theatrical interpretation of Greece, as it was before the Medic wars. I was anxious to make the attempt and after having thought over and over again about the *Oresteia* I fell in love with it and decided to try to tackle this new problem.

GREECE IN THE AGE OF AESCHYLUS

Between the *Cid* (1636) and *Athalie* (1691) (which was not even produced) there is a span of approximately sixty years. Between

Cervantes (1547) and Moreto (1618) there are sixty to seventy years, between Marlowe and John Ford there are approximately fifty years, between Aeschylus (525 B.C., and Euripides (480 B.C.) there is barely fifty years. This means that golden ages are very short; they cover at the maximum, three generations, they stretch from a grandfather to his grandchildren, and yet they can embrace the whole range of a given civilization. When Athens was destroyed by Xerxes in 480 B.C., Aeschylus was 45 years old, Euripides was about to make his appearance in the world, and Sophocles was still a small boy. These are dates which surely matter; the date of the battle of Salamis is of capital importance. The man who has lived his youth and a good deal of his life in a spiritual atmosphere which has ceased to exist is markedly different from the man who is as new as the newly carved marbles of the age of Pericles. There is always a world of difference between pre-war and post-war generations. Aeschylus announces changes in Greek civilization; he heralds a new age. By the time of Euripides's arrival, everything is ready to be put to use. Aeschylus is the man of a renaissance, and consequently great problems are dealt with seriously, for people are then aware that time is pressing, that life moves on, and changes and anxiety increase, therefore men are compelled to be careful over what they do. One has the feeling that the Medic wars separate two countries which are completely different, and perfectly distinct one from the other; Salamis marks a complete metamorphosis; Aeschylus is the only one of the three great poet dramatists who took part in it; he is the only one who is also the repository of what existed before; he is therefore an old master who still holds the keys of the old civilization. It is he who ensures the transition between an archaic and naturally religious Greece which does not distinguish between the sacred and the profane, and the Greece of the fifth century, which the world admires. The *Oresteia* belongs to the lists of masterpieces which are part of ages of renaissance, like *Hamlet* for instance. We know that the *Oresteia* is the last work of Aeschylus who had only three more years to live; he died at Gala in 455. He was 67 years old when the choir-master Xenocles of Aphidna was entrusted by the archon with the production of his new trilogy. It seems barely worth while mentioning the fact that the satyrical drama which accompanies the trilogy is *Proteus*. What a happy time for the theatre in the days when the archon chose from among the wealthy citizens the choir-master and the producer of the great celebrations to Dionysos. These choir-masters felt that it was an honour to finance a production, or to support the members of the choir for a year; and to look after the costumes, the rehearsals, musicians, actors and all the banquets.

ARGUMENT OF THE ORESTEIA

This trilogy was composed in 458 B.C. and comprises: the *Agamemnon*, the *Choephori* and the *Eumenides*. Aeschylus was 67 years of age, Sophocles 37; the same difference in years separated Corneille from Racine; Aeschylus won the first prize. He uses as his theme a story which is supposed to have taken place 600 years before his time, and he gives to this story a topical touch. Will this topicality be eternal? Has it some value nowadays? I think so, but before going any further, let us examine the data of the situation. The genealogical tree is well known; here it is: Atreus had a brother called Thyestes who had three children—Tantalus, Plisthenes and the famous Aegisthus. Atreus had two sons: Menelaus who married Helen of Troy and Agamemnon who married Clytaemnestra and had three children: Orestes, Electra and Iphigenia. Atreus fought for the crown of Athens against his brother Thyestes whose children he killed and served at a dinner to their father. Only Aegisthus escaped, and of course he hated Atreus and his family. Helen, as is well known, preferred Paris to her husband Menelaus, who with the help of his brother Agamemnon roused the Greeks to seek revenge upon the Trojans. In order to obtain favourable winds Agamemnon sacrificed his daughter Iphigenia. So here we have fratricide, treason, injustices and cruelty. The gods are angry, the humans are full of hate, Aegisthus wants to avenge his father and his brothers, Clytaemnestra wants to avenge her daughter. During Agamemnon's absence Aegisthus and Clytaemnestra become lovers, and Aegisthus rules in Agamemnon's place and occupies his palace.

THE AGAMEMNON AS THE TRAGEDY OF ANXIETY

Ten years have elapsed since the Greeks set off for Troy, and we now hear that they are returning. But the joys of victory and homecoming are spoilt by the anxiety which weighs upon the people's mind; twelve old men who form the chorus symbolize this anxiety. Clytaemnestra prepares to receive Agamemnon in her own style and as she thinks fit. The herald precedes the king who soon arrives and is welcomed by Clytaemnestra with the pomp used only for gods; the anxiety increases, and while Agamemnon is in his bath, Clytaemnestra kills him, together with his Trojan prisoner, Cassandra, given to him by his army, who had the gift of knowing the future and therefore had already prophesied all, including Clytaemnestra's deed. Aegisthus, who had kept out of these actions, comes forward and rejoices at the way he has been avenged. The choir is indignant at the arrogance of Aegisthus and quarrels with him, and the drama, which up to this point is a strictly human drama, ends with the chorus's wish: 'May some god bring back Orestes.' Clytaemnestra had sent Orestes away from Argos, and if he came back he would obviously avenge his father.

THE CHOEPHORI

Apollo, the god of justice whose law is the law of retaliation, death for whoever has killed, has ordered Orestes to return to Argos. It is dawn, Orestes stands by his father's tomb; the chorus is composed of twelve young women, and Electra, Orestes's sister, is among them and shares their life; they all hate the adulterous and criminal queen. Orestes makes himself known to his sister. Through a kind of magic ceremony the women of the choir excite Orestes towards revenge, and as soon as he is ready for it, he goes to the palace disguised as a peasant, finds Aegisthus, kills him, and when Clytaemnestra comes to the latter's rescue, he kills her too. He has obeyed Apollo and avenged his father, but in so doing he has shed his mother's blood and a law older than that of Apollo condemns him to be hounded by earthly divinities called the Erinnyes whose eyes shed tears of blood and who, like dogs, are going henceforth to cling to him without pity. He runs away and they pursue him.

THE EUMENIDES

Orestes has sought refuge in the temple of Apollo at Delphi under the protection of the god who has seemed faithful to him. To begin with, he must purify himself by a long voluntary exile over lands and seas and through the fraternal contact of men. After that he will go and implore the justice of the goddess of wisdom— Pallas Athena. But the Erinnyes have not given up their prey and they threaten to revenge themselves upon the country if they are deprived of it. Apollo defends him in the name of the most powerful god. Pallas Athena must settle this quarrel between ancient divinities and young gods; she has recourse to human wisdom; she summons for the first time a jury of men; she inaugurates an areopagus and therefore glorifies human intelligence. Thanks to her, Orestes is not only acquitted but reprieved, and as a token of gratitude he promises peace between Argos and Athens. The only thing that remains to be done is for Pallas Athena to use the magic power of her persuasion and turn the furious Erinnyes into beneficent divinities. She manages to overcome the obstinacy of these infernal divinities and the trilogy ends with a song of hope and general reconciliation. Thanks to Pallas Athena's wisdom and to human intelligence, old and new gods, old and new civilizations are reconciled for the greater joy and prosperity of the Greek people. The *Oresteia*, free from anxiety, is a work which celebrates the 'renewal'.

STRUCTURE

Before dealing with the spiritual aspects of the *Oresteia*, let us have a look at some of the structural problems connected with it. They are the problems concerning the text to use, the chorus, the characters, and all the other ingredients to be used for the presentation, that is to say the décor, the costume, the masks, the mime, techniques of the performance—song, diction. In short, all that an actor ought to know in order to serve a great work.

THE TEXT

We decided to use André Obey's adaptation. We did not choose Claudel's translation for very simple reasons. He had translated *Agamemnon* at the time when he published *L'Arbre*,[1] that is to say at the end of the nineteenth century, and he had translated the *Choephori* and the *Eumenides* thirty years later. The style of the two translations is different, and Claudel with whom I discussed this problem was very much aware of the differences. He would have liked to bring the *Agamemnon* into line with the other two, but as he said, owing to his great age 'his inner man' was in a state of 'suspended animation'. I believe that the *Oresteia* must be produced in one single performance, since one must endure three hours of tragedy before Pallas Athena liberates us from 'sterile

[1] The tree.

anguish' in the last quarter of an hour. It is just like a mountain climb through mist which only lifts on the summit where the sunshine spreads over the vast horizon. In Claudel's translation the three plays could not be given in one single performance. I therefore decided to use André Obey's literal translation and with the help of Paul Mazon we undertook to produce a dramatic and concise text. After having timed the Greek text, we endeavoured to give the French text exactly the same length. If a speech lasted twelve seconds in Greek, it had to last no more than twelve seconds in French. We felt that by so doing we should gain in intensity and density and we should avoid the sorrow of having to make cuts in the course of rehearsals and performances. All in all the *Oresteia* has the length of *Hamlet*, that is to say three hours and a half. We constantly kept two things in mind: dramatic effectiveness, and poetic equivalence. According to Paul Mazon's indications, the dialogues are spoken; they are therefore written in a dramatic form, while the chorus parts are written in poetic form since their use is essentially lyrical. As far as the spoken scenes are concerned, the only thing to do is to avoid the alexandrine which seems to be the natural way of translating the anapestic lines of Aeschylus. The problem of the chorus was far more complicated.

Convinced as I am that the choruses have been written to obtain incantatory, rather than poetic effects, we carefully avoided altering their structure. We simply endeavoured to preserve the exact construction of the strophes and antistrophes, the position of the epodes and the symmetry of form which links the strophe with its antistrophe. For about a year, thanks to the precious help of the Rev. Fr Festugière and friends from the Sorbonne, we took to pieces one by one the 1,500 lines or so which compose the choruses of the *Oresteia*, while rhythming the beats of the various Greek metres on a table around which we were working. We did not try to fit the French words in the Greek metre, for that method simply produces bad French verse without rendering faithfully the Greek verse. We followed, on the contrary, the principle of poetic equivalence. Let us take an example: the parados of the *Agamemnon*. The chorus leader's speech is anapestic, interwoven here and there with dactyls and spondees. We decided to translate this first tirade, mostly in an anapestic rhythm, into a rhythmical prose broken here and there by a versified 'jewel phrase'. The first strophe which follows, as well as its antistrophe and the epode, ends in each case with a penultimate line of four iambs and the last line is made up of dactyls. We therefore tried to translate them into a French line of four iambs, which give a rhythm which makes it possible to sing this line so that the last line of dactyls which is chanted might lift like a plane. When the rhythm was mostly iambic we rendered it by the alexandrine or by the six-feet line; in places where it is mostly trochaic we used the ten-feet line. When we came across a paeonic rhythm based on cretics we generally opted for the alternative of eight feet, six feet, etc. In brief, after working out the correct prosody of all these lines, we tried to replace them by their poetic equivalence but always conforming to the structure of the choruses which seemed to us to be above all physical, that's to say magical. These choruses are in turn spoken, according to a chanting rhythm with or without music.

Then comes the problem of the movements of the chorus on the stage. I found some information concerning that problem in books lent to me by Jean-Louis Bory. We tried to respect the agreed conventions which are that the chorus should come in at the right side of the stage either one following the other, in four groups with three people in each group, or in three groups with four in each for *Agamemnon* and the *Choephori*, and five groups of three people in each or three groups of five in each for the *Eumenides*. Sometimes I divided the chorus into two groups; one group was led by the choir-master, and the other by its 'parastate'. We tried circles and semi-circles and I trusted a good deal in my improvisations. Bearing in mind the archaism of the work, I decided that the actor should use as an acting area the orchestra pit as well as the proscenium. We did not forget the fact that in the Greek theatre the orchestra is the semi-circular space from which the tiers of seats rise, while the proscenium is what is now called the stage. Between the orchestra and the proscenium there was a curtain which could go up and down through a gap in the floor as on the Italian stage.

THE CHARACTERS

We were taught at school that Aeschylus is the true father of tragedy and that, thanks to the lessons which he had learnt from Thespis and Archilocus, he had carried tragedy to its perfection by introducing two or three characters on the stage. We were told that his theatre was essentially a matter of structure and that characterization was not very important. I am, on the contrary, inclined to think that the *Oresteia* contains characters of a Shakespearian subtlety. I have been struck by the plain human aspect with which he invests some of them. Even Agamemnon, who represents above all the totemic aspect of family, kinship and race, expresses himself at times like a 'petit bourgeois' who dreams 'of spending the last years of his life in quiet comfort'. But the most accomplished character from the psychological point of view is Clytaemnestra. She is truly one of the great characters of the theatre; she is a wounded mother who has the right to avenge herself, she is a sensuous, adulterous woman, a great lady conscious of her wealth, yet not without a touch of the parvenu; she is a wife jealous of her husband's concubines, a queen harassed by the fatality which weighs upon her race, and she is a woman who indulges at night in strange magical rites. She is, all in all, a very complex character. Besides that all the other characters of the *Oresteia*: Electra, Orestes, Apollo, Pallas Athena, Cassandra, the herald, the nurse and the hall porter, show that Aeschylus had a knowledge of the human heart comparable to that of Shakespeare. The verisimilitude of these characters should have been an encouragement to act them without masks; let us have a look at this complex problem.

The masks were supposed to be first and foremost an enlargement of the face, with a kind of speaking trumpet in the shape of the mouth, so as to enable the voice to carry. These reasons could not be of much value since the *Oresteia* was to be performed in a theatre; yet we decided to adopt the use of the mask for far more important reasons. The human face reflects the human soul and the mysterious links which might connect a human being with the supernatural world. From his earliest childhood man likes to impersonate parts, and to impersonate somebody is to change face; it is to adopt somebody else's face. The attempt to wear another man's face aims at trying to get out of oneself, and in that line of thought, the action of placing on one's face the mask of another face is something far more striking and stimulating than the act of making up to play a given part. A mask confers upon a given expression the maximum of intensity together with an impression of absence. A mask expresses at the same time the maximum of life and the maximum of death; it partakes of the visible and of the invisible, of the apparent and absolute. The mask exteriorizes a deep aspect of life, and in so doing, it helps to rediscover instinct. This kind of simultaneous exteriorization of the inner and outer aspect of life, of the relative and of the absolute, of life and death, makes it possible to reach through incantation a better contact with the audience. That is why we chose the use of masks. But we did not try to imitate statues. There is in the look of masks something visionary, while on the contrary statues have a kind of fixed and blank stare. Although ancient masks were supposed to be made of linen we preferred leather, and we asked a sculptor from Padua, called Sartori, to make for us the frames of our masks which with the help of Petrus Bride, Felix Labisse and Marie-Hélène Dasté, we dressed up and painted, trying to emulate African tribes preparing for religious festivals rather than conventional Greek masks.

CASTING AND DÉCOR

The books which try to give us an idea of everyday life in Athens in the age of Pericles and before the destruction of Athens in 480 B.C., tend to give us the picture of a city composed of official monuments and small and poor dwellings in which lived the common people. One cannot help thinking that these monuments which have survived time, were very much like the splendid houses surrounded by native dwellings which one finds in North Africa or Brazil today. The study of ancient vases belonging to the age before Aeschylus shows colours which are also seen in African vases which we found in Dakar. In fact, the *Oresteia* which takes place in Argos (let us not forget that we are in 458 B.C. and that Mycena has been destroyed in 465 B.C.; Aeschylus has set his action in Argos with the obvious aim of facilitating the alliance between Argos and Athens) is something which is supposed to have taken place in the eleventh century B.C. Therefore, as far as the costumes were concerned, it was essential to go back to archaic times. Marie-Hélene Dasté who was dealing with them followed the models found on the archaic vase of the Louvre collection; she was also greatly helped by the staff of the Louvre; we felt that by combining their knowledge with data gathered from Africa and the East, we could not possibly be unfaithful to the spirit of Aeschylus. For the décor we used mostly wood. One must not forget the fact that the age of stone and marble is part of the age of decadence. In the great age theatres were made of wood. The

orchestral circle was our magic circle; in its centre we had the
altar; the proscenium was a kind of second slope, and between
the proscenium and the orchestral pit we had a large flight of
steps. The palace was simply represented by a monumental
door.

Aeschylus does not respect the unity of place; the action moves
indeed from Argos to Delphi and Athens. Bearing that point in
mind, we decided to use Agamemnon's palace only when he takes
part in the acting and then to replace this by his tomb which
dominates the stage during half of the *Choephori*.

MUSIC

The *Oresteia* being a work which marks a transition between a
semi-oriental antiquity and the Hellenic age westward bound, we
decided that the choral music should be closer to oriental rather
than to western music, which only becomes predominant at the
moment when Pallas Athena turns the Erinnyes into beneficent
divinities. Pierre Boulez who composed the music studied Japanese
and Tibetan music and applied to it his pet theory of the twelve-note
series; he produced a kind of music which on the whole attuned
the *Oresteia* to the orient. As for the double flute we simply
ignored it, we did not wish to have the pseudo-reconstruction of a
flute-player heralding the entrance of the choir with a useless
instrument.

CHOREOGRAPHY

The *Oresteia* is full of choreographic problems. How did the
actors move? With what gestures did they accompany their natural
or their rhythmical speeches? What kind of dances did the chorus
perform?—so many questions about which we know nothing. Yet
it seems impossible to believe that a character like Agamemnon
who is like a totem of the race, should move about in an ordinary
way. If he did so, there would be an obvious discrepancy between
his behaviour and the kind of diction which the work requires.
There are numerous studies on Greek choreography, and we even
discovered a very interesting thesis dating from the middle of the
nineteenth century in which the author, after studying texts and
vases, gave a good account of Greek choreography which according
to him rests on classical dance. This seems to be a conclusion
with which we cannot agree. The author of this thesis notes that

the Greeks knew the five positions of classical dance and particularly the fourth position. Anybody who has watched European folklore dances or African or Brazilian dances has noted that peasants and natives quite naturally take up the fourth position crossed, either on the tips of their toes or on the heel, and by a twist of the bust achieve a fast whirling movement while maintaining the fourth position crossed; this is therefore a step from primitive dancing which has no connexion with classical dancing. If one tries to reduce the Greek dance of Aeschylus's plays to classical dances, one reaches a form of serenity and western sophistication which is out of tune with the feverish excitement of the text. Yet, with these few exceptions, the thesis in question is a very useful work. Comparing museum pictures with certain primitive dances which we have witnessed, we felt that we could discover in them the inspiration for the dances painted on Greek vases. We discovered among them not only African steps (particularly when the dancers are in a trance) but attitudes from Russian and Spanish dances. The appreciation of these dances in our times presents certain difficulties. In the time of Aeschylus the whole population could dance. The art of dancing was taught through two operations. First of all, every child who went to school was taught how to dance; this was done by the pedotribe or gym master. Dance was a part of education. In Brazil, which I mentioned before, there are schools of education for 'samba' or foot dancing which endeavour to develop the flexibility and the bodily skill of the child. The speed of the foot movements developed in these schools is such that we Europeans cannot follow them. Besides this general training undergone by all, the members of chorus, who generally came from the best families, spent the whole year preceding a performance, practising under the guidance of the dancing master and they reached an extremely high standard of professionalism which spectators were able to appreciate. In our times that is no longer the case; yet when we produced the *Oresteia* we bore in mind all these facts.

We have now mentioned some of the ingredients required for a good performance of the *Oresteia*: singing, diction, breathing, gurgling in the Chinese style (for the Erinnyes sequence), the art of gesture, the dance, trances, mask, rhythm, etc.: we, who love total theatre, find in this the fount of our theatre, what we are looking for. Yet, however interesting all these technical problems might be, what impelled us to produce the *Oresteia* was the fact that besides the dramatic skill involved for its production this work is full of important ideas.

THE IDEAS

THE DRAMATIC RHYTHM OF THE ORESTEIA

The dramatic rhythm or tempo of the *Oresteia* is something unusual. The action unfolds according to a pattern, as follows: first a slow, heavy, anguish-laden period of smouldering or preparation; after that the action flares up in sharp, brief bursts; then finally a third stage, which is a return to a heavy and anguish-laden atmosphere which connects with new preparations of a similar nature.

This rhythm of action, which is not in accord with the tempo of the life of our times, seems to suggest certain observations. This kind of ternary rhythm of action, comprising the preparation, the action itself, and the consequences, seems to correspond to the rhythm of every important act which one meets in life. The theatre is the art of life, that is to say it is fundamentally the representation of the act, and the essential act is the act of love, or rather the act of fecundation which follows exactly this ternary rhythm—slow preparation, the act itself, brief and sharp, then the consequences slow and rich. If we examine a storm we find again the same pattern. First the atmosphere is heavy, laden with electricity; soon the clouds gather, light darkens, the tension is well-nigh unbearable, it is what one might call the neutral stage. Then lightning flashes, and thunder fills the sky with its roar; this is the masculine stage. Finally rain begins to pour down endlessly; this is the feminine stage. It seems to me that most acts of life follow this kind of pattern which is also the pattern adopted by Aeschylus in the *Oresteia*: the neutral element heavy and slow, the masculine element sharp and brief, the feminine element, slow and heavy. Nowadays when our age knows only agitation and no acts, this ternary rhythm seems rather strange. This love of agitation accounts for complicated patterns of plot and counterplot which are the characteristics of most plays and are in fact the result of excitement and nervousness and not of true virile power which only knows itself in the act. The lesson which the *Oresteia* offers us is that which emerges from a true master of action; it is the rhythm of the *Oresteia* which is normal and in accord with life and not the sterile, empty agitation of most plays which are offered for production now.

The pattern of international life seems on the contrary to follow the rhythm of the *Oresteia*. First slow preparation of what is described as the cold war, with many conferences and situations such as Munich, then the violent explosion of conflict, followed by a slow endless aftermath which merges with the atmosphere of cold war which is the preparation for the next conflict.

Let us try to enter the extraordinary universe of Aeschylus. It was previously stated that the theatre is the art of justice, the word here being given its universal meaning. Men torn by their passions behave in ways which risk upsetting the equilibrium of life and may drag the rest of mankind into death. That is just what happens on the stage when men in conflict struggle for the triumph of their views. They plead, they argue and fight; each one of them thinks that he is right and that he is struggling for a good cause. It is obvious that they can't all be right in the end, and that if some are right some must be wrong. Who, then, can decide as to who is right and who is wrong? Life and life alone can do that, and at the dénouement it settles the various accounts, dispenses justice and restores the equilibrium of our times. The spectator who for three hours has been tossed about between distress, terror, anxiety, pity and tears, to be finally confronted with a kind of settlement of conflict or justice, leaves the theatre cleansed from his own passions, that is to say, revitalized and strengthened. It is obvious that without such a feeling of final justice, the theatre loses its strength and its vital importance. There is no better illustration of the ideal of justice than the *Oresteia*. The most sordid story of family crimes and revenge offers also the most striking examples of justice. Orestes has killed his mother who had killed her husband. Each one had some reasons for doing what she or he did; but how is Orestes going to emerge from this situation? Will he be judged according to the rules of ancient justice and handed over to the divinities of the earth called the Erinnyes which belonged to the ancient civilization, and which with their human sacrifices are also part of the civilizations of Mexico and Peru; or will he be judged according to the rules of the new justice which rests on reason, intelligence, pity and forgiveness?

Two religions, two worlds, are in conflict because of a human story. On one side the ancient ruthless world of the Erinnyes, on the other the new world, the world of young divinities like Apollo and Pallas Athena, endeavouring to win over the reigning god Zeus. This apparently insoluble situation is brought to a satisfactory end through human wisdom called in by the divine persuasion of Pallas Athena, and this reconciliation will show man that life is possible even in a divided world and that contraries can be resolved and become a source of inspiration to the world. Thanks to Pallas Athena's divine wisdom, the bloodthirsty Erinnyes are transformed into the beneficent Eumenides. The meaning of justice has changed and harmonious life is possible. This is something which makes the production of the *Oresteia* in our times worth while. As for the civilizing effect of the *Oresteia*, such as the various transitions from family to clan life and the ordered life of a city, I leave this problem to specialists; I should only like to say a few words about man's position in life. Man, according to Aeschylus, lies half-way between the plane of animality and that of immortality. He began life in extreme misery and his continuous efforts are imprinted with pathos. If he has succeeded in evolving actions of good and evil, which in fact do not exist, it's because he has been unable to understand the world and to grasp physically God's wishes. If man could understand God's wish and will, he could rise to the rank of the immortals, but for that he must spend his life in suffering, for there is no understanding without suffering.

Aeschylus's concept of destiny is different from that of Sophocles. With him, destiny dominates justice, with Sophocles justice and destiny are separated. For Aeschylus, destiny is nothing else but justice brought about through divine will. Any given destiny is the result of certain component factors: individual errors or failings, the gods' reactions, and hazard. Man has the power to contribute to the making of his destiny since he is not submitted to an arbitrary will, but on the contrary makes his own destiny through his faults and the way he uses hazard; he is therefore relatively free. There is in the *Oresteia* another theme which is one of the reasons why we were keen to produce it, and it is the theme of anxiety. 'Oh, gods, free me from my sterile anxiety' says a member of the chorus. This seems to be the starting point of the whole of Greek tragedy which rests essentially on the anguished awareness which man has about his place in the world. Every morning we awaken with this load of anguish and we endeavour to get rid of it as soon as possible. My prolonged contacts with the exciting world of Kafka lead me to believe that anxiety is something which is inherent in man, and which although it has been fully exploited by some artists in our time is the most ancient and most basic feeling of the human condition. I should be tempted to say that anguish corresponds to an excremental aspect of the mind— just as there are physical excrements there are spiritual excrements, and anguish is something as sterile as excrement. Therefore one must get rid of it in just the same way as one gets rid of its physical counterpart and those who delight in it are comparable with those who delight in the physical excrements.

The aim of the *Oresteia* is to free us from this anguish, and that is why it is a work which rests on hope. In that other masterpiece *Hamlet*, the hero dies from his superior anguish, but before dying he prophesies the renewal of life; thanks to the symbolic importance of Fortinbras who represents action in its virility, one is freed from anguish. That is why *Hamlet* is one of the masterpieces of any period of renaissance. In the *Oresteia* the idea of renewal is even more clearly suggested than in *Hamlet*. As soon as Fortinbras arrives on the stage, the curtain falls, and the renewal is announced but not carried out. Aeschylus devotes one of the plays of his trilogy to this very question. The *Eumenides* deals with the problem of sterile anguish and shows how a civilization can be developed, and how humanity can renew its strength. Aeschylus, who had known the ancient civilization of painted totemic statues, helped the world of his time to pass from the wooden gods to the marble gods of Pericles. He tried to reconcile the old gods with the new ones and he heralded the modern world. He showed that man before being a moral animal is a political animal; he introduced on the stage the democratic principle of the vote, and owing to a vague premonition of things to come, he drew attention to the importance of pity and forgiveness in human relations. It is difficult at this point not to follow Claudel's example and in spite of the twenty-four centuries which separate us from her, not to look upon Pallas Athena in the same way as we look at the Holy Virgin's image in our churches. Such is, all in all, this magical work imprinted with the need for reconciliation, renewal and the abolition of anguish, and pervaded with hope, to which we have offered our devotion and our services. It is a work which urges upon us the reconciliation of opposites; it asks us not to divide life, which is essentially and naturally religious, into a physical and a spiritual aspect; it teaches us that we must suffer in order to understand, and that we must try to protect our civilization from the permanent miseries which threaten it and which are despotism and anarchy. Such was the good advice offered to us twenty-four centuries ago by Aeschylus, father and founder of the theatre.

Menander

Menander has only begun to be known in our century; he is a modern discovery. Previously he belonged to legend and to the very vague notions we had of him through Terence. Let us try to place him. He was born in 342 B.C., in Athens of an upper class family, he despised democracy; he died while bathing at Phalère in 290 B.C., aged 52. He began to write when he was 20, and he wrote about 105 comedies, apparently more appreciated by the critics, that is to say by the intellectuals, than by the public. He was only crowned eight times. His most direct rival was somebody called Philemon, to whom Menander, who had no doubts about his talent, is supposed to have said once: 'Tell me frankly, Philemon, aren't you a little ashamed when you are proclaimed the winner against me?' The excitement of those prize-day ceremonies is not difficult to conceive; we have only to think of the atmosphere of some first nights in Paris; I am reminded of the first night of a Mauriac play which hadn't been too successful. On that occasion Bernstein went on the stage in order to say a few words to Mauriac as 'an affectionate colleague'. 'Well,' said Bernstein, 'are you satisfied?' And Mauriac, who was aware that things had not gone too well, said with his usual wit, 'Not as much as you are!' The atmosphere of upper class manners and literary feeling connects Menander with our time. Menander with his intelligent, aristocratic and refined mask and his bitter smile; Menander with his mistress—Glykera the sweet; Menander, Aristotelian philosopher and pupil of Theophrastus; Menander the epicurean leader of the theatre, and the man of the very refined Governor of Athens— Demetrius of Phalera, who used to dye his hair to fair, put rouge on his cheeks and perfume himself with myrrh; Menander belongs to that great spiritual family whose essential qualities are grace, sensibility, refinement, intelligence. It is the family of Boileau, La Bruyère, Marivaux, Proust, Henri de Régnier, Vaudoyer, Gérard Bauer, Cocteau, Mauriac . . . etc. Menander is therefore very close to us, and the discovery of one of his comedies makes me wonder whether there is not some lesson to be drawn from him.

We were told at school that the great classical age of Greece ended with the appearance of Alexander in 336 B.C. We must note here that the period which precedes the battle of Salamis in 480 B.C. (a most important date to my mind), that is to say the age of Aeschylus, is only now beginning to attract the attention of philosophers and historians. The only Greece we seem to hear about in our schools is the Greece of marble statues, of harmony, equilibrium, control and taste. We know little or nothing about the Greece in which anguish prevailed. And yet! . . . Claudel has written some excellent pages on this very subject. We were told at school that the Alexandrine period only begins round about 295 B.C., after the popular and demagogic movements of Poliorcetes, and which is something comparable to the dictatorships of our time. We therefore have between the great classical period of 336 B.C. and the Alexandrine period of 295 B.C., a period of transition which contains the life of Menander. The Peloponesian wars inaugurated the golden age, while the Medic had left the country exhausted, with its political structure falling to pieces and the people losing more and more the sense of belonging to a community. Tragedy, comedy and satyrical dramas, whether they criticized or extolled the life of the state, carried with them a social value. All these works were part of history and today we would say that their authors had an historical sense. The gods were sharing in the daily life of the people, the theatre was an emanation of society; it was a popular art, its impact was total and it affected the whole of society. The audience comprised representatives from all classes of society, all sitting together and forming a complex and lively jury appraising the politics and the morality of gods and men. The fourth century is imprinted with fatigue; the city declines and the memories of its glorious past are a strong contrast with the inertia and apathy of the new generation. The politicians are merely interested in their own interests and only a handful of them try without conviction to awaken the civic spirit of the people.

One is struck by the similarity of that period to the age in which we are living now. Still, although it looked very much like a period of decadence, it was merely a period of transition. That period which covers the last forty years after the fourth century must be viewed, like ours, on three planes. First of all, the gods have disintegrated, and intelligence is no longer creative; Pallas Athena, who is merely intelligence and nothing else, ceases to be Pallas Athena. Religion, which previously bound together the various families, has now broken down, and the families become independent units and self-sufficient little worlds. The notion of motherland disappears; the people, tired by taxations and wars, and lacking a mystical concept of life and a sense of civicism, become self-centred. The children become the important preoccupation of society, and women become its main force. A hundred and fifty years earlier, Aeschylus, already aware of the growing effeminacy of society, was expressing his indignation with the words: 'This man is a woman.' Michelet in his important book entitled *The Bible of Mankind* states that the growth of the effeminacy of civilization began in the sixth century B.C. This effeminacy was to be consecrated by the Holy Virgin Mother in the year one of our era. In the age of Menander the divinity which matters is Adonis and not Pallas Athena.

The political inheritance is no better. Apollo and Pallas Athena who in the times of Aeschylus were young, progressive gods, had instituted the Republic, the vote and the supremacy of democratic institutions. A hundred years later Athens, having passed from a growing, expanding power to an imperialist power, tries to dominate the world and is lost in self-admiration: her institutions decay. In the age of Menander, the people, with their usual common sense, turn away from venal politicians dazzled by a great past and from orators who are corrupt. Demades, a man from the people who strove with all his might to restore the health of the state, said, 'I have in my hands the wrecked remains of the Republic; it is no longer the state of our ancestors, but an old woman, doddering about in slippers, and drinking infusions.' One is reminded of our present-day political leader who on his accession to power said: 'I have come to liquidate a bankruptcy.' When this same Demades was asked why he did not want to wage war, he replied: 'I am waiting for the day when young men are ready to wage war, the rich consent to pay their taxes, and the orators cease to rob the people.' Faced with the disintegration of faith and political corruption, the reaction of the people, who had remained untouched by corruption, was to follow their instinct for self-preservation, and to devote all their energy and love to the task of maintaining the family, something which was both logical and wise. An examination of the life in Athens in these times shows that intellectual and artistic life had anything but decayed in the way that political and civic life had done. Great painting had disappeared, but sculptors like Praxiteles and Scopas, philosophers like Aristotle and Theophrastus, together with unknown poets, show that on the plane of intelligence and art Athens maintained its vitality. Politicians and generals were the cause of the ruin of the state. Here the parallel with our present situation is striking. Our intellectual and artistic life, though it might show an excessive interest in epicureanism and cynicism, is nevertheless very healthy. It is the moral, political and military confusion which threatens the destruction of our country.

Aristophanes in the fifth century was enjoyed by a whole people full of vitality and inspired with religious and patriotic feelings. A hundred years later, Menander is the comic author of the refined, intelligent and philosophically-minded bourgeois society; he is the master of the new comedy. In France it is only during the Middle Ages that we find exactly the same situation as that which prevailed in Athens during the life of Aristophanes. Then the whole of society participated in the life of the theatre. Nothing resembles more the spirit of Aristophanes's comedies than the satirical farces of the Middle Ages. After the Renaissance the spirit of Menander reappears; Terence and his disciples will lend it their voices. In our time we are still living under the aegis of Menander; the mould which he made 300 years before Christ has not yet been broken. Here we have a man who during a fête unknowingly seduces a woman who later becomes his wife. Once he has married her he discovers that his wife has already had a child before she married him, and he cannot bear it. Happily the situation is saved by a skilful valet and a sympathetic courtesan. In another play, we have a father who is his son's rival in love, and his name could very well be Harpagon; in another, an army officer is much angered by the fact that a dashing young boy is fluttering around his wife; well, it just happens that this young puppy and the young wife are brother and sister and do not know it. In another play there is a wonderful slave overflowing with the milk of human kindness who plays the low character, and the seducer. One can safely say that the situations and characters which are the foundation of western comedy from the seventeenth century onwards, have been suggested by Menander. Terence, who knew Menander's work well and did not shrink from copying him, acted as the middleman.

Was Aeschylus known in the age of Racine, and did the latter think when he took his subjects from Euripides that he was drinking at the very source of tragedy? Who has influenced the Elizabethan theatre? It is Seneca and not the Greeks. The comic writers of the last three centuries never went any further than Plautus and Terence, that is to say Menander, for their inspiration. Is it possible to say that Aristophanes, Sophocles and Aeschylus are relatively recent discoveries? It seems that our secondary education has rested for centuries on the period of Greek civilization which was dominated by a society which was intellectually and artistically alive but completely worn out on the religious and political planes. Nineteenth-century French bourgeoisie instinctively went for its roots and justifications to Athenian bourgeoisie. The theatre which is the emanation of a whole people, the theatre of Aeschylus, Aristophanes and the Commedia dell'Arte, the mystery and morality plays, the satirical dramas together with Spanish popular drama, has only been known recently. We must remember that in the age of Menander and in Roman days, the actors still wore masks, therefore their family or bourgeois theatre was not realistic, for the mask cannot fail to impose a certain transposition. In fact it is probably the 'slice of life' aspect of this theatre which led to the rejection of the mask and to a dilution of style in the representation of Menander's plays. Might one risk the observation that Menander's theatre retained its appearance of greatness only because it was acted with masks? These brief remarks about Menander imply no condemnation on my part. I have simply been struck by the similarity between the two tragic ages. My position is that of a craftsman and my role is to ask questions. What rewarding answers might we not get if an historian-philosopher seriously undertook to answer these questions! I can't help hoping that, thanks to the recent discovery of one of Menander's comedies, such a wish might be fulfilled.

Shakespeare and the French[1]

From the second half of the eighteenth century onwards, Shakespeare has been regularly played in France. Voltaire is supposed to have been one of the first French writers interested in Shakespeare; we shall see later the various stages he went through. The most recent lovers of Shakespeare were Antoine, who produced practically every play, including *Titus Andronicus*, Gémier who is supposed to have been an extraordinary Shylock, Charles Dullin who produced *Richard III*, *Julius Caesar* and *King Lear*, and Gaston Baty who produced *Macbeth*, *The Taming of the Shrew* and *Twelfth Night*. The latter play was also produced by Copeau. Then came the Pitoëffs who produced *Hamlet* and *Romeo and Juliet*. Last but not least the Comédie Française gave *Coriolanus* in 1937, and in 1945 *Antony and Cleopatra*, which I directed. Finally, Jean Vilar produced *Richard II*, and quite a few new companies have followed this lead and produced *A Midsummer Night's Dream*, *Much Ado*, etc. And of course here I have only been concerned with Shakespeare played in French translations. All these examples show that in France Shakespeare is given practically as often as Racine and Molière, and is therefore a necessity to us. Yet Shakespeare's entry on the French stage begins with a crime. In order to cross the Channel he has to be shorn of his poetic garb. The poetic atmosphere of his art which rises towards suprareality and ideal forms, is cruelly dispelled by the cold light of our severely rationalized language. Shakespeare, whose thought belongs more to poetry than to pure reason, has his wings severely clipped by the logic which destroys rhythm and music, and seeks to pierce the most shaded and mysterious recesses of his poetry. This is altogether a very great handicap which seriously hampers even those who love Shakespeare. When he is shorn of his poetic appearance, there are people who only see in him the representative of a barbarous age, dealing in ghosts, female pimps, murderers and plotters. Such has been for many centuries the opinion of many French purists, and such would normally be the opinion of most French people who are so form-conscious; and yet the descendants of Malherbe, La Fontaine, Boileau, Voltaire and Chénier, love

---

[1] Text of a lecture given during the Edinburgh Festival in September 1948 before the performance of *Hamlet* in French.

Shakespeare even if he has been rendered somehow ungainly and lame by translation.

The three books which I always keep by my bedside, and which I should wish to take with me if I had to leave hurriedly without any warning as so many had to do during the dark years of the occupation, are the Bible which contains our sources, Racine with his artistic beauty and Shakespeare which contains life. Today I should like to add a fourth: Molière for his studies of men. Shakespeare is always ready at any moment to offer us an injection of life; he is by far the best 'blood donor'; he revives us whenever we need it and that we do often enough. France's spiritual life could be represented by a passionate yet brotherly conversation between three people. What a remarkable trio that would be! Let us imagine the passionate Pascal clashing against the logical genius of Descartes, with Montaigne as a smiling referee, or let us imagine La Fontaine caught between Ronsard and Malherbe, or coming to our times, let us imagine Gide encouraging Valéry to bait Claudel! These examples show that we have in France three different attitudes which are in constant conflict. The three attitudes summarize French thought. For the foreigner it is the Cartesian attitude which best represents France, generally described as Descartes's country. This statement is often followed by well-known tags such as: 'Enfin Malherbe vint; ce qui se conçoit bien s'énonce clairement',[1] etc., or this sentence which has dominated French art: 'Art separates what Nature confuses.'

One of the most striking features of French life is the luminous clarity of the French genius which can lift to their highest pitch logic and common sense. If logic and common sense are the hallmarks of the French character, taste, control and subtle discrimination are the hall-mark of French art. How can one account for these traits? Are they due to France's geographical position and to her temperate climate and her varied landscape? Indeed in France everything is varied and temperate, and wherever we look, whether northward or southward, whether we look at forests, mountains or rivers, we never have the opportunity of seeing anything which horrifies through excess in one direction or another. Everything is varied, and temperate; the result is that wherever he goes, the French artist moves about with a rubber or a file in his hand to

---

[1] At last Malherbe came; what is clearly thought out, can be clearly expressed.

polish and repolish ceaselessly. France is the land of thrift. 'Thrift, thrift, thrift, Horatio.' All this makes France one of the very few countries where a genius like Racine could be born; Racine the acme of taste, control and discrimination, whose vocabulary does not exceed 1,500 words and whose alexandrines could not be improved. Valéry once tried to do so, and after three days gave it up. Racine deleted from his masterpieces only what ordinary minds could have left in and he draws from his audiences the tears which fall from Orpheus's lyre and which are prompted more by admiration than by pity. But one must not forget that the love of control and measure above all things, together with a tyrannical passion for taste can become a weakness through which art could become anaemic and die. Constant rubbing and filing can end in rubbing out the edges, in thinning out the material and in conferring upon it the worn-out, thin look of an old coin. The fear of ridicule and excess of refinement and polish can lead to dryness and lack of life. That is the moment when we can only be saved by calling upon Shakespeare with his exuberant life, his fecundity, and his genius.

France, exhausted by '*le Grand Siècle*', was in need of rejuvenation; her blood had become too blue. The trees of the French garden had been overpruned and they had lost their sap. Shakespeare's appearance on the French stage was eagerly welcomed by those who, later, made possible the romantic revolution. They took to Shakespeare as if he were the long awaited wholemeal bread. Voltaire, who had introduced Shakespeare, was swept by a great enthusiasm, which later he tried to temper with criticism. Having praised before the fecundity, the sublime power of Shakespeare's genius, he proceeded to reproach him with lack of tact and ignorance of the rules; and he ended by describing Shakespeare's tragedies as works which contained splendid and majestic scenes but were in fact nothing but monstrous farces. There certainly was gold in them, but according to him it was still too mixed up with the dross, and his final conclusion was that one had to keep a firm check on such a source of mediocrity, triviality and long and tedious improbabilities. So the classical corset was again tightened up on a chest which for a while had breathed freely and which now was made to pay for the folly of having deified 'the drunken savage'. Taste was again in conflict with genius and life, and the pattern of Voltaire's behaviour was repeated by many of the following generations who, like him, oscillated between enthusiasm and coldness.

The truth is that the Frenchman is less a gardener than a horticulturist. When he realizes that his beautifully planned garden has too many gravelled paths, he is overwhelmed with nostalgia for an English lawn; so he plants a lawn; but as soon as it has grown, he covers it with geometrically laid out flower-beds 'in the French style'. This is part of the age-long debate between good taste on one side and genius on the other; and the Frenchman constantly knocks his head against both.

Taste and genius exist in every age, but it is only at certain given moments in the life of nations that they harmonize; then the lyre only produces the sound which it ought to produce. These moments are as rare as the meeting of stars and they only have a very brief duration. They form our golden ages, the ages of our masterpieces; in such ages we have: *Andromaque*,[1] *Hamlet*, *Britannicus*, *Macbeth*, *Bajazet*, *Antony and Cleopatra*, *Phèdre*, *The Tempest*, and Racine and Shakespeare rise above the problems of genre into a world which is their own. There, Shakespeare's restraint is as elegant as Racine's, whose cruelty has nothing to envy in Shakespeare's. It might very well happen that if there were an international competition, Racine would be given the prize for taste and Shakespeare for abundance; but that simply means that the world is conventional and loves labels, and nothing can alter that. Yet it remains true that when we are tired of looking for rare things, Shakespeare is the supreme refuge to bring us back to life, to revive our hearts and to return us to the human world. You might ask, 'Why Shakespeare and nobody else? Is he the only one to possess such virtues? Is there not in the French patrimony a writer who blends taste and genius perfectly and who, like Shakespeare, has ferocity and strength and is fully immersed in life? What about Molière, why do you prefer Shakespeare to him?' My reply would be: I do not prefer Shakespeare, but the point is that Molière is ourselves, quotations from his plays are part of our minds since our earliest age; we have grown up with him, yet I must admit that at this moment I feed more on Shakespeare than on Molière. The probable reason is that Shakespeare has more in common with us and that his situations and themes are closer to ours than those of Molière. Such a remark does not take anything away from Molière who in genius and taste is equal to the greatest.

[1] *Andromache.*

Shakespeare is topical to our time, he lived as we do now, in an age of transition, an age of revolutions and calamities in which the old faith had been lost, and the new one had not yet appeared. His world was, like ours, in the throes of doubt. Molière on the contrary lived in an age of prosperity and brilliance, in an orderly society dominated by monarchic authority. Wealth, prosperity, order, authority, all these notions are very remote from us; Molière stands for equilibrium and at this moment we do not know what equilibrium is. If therefore I am prepared to take with me Shakespeare, leaving behind Molière (though I should very much like to take both), it is because at this moment, and I mean at this moment, and not in fifty years' time when things will be different, Shakespeare is more modern than Molière. He is closer to us, and the conditions in which he lived are also closer to ours. In order to make this point clear it is hardly worth while recalling the long imprisonment of Mary Stuart and her end on the block, the great Elizabeth dining to the sound of bugles and drums, Murray's vices in Scotland, Rizzio's and Darnley's murders, Dunbar's flight, or Morton put to the torture. It is hardly worth mentioning the Low Countries and their suffering, or Spain where Philip II, dying, said to his doctors: 'Why do you fear to draw a few drops of blood from a man who has spilt so much?' It is hardly worth while mentioning Wallenstein in Germany, the Cenci in Italy, St Bartholomew's Day in France, Charles IX, Henri III, the barricades, the death of the two de Guises at Blois, the death of Henri IV, etc. All these things testify to the troubled state of the age in which Shakespeare was living. The genius of the age fed his genius, and more than anyone else he immortalized the turmoil of his time. The Middle Ages were fading away, and with them the faith which united the western world; the religious reformation begun under Henry VIII was still in progress, and the political revolution which reached its climax with Charles I was about to begin; the modern age was about to be born, and Shakespeare was, as we are now, struggling in a vale where murders and catastrophes were parts of life, and where all human values were again questioned. At the age of 26 in *Henry VI* he makes a father who has killed his son say:

O, pity God, this miserable age!
What stratagems, how fell, how butcherly,

erroneous, mutinous, unnatural
this deadly quarrel daily doth beget!
                                    —*Henry VI*, III, 2.5

To us, who still have present in our minds the memory of Buchen-
wald and Auschwitz, the retreat of Dunkirk or the horrors endured
by Coventry and Hiroshima, these cries of despair easily find an
echo in our souls. We must confess that we feel rather remote from
the antiquated common sense of Chrysale and the arguments of
les Femmes Savantes.[1] Shakespeare's age is, like ours, an age most
aptly described by Hamlet's phrase, 'The time is out of joint.'

What does Shakespeare do in such a situation, what example
does he offer us; does he forsake his age for the shelter of an ivory
tower? No, he replaces the poet in his true function which is to
be the summary and brief chronicle of his time, by borrowing
subjects from life to give to his age its style. Had he emerged like
us from the Second World War, and had he lived, as we do, through
the anxieties caused by the behaviour of the two world powers
which are holding peace in their hands, I doubt if he would alter
in any way Enobarbus's words when he says about Antony and
Caesar who are now face to face:

> Then world, thou hast a pair of chops, no more;
> And throw between them all the food thou hast,
> They'll grind one on the other . . .

'What we must imitate from this great man,' said Stendhal, 'is
his way of studying the world in which we live and the art of offering our contemporaries the kind of tragedy which they need (but
which they dare not ask for, terrified by their habits and their
mania about taste). What matters is not so much to write plays
which resemble Shakespeare's as to study the world in which we
live in just the same way as Shakespeare studied his; for we too
have conflicting paths and conspiracies, and we too have men who
today laugh and joke in drawing-rooms and will be in prison a
week later, or men who laugh and joke with those who, a few days
later, will choose the jury which will sentence them to death.' The
age of Stendhal was like ours, in tune with that of Shakespeare.
Therefore Shakespeare with his social message which corresponds
to our time can be considered as something like the patron of the
artist who is committed, and, the more one thinks about this point,

---

[1] The learned ladies.

the more truth one finds in it; yet we must of course be very careful about this kind of assertion. True, Shakespeare walks about the streets of the cities of his time, but it is in order to bear witness and not to take sides, and that is of supreme importance, for, if we do not bear this point firmly in mind, we might discover that our age, which is thoroughly infected with politics, has managed to ascribe to Shakespeare a definite political party and ideology. We have only to think of the protracted anguish which followed the production of *Coriolanus* at the Comédie Française in 1937 at the time of the Popular Front. Shakespeare was very nearly transformed into an apologist of fascism. Shakespeare is an artist and as such he has no politics. When, for instance, in *Henry VI*, Part II, he deals with Jack Cade as the representative of the masses in rebellion against the privileged classes, he remains above the masses and above the privileged classes; he does not take sides. If he concedes a point to the privileged classes by making Jack Cade foolishly say: 'But then are we in order when we are most in disorder' (*Henry VI*, Part II, Act IV, Scene 2), he follows that by paying homage to the eternal greatness of oppressed people, through the words which he puts in the mouth of Jack Cade dying in the garden of the wise Iden: 'For I, that never feared any, am vanquished by famine, not by valour.' (Act IV, Scene 10.) Shakespeare teaches us that politics bring out futile hatreds, and Stendhal used to say that: 'Any political admixture in a work of art was like a pistol shot in the middle of a concert.'

With the exception of a few examples of jingoism which could irk a rather sensitive Frenchman, Shakespeare's art is always above politics. He always manages to avoid propaganda, even in his most 'official' plays. He never preaches morality or politics; he is only concerned with justice, and that is why he is a great dramatist whose wisdom is enriching. For him a dramatic subject is first and foremost a problem of mechanics involving conflicting human forces; the dramatist must control the conflict and find a solution. A dramatic theme is a kind of complicated clockwork mechanism which has more or less broken down under the impact of the passions which are part of it, and which has to be repaired and made workable in the course of the play. The balance-wheel of the mechanism is out of order and must be adjusted or put right. The complicated clockwork, its balance-wheel and its problems represent life in the broad context of the universe. The equilibrium of life is as unstable as the mechanism of a clock, and life, like man, endeavours to stand up, in spite of the law of gravitation. The conflicting forces, the passions, the balance-wheel out of order, are the images of men who oppose one another, who fight and plead for their rights, who use all kinds of means, in bad faith as well as in good faith, simply because their hearts are swamped by their passions, and their heads are cracked like old walls by the fury which sweeps them away. To find the solution to this problem of mechanics, to repair the clock by adjusting the wheel, means in terms of drama to settle all accounts, to cleanse man from his passions, and to restore health and life which in the end will be all the better for what preceded. It is in fact to perform the act of true justice. That is the real task of the dramatist, and it is the basic social function of the theatre.

The theatre is only useful to society if it cleanses men, adjusts and restores them, and it can only reach that aim by being, above all, the art of justice. It is in the name of justice that we witness the entry in the lists of young Henry Richmond, the future Henry VII, who to the trumpets' sound, and like St George, comes to defeat the monstrous Richard III. By his deed he brings justice to the most beautiful piece of historical pageantry which exists in the theatre, something which is comparable to our best tapestries, and which is a splendid slice of English history from Richard II to Richard III painted by Shakespeare. The blood of Richard III finally washes away the plot of Bolingbroke. The same aura of justice surrounds Fortinbras when he arrives on the stage at the end of *Hamlet*, bringing to a world of death and suicide a breath of new life and a positive solution to what looked like an insoluble problem; it is the fulfilment of Hamlet's prophecy before his death: 'I do prophesy the election lights on Fortinbras.'

Richmond, Fortinbras, are the characters who enable Shakespeare to develop for us Richard II, Henry VI and Hamlet, and at the same time to preserve justice; they are the axles of the scales and we could not do without them; they anticipate the angels of judgment day. A tragedy can only end, not by the death of the hero but by the complete solution of the problems dealt with; a play is a complex of parts and not one single part; a tragedy can only end with the appearance of the one who administers justice, and not simply through the death of a victim. The fanfare which meant the close of great tragedies is reminiscent of

the trumpets of judgment day. To deal with the real, to give a
style to an age, to go down in the street as a witness and not as a
militant propagandist, to restore morality to its proper place, all
in the name of justice, such are some of the aims of Shakespeare
which one might also describe as his social message. But he does
more than that, he brings on a new hero; he adds to the gallery of
tragic heroes a new one, one who is specifically his creation, and
who does not belong either to antiquity or to the Middle Ages; it
is the Renaissance hero, the hero who, tired by the mediocrity of
life, tortured by madness, is assailed by the highest form of doubt
and is so exactingly scrupulous as to put all in question. He is
chaste, pure, admirable, fascinating; his name is Richard II,
Henry VI or Hamlet. He is the hero who fails to save Macbeth
and so lets him go to his death; he is the one who gets hold of
Antony, he is the voluptuous victim of the Sonnets, and if he is
not Shakespeare himself, he is the most typical hero of a period of
renaissance, whether it is Shakespearian Renaissance or any
other renaissance. Shakespeare communicates to us the experiences of this hero, and with him we see that paradise has once
again been lost and with it faith. Everything is again put into
question; men have to endure the test of doubt and live through
the drama of belief, and the Shakespearian hero preserves through
all his trials a chaste nature, a scrupulous intelligence and a noble
heart. Whenever confronted with action he doubts its necessity,
for in ages of conflict a morality of action is an encouragement to
mediocrity, cupidity and injustice; everything is dirty and vulgar,
all flesh is threatened by worms whether it is alive or dead, therefore every gesture is a crime against human love and true friendship: and one cannot go on acting without soiling one's very soul.
That is the problem:

> How so ever thou pursuest this act
> Taint not thy mind,
> Taint not thy mind!

The moment the consequences of an action are in doubt, the
moment one asks oneself whether the action one is about to
perform is not only useful but just, everything collapses. As soon
as a man becomes lucid, as soon as he ceases to act according to
his faith, without the slightest reflection, even if it is only 'for an
eggshell', or even if there is 'no cause why the man dies', every-

thing grows blurred. Night and day, morning and evening, sun and moon, joy and hatred cease to exist as such; a kind of twilight hour, in which Nature herself seems to be at a loss, wondering whether 'to be or not to be', descends upon our earthly world and heralds the coming night. It is an ambiguous world very much like the one we are living in now, and the Shakespearian hero generally finds himself caught between light and darkness, between the real and the unreal, between being and not being, in a most ambiguous and dangerous, albeit superior position which if one becomes conscious of it, makes action impossible.

> . . . Thus conscience does make cowards of us all
> . . . And . . . enterprises lose the name of action.

This incapacity to act feeds the *taedium vitae*, the bitter intoxication of despair and the longing for suicide and death, through the bare bodkin 'which could bring about *quietus*':

> How weary, stale, flat and unprofitable seem to me all the uses of the world. Fie on't! O fie!
> . . . .
> I do not set my life at a pin's fee
> . . . .
> Since no man has ought of what he leaves,
> What is't to leave betimes?

But despair is only a transient phase, which leaves the hero's soul uncontaminated, and by submitting to his fate in time, he wins a transcendental victory. The hero has lived too long with his eyes fixed on the window which opens upon the infinite, to miss his moment of illumination and to fail to see from under his closed eyelids the glimmering lights of infinity beckoning him to their bourns. Having rejected suicide, he accepts death as a kind of solution to the problems which beset him, and he can prophesy the advent of action in a world which will bathe in a new faith. The trial by doubt is ended; the hero has been on the verge of the void, and now he knows that his sacrifice, accepted in the perfect lucidity of his mind which has trodden every corner of the maze of doubt, will bring forth a new world and a new faith.

Such is, as far as I can see, my understanding of the fascinating and complex Shakespearian hero, whom I like to call the hero of superior doubt, which for me is best represented in its purest and most chaste state by Hamlet. But we shall never repeat often enough that everything in Shakespeare is certainly complex; great poet that he was, Shakespeare could not fail to touch upon all the aspects of the problems which beset man and which as soon as they are observed become as varied in their aspects as Hamlet's cloud; 'they can look like a camel, like a weasel, like a whale'. The Shakespearian hero is the great human contribution to modern civilization; he is his spiritual message to us all. Besides his social and spiritual message, is there a kind message which in spite of the loss of his splendid language, the great and universal William sends to us Frenchmen, or rather to us men? I think there is, and it is a message on the plane of art. Shakespeare gives his art the apparent confusion and complexity of Nature. He composes musically, and most of his great works are composed like symphonies; one of the most musical of his compositions is *Antony and Cleopatra* which I used to love passionately. My love of this play brings to mind the extraordinary skill with which Shakespeare plays with words. He squeezes the last ounce of life out of them, he turns them inside out in the most brilliant puns, of which he is the supreme master; all sorts of puns, earthy, coarse or refined, they all spring from the very roots of the words. This leads to a final remark about poetry and about Shakespearian realism.

Shakespeare's poetry generally begins to soar when after having started from reality it rises above it. Let us take the example of *King Lear*, which is the play which moves us the most. Whenever I hear the words: 'My God, make me not be mad. . . .' I burst into tears. I saw Laurence Olivier play the part of King Lear, and he was unforgettable. The way he played the part was for me a revelation. When he came on the stage, crowned with flowers, I noted that Olivier had followed realism as far as daubing his feet with blood, which for us spectators looked like real blood. Looking at them, I suddenly realized that the blood on the feet made it possible for Olivier to forget about trying to show that his feet were bruised and sore and on the contrary to concentrate all his energy in rendering the sublime and serene poetry of Lear. Realism, pushed to its extreme limit, frees poetry. In France Lear would have had no blood on his feet, and the actor playing this part would have been compelled to show that this part of his anatomy was troubling him; this would have been a kind of stylization which would have detracted from his concentration on rendering the turmoil of his mind and soul and therefore from the poetry. Shakespeare offers us the best examples of poetic realism: he is one of the three or four universal geniuses. He soars above nations and it is quite natural that whenever we wish to draw him to us, we should look for what is universal in him. We are instinctively inclined to denationalize him and to leave behind his national garb; the English follow the opposite process, and it is right and natural that it should be so. For England he is universal, no doubt, but he is British born, and Rosencrantz and Guildenstern are students who belong more to Oxford than to Wittenberg. We all like to pull Shakespeare to ourselves; we take a leaf from Bottom's aesthetics, Bottom who in *A Midsummer Night's Dream* nimbly manages to produce 'Pyramus and Thisbe' by representing a wall with one hand, and a moon by using a lantern and a faggot. We take away from Shakespeare his props and crenellated walls, and we try to draw him towards the abstract, producing him with curtains and costumes which do not belong to any definite period. The English people try with all their might to hold him back in the midst of their chivalry and to prevent him from crossing the water; we on the other hand try to draw him to us. Can we be blamed for that? I think not, for Shakespeare is for us a vital need.

La Commedia dell'Arte[1]

Whenever I think about the Commedia dell'Arte, I think of my master Charles Dullin, all huddled up on his wicker chair and surrounded by his pupils. His sparkling eyes were either trying to pursue his thoughts or to follow the strange flights of his imagination. We, his pupils, swallowed with gaping mouths the nutritious art of improvisation which he was at that time pouring into us. Already deformed by illness, and accentuating still more his deformity in his urge to make us grasp the Commedia dell'Arte, Dullin worked like a flesh and bone reincarnation of a drawing by Jacques Callot. Whenever he discussed the various characters of the Commedia dell'Arte, particularly when he dealt with the enchanting characters of the first and second Zanies, his mouth watered and his thin lips curled up in an indefinable smile. Like a sorcerer he conjured up for us the mystery of those long words

[1] This is the text of the preface to a book about Commedia dell'Arte, by Duchartre.

like: Commedia dell'Arte (with two m's), improvisation, Zani, Pulcinella, etc. It would be excessive to say that he gave us the secret of these things, we probably did not deserve it, but he made us grasp the poetry which emanated from them, and to which he added his own personal poetry, which I shall never forget.

Later he took us through our first steps in improvisation, just enough to show us what a difficult art it is. I particularly enjoyed representing animals. I loved to restore to animals their humanity, and at the same time to denounce the animality of man. This clerk in a ministry, for instance, what is he made of? Is he simply dust and lustring, is he a crow or a mouse? These two ladies jabbering along the Promenade des Anglais in Nice, are they not ostriches in a zoo? Soon each one of us looked like the animal which corresponded to his own nature. Here from a collar and tie emerged a ram's head, there a horse; behind me a lion, a she-cat in practically every corner of the room. My friends thought I looked like a wolf; a young woman saw me as a puma . . . but there was something feline in her. . . . Thus was born in us the love of metamorphosis without which there is neither poetry nor art; at the same time the great problem of character loomed ahead. But the boundless universe of the Commedia dell'Arte retained its mystery: in spite of Dullin's precious guidance, we would have been unable to assume the appearance of a 'Capitan' by Callot or to put on our heads the black and hairy mask of Harlequin in order to produce laughter. The Commedia dell'Arte remained for me an enchanting but closed world which I hoped to visit one day. I was strangely attracted by this extraordinary form of theatre which behind Gilles's impenetrable mask and Scaramouche's vinous moustaches, kept its secret. The sight of the famous painting: *Departure of the Italian Commedia* has always caused me a very painful feeling, something like the strong sense of shame which one experiences when one finds oneself unwillingly involved in an act of injustice. The revocation of the Edict of Nantes and the expulsion of the Italian Commedia are two horrible deeds.

In Dullin's school we used to peer at the prints representing figures which defied the law of gravity; we weaved strange characters into our dreams; we should have loved to have had feet slim and pointed like those rubber-like dancers, the exuberant gusto of their fat old men or the lightning wit of the first Zani. We should have loved, above all, to share the nomadic life of these pleasant, philosophic scoundrels. More than twenty years have elapsed since those days, and we have never stopped exploring documents and reading books on this subject. Above all we have shed our clothes, donned the slip and practised our exercises in practically every theatre where we have been. We have done so on the proscenium of L'Atelier, in the Comédie Française, in Mounet-Sully's hall, at the Marigny, in a hall that we called La Roseraie, in brief wherever we took part in a play. We tried all sorts of masks, from the simple silk stocking which one puts on the head, to masks made of wire, cardboard or rubber; we have tormented our bodies working on the parallel bars, we have acquired bumps on the head, displaced vertebrae and done all sorts of things; we have tried everything, and I can say that I am not yet sure of what exactly Commedia dell'Arte is. Will this mystery ever be cleared up? As far as erudition on the subject is concerned, I must confess that I have made no headway at all. As for experience, it seems to me that it has to be started anew over and over again. But when it comes to love, faith and convictions about Commedia dell'Arte I could fill up reams of paper or talk for hours. Of course I am not quite sure whether what I might say would be labelled Commedia dell'Arte with two m's, Italian comedy or theatre of improvisation; all I know is that there is a type of play which consists essentially in representing life, only by using the human body. There is in my opinion a kind of performance which consists in taking four barrels, in fixing up on them planks in the shape of an apron-stage, climbing on these planks, and with the help of one's body, breath, voice, face and hands, re-creating the world. Call this what you like, this re-creation of the life which surrounds us aims at attracting and holding the attention of the passers-by who stop and watch. There is a game which consists in making an appointment each night with these passers-by or spectators and, by communicating and conversing with them, re-creating the world through one's own means. This game which you may call what you like establishes a to-and-fro exchange between performers and spectators, an exchange of hearts and a harmonization of tempo of breathing, which brings comfort to all and renews our faith in life. In order to take part in this game, we must open our eyes and ears and all our senses and use our 'radar' instruments to capture everything human. Then we witness the appearance of all sorts of natural and supernatural characters.

There is the wind, fire, water, a tree in a forest, illness, hunger, death, war, harvest, there are animals and there is man who merges into nature while nature plays at being man. The sun has set, the moon is about to rise and this is the hour of metamorphosis. The spectators lined up like the coils of a magnetic battery are ready to become the public. The actor feels his character glow within him; his everyday life fades away, disappears, his body creaks and alters under the force of the character who has lived in him for years. This character is himself, that is to say the prototype of his category, it is himself exteriorized. For twenty years the actor who is now on the stage has been constantly reconstructing his essential character to whom he belongs, since this character is his true mould or essence of his personality. For twenty years the actor has massaged his muscles, his joints, looked after his health, sculptured his cheekbones, drawn the twist of his mouth, or given the right tilt to his head, and by now he knows each beat of his heart, each breath of his lungs. He has examined carefully the relations which might exist, in all sorts of circumstances, between the character who is his 'true self' and other prototypes of mankind. His memory is an encyclopedia of tirades with which he can meet any dramatic situation, he is therefore fully armed and fully prepared for any situation.

There are three ways, or rather three styles, of facing up to a theatrical performance; an actor may act 'à la broche', 'à la souffle', 'à la canne'. In the first case 'broche' is an abbreviation for brochure, and it means that the actor has learnt his part by heart and can recite it; in the second case, 'souffle' stands for 'souffleur', the prompter, and it means that the actor relies on him; in the third case 'canne' stands for 'canvas', that is to say the floor of the ring or public stage upon which the improvising actor performs; it means therefore to act out of improvisation. In this case the actor has anticipated everything and he can meet any situation, and of course it is only when one has perfect control of one's body, feelings and mind, and when one is fully prepared to meet any situation, that one can talk of improvisation. The Commedia dell'Arte can therefore only be practised by the 'Complete Actor', and it is the kind of theatre which compels the actor to get to the pitch of his 'own true personality'. It is the kind of art which shows that freedom lies beyond silence and not within. An ignorant actor could not improvise for long; only somebody who

knows a lot can invent new words: Homer, Dante, Claudel. The
Commedia dell'Arte, which is the true art of the theatre and of
acting, denounces the absurdity of life and endeavours to restore
its equilibrium. The Commedia dell'Arte, which I cannot claim
to know fully, seems to me just as old as man. How many 'doctors'
do we not meet in life, and is the second Zani with the white mask
not the modern lamplighter? Don't we meet everywhere these
extraordinary characters which Callot had already fixed on copper?
But in the end it is the actor who, through his technique, transposes these characters into his magic world which has done away
with gravity, and in which imagination is free to move about
and to enjoy itself.

Why *The Cherry Orchard*?

In my opinion, *The Cherry Orchard* is Chekhov's masterpiece; I
think that of the four great plays which he has written, this is the
one which comes closest to universality and to generalizations
which embrace all men. While it reflects striking aspects of the
Russian soul it also contains aspects of feelings and thoughts which
pertain to all mankind. *The Cherry Orchard* is born from silence,
it is a vast pantomime unfolding in the course of two hours and
being adorned every now and then with bursts of poetry in the
same way as a necklace is livened up here and there with beautiful
jewels. It is a setting of brief retorts which frame a very rare silence.
The Cherry Orchard flows slowly like life; it is a kind of pure spring
in which one hears the murmur of souls. Few plays can give such
a physical 'impression of the passing of time'; this effect is obtained
through the fact that starting from silence, the play reproduces
most vividly the present; and the theatre is above all the art of the
present. In life the present is what is most difficult to get hold of.
Therefore it is not surprising that *The Cherry Orchard* should be
a play very difficult to grasp; its action takes place in silences, and
the dialogues, with the poetic tirades which shine like jewels, are
like music only meant to make silence vibrate: silence struggles
with time which in front of us or behind our backs continuously
transforms the future into past and memory. We say, 'Time passes',
but what does this mean since time is nothing but action? Should
we not say time pushes life as if through a strainer? Thanks to its
magic strainer, time turns what is coming to us and does not yet

exist concretely, into something finished and which therefore will only exist in memory. Coffee is a solid powder, but the filter strains it through and it becomes a liquid. What is time doing? Oh! it is at work. Ah! what is it working on? It is passing, and it is this mysterious passing or straining which makes our present. Existence is made to vanish by the extraordinary conjurer time. At a certain moment someone in *The Cherry Orchard* says, 'You see this card game', and at once one thinks that this card game is life. 'Take a card', that is the moment lived. 'Look at it, and put it back in the pack'; that, you think, is action in the present. 'It's in your pocket and with your handkerchief over it, my dear chap'; the present is past, finished! That's what happens in *The Cherry Orchard*. It is a play about the passing of time; therefore whether the characters are Russian or Japanese does not matter. Like some plays of Shakespeare and Molière it is a play which has universal value and which belongs to all mankind. But just as that English genius has described better than anybody else the approach of madness, and just as French insight is at its best in describing the problems of the human heart, the Russian genius seems to be better fitted than any other to deal with the present or the lived moment. Is Russia not placed astride the east and the west in just the same way as the present is astride the past and the future? Yet the universal values which are found in *The Cherry Orchard* cannot detract from the great homage which is due to the Russian soul for having revealed to us this subtle and profound experience of the passing of time. The structure of this play, which is built on silence and which takes place in the present, is fundamentally musical. The present, of course, is something so elusive, so fast changing, that the author never has enough time to develop a given theme, and so he must always pass on to the next. There is no time to stop, so we pass from an everyday incident to a sentimental sensation, from this sensation to a general thought, from that to a joke, from that to reflections on society, etc., without ever exhausting any one of these moments which are in fact only means of avoiding the danger to which one ceaselessly returns. We are confronted by a succession of moments of torpor interspersed with sharp awakenings and vain attempts to avert a magnetic attraction towards suffering and disaster, in the same way as one tries to keep oneself awake because one is afraid of dying in one's sleep. Each of these unfulfilled and incomplete moments leaves behind a state of anxiety which is really the true subject of the play. One cannot help thinking that if a composer applied these subtle methods of composition to his art, his music would probably be ultra-modern. The themes are no sooner stated than they fade away as if burnt out, and there is an air of incoherence between the various themes which is in fact the result of the most careful and methodical planning. The dramatic movement is extremely subtle, and built as it is on a musical analogy, it is a slow movement.

This is one of the reasons why I like *The Cherry Orchard*. The dramatic tempo of the play is a matter of density and not of velocity, or of speed of acting and unfolding events; it is effective when every instant is filled to capacity. It is often said, and it is even confirmed as far as *The Cherry Orchard* is concerned in the *Dictionnaire des Oeuvres*, that there is very little action in Chekhov. What this really means is that there are no complicated plots or abundance of incidents; but that does not mean that there is no action. Action must not be confused with plot. 'Let whatever you do be always simple,' said Horace, and Racine added: 'Invention consists in making something out of nothing.' The action of *The Cherry Orchard* is taut, and it embraces the whole play, for every one of its moments is well filled and has its own density which does not lie in the dialogue but in the flowing life. The subject of the *Three Sisters* could be summed up in the following way: we should like to get to town; will we go to town? we shan't go to town. There is one single catalyser ('the object' as Stanislavski used to describe it) meant to bring about the progress of this simple and unique action: soldiers. In *The Cherry Orchard* the catalyser is the domain which gives the play its title.

Act I 'The cherry orchard' runs the risk of being sold.
Act II 'The cherry orchard' is going to be sold.
Act III 'The cherry orchard' is being sold.
Act IV 'The cherry orchard' has been sold.

The rest of the play is made up of life itself. The house is asleep in the night, waiting; people arrive, have some coffee, read a telegram, then go to bed. The morning comes, the birds awaken. In small groups, the inmates of the house sit in turn on the same bench, like flights of swallows on the same telegraph wire. Some Jewish musicians pass by, playing; the moon rises; some dancing takes place; another telegram is read, then a few glasses of kvass, a game at cards; five people arrive from town. The time has now come to leave 'the cherry orchard'; clothes have to be packed up, furniture has to be brought together; one hears the jingling bells of the horses in the courtyard; the shutters are closed, a last glance at the old walls and all is over. This house, which two hours before was like a pregnant woman about to give birth, is now an icy tomb from which life has fled. This life composed of silences, these mysteriously fleeting themes, this sorrowful and anguished unfolding of the action, confront French actors with entrancing problems. The French actor is used to basing his acting on the text which, in the French theatre, generally contains the action; here in this case, acting must find its basis outside the text. When the action is contained in the text, it unfolds at a quicker tempo than when it is outside the text. The French actor is therefore used to a quick tempo. *The Cherry Orchard* has a slow tempo, even for Russian actors, and besides that, Russian slowness is not the same as French slowness; therefore *The Cherry Orchard* must be produced according to French slowness and not Russian slowness, but this slowness constitutes for French actors an excellent discipline in the art of conveying the density of life. There are few plays more entrancing than this play. There are not many actors who get thoroughly immersed and lost in this play, but when that happens, those who do so live the best moments of their artistic lives. It is the same for a whole cast; *The Cherry Orchard* is one of the few plays in which a whole cast could really get so profoundly lost as to cease to believe that they are in a theatre, and believe on the contrary that this family truly exists and that they are in real life, and such an extraordinary metamorphosis takes place in the name of poetic truth. This play belongs neither to the naturalism of the beginning of the century nor to realism, it belongs to truth, and truth always has two faces, a real one and a poetic one—its appearance and its inner meaning, and that is the basis of poetic realism as in Shakespeare.

These are some of the points I should like to bring out in a production of *The Cherry Orchard*, and I should add that the love I bear to the play is my excuse for the personal way in which I may approach it; true love is better than respect. *The Cherry Orchard* reminds me of a nest of tables which stretch indefinitely one into the other; it starts from any familiar everyday subject, to move to the universal and the general; it is something like a

Japanese flower which begins unfolding in a glass of water as soon as the appropriate tablet has been thrown in; it is also a kind of parable, which starting from everyday life rises to the metaphysical plane; it starts from individuals in their own universe and it rises to the general plane where individuals are seen under the angle of universality, and that is what makes it a great play.

Let us have a look at it in detail. In the centre we have a woman full of charm, generous and unconscious to the point of amorality. She represents that type of human being which is weak, passionate, most attractive by the combination of virtue and weakness which makes the true hero. Her heart in her hand, a sinner full of love, distributing her money freely, Liouba is the symbol of humanity, the eternal human being. Around her, there are three men who form the three angles of a triangle and represent the three age-long social currents which never cease to battle against one another. Gaiev personifies tradition, ancient civilization and the old generation; he stands for an age which has lost its vitality, which is now fast fading away, and which one tries to hold back with all the nostalgia of a good thing which has been lost and yet remains worthy of love. At the top of the second angle, we find Lopakine, the son of a moujik, the hard-working business man, proud of his newly acquired strength, and also somewhat ashamed of the imperfections which he still drags about him. He too loves and esteems the age which is just fading away and would like to save it, but social evolution is irresistible and he finds himself more or less compelled to buy 'The cherry orchard', symbol of an obsolete world; it is he who has the idea of utilizing it in a modern way, by dividing the property into plots of land for building new houses. He announces in prophetic tones the first revolution which was to break out a year later (we are in 1904). If Gaiev represents the past, Lopakine represents the present. Yet nothing stands still, all things are meant to disappear, that is why Chekhov confronts Lopakine with another character who is the third angle of the triangle, and who is Trofimov, the eternal student. Trofimov has a kind of undeveloped prophetic gift which enables him to tell Lopakine that the present occupiers of his newly built houses will be their owners tomorrow; Trofimov, who is the potential revolutionary, announces the 1917 revolution and the fact that every social revolution is followed by another. We cannot help thinking about the permanent state of revolution of Trotsky.

These various social positions are examined and developed, with a control and a tact which call forth the admiration of the most delicate sensibilities. The social aspect of *The Cherry Orchard* is dealt with by a fairy-like hand and therefore is all the more effective. Like the Chinese methods of acupuncture, the prick is small but the repercussions are of enormous importance and go far beyond the 'Russian case'. They affect every one of us, both in space and time; it is something that is valid for all men at all times. If the individuals who are studied become sociological cases, sociology then becomes a science which is of interest for the eternal individual. Trofimov explains how this kind of development takes place; he says: 'If we wish to begin to live, we must first of all redeem our past and tear ourselves away from it; but one cannot do that without great suffering, and one cannot redeem anything without a frightful and obstinate effort.' This sentence is obviously addressed to a whole generation, and to a whole society and also to the religious notion of redemption, but it is also addressed to every individual throughout the ages and in its most general aspects. The human being, like societies and civilizations, comes to life, lives, dies and renews itself. Is it not said that every three weeks all the cells of our body are renewed, and that therefore every three weeks our being is something different from what it was previously? Chekhov deals with three types of human beings: Gaiev the one who is about to disappear, Lopakine the one who is due to replace him in the present, and Trofimov the one who already prepares for the one who will replace Lopakine. They are the past, the present and the future. However attractive our past might be, however much we might cling to it, we must become worthy to receive the future, and in order to be so, we must have the courage to tear ourselves away from our past; it is the price we must pay for the right to live, it is the redemption and the ransom exacted by life; 'good night, old life, good morning, new life'; and though the eyes may still be reddened by tears, a new smile begins to break. That's life, and that is the lesson of *The Cherry Orchard*. That is the meaning of the three men who gravitate round Liouba Ranievsky, the moving symbol of humanity on the march, on a plane far above any social plane. *The Cherry Orchard* is neither a realistic play nor a social play; Chekhov is too great a man to tie himself to one single plane; it is the play of a great poet who, owing to the depth of his feelings, and an extraordinary vision, goes beyond the

social, which is given the importance that it deserves, to the very
sources of existence.

Another lesson which can be learnt from *The Cherry Orchard* is
that Chekhov shows us what a true artist is. We rather tend to shun
that word because of hypocritical modesty, but we nevertheless
know that an artist is a witness for his time and therefore he must
try first and foremost to be the servant of justice. We cannot be
partisan and just at the same time; a true artist can only be
partisan of justice and nothing else; he can only be committed to
justice and to nothing else, and such was Chekhov's love of justice
that it is said that he was respected and admired by the two camps
which existed in the Russia of his time. In *The Cherry Orchard*
we love Gaiev and we love the good old days, but we also love
Lopakine and would hope to help him to refine himself and to
bring to him what he lacks and what at times gives him a sense
of shame. At the same time we cannot but approve of the ideas of
Trofimov; we regret his slackness, and would ask him to be
more realistic in his revolutionary plans. Chekhov's art is an art
devoted to justice, therefore to great art, and *The Cherry Orchard*
leaves behind it a great feeling of impartiality. Chekhov is an artist
because he gives us a lesson of tact, control and above all of restraint.
One cannot be a great artist without a strong sense of pudicity.
The lack of pudicity can only be excused on the ground of simplicity and candour; but of course one must not confuse restraint and
prudishness. Chekhov teaches us the art of economy. One cannot
take away anything from *The Cherry Orchard*; whatever could be
left out has been left out by the author. One is reminded of Charlie
Chaplin's admirable remark about one of his films: 'When a work
seems finished, you shake it like a fruit tree so as to keep only the
fruit which cling solidly to the branches.' 'Never put anything in
a play which is not absolutely necessary,' said Racine. With
Chekhov the stage directions themselves are important and must
be examined with great care; in one of his letters he said: 'One
finds often in my plays the stage direction: "through tears", but
that is intended to show the state the characters are in and not the
tears.' All his characters, like most of Shakespeare's characters, are
ambiguous; Lopakine the terrible is also a shy, undecided and
good man; Madame Ranievsky, the victim, has also a very passionate nature; Gaiev who represents tradition is lazy; Trofimov,
the revolutionary, is a spineless, impulsive character. All Chekhov's

characters are complex, they are not wooden, they are all very much alive and with throbbing hearts. *The Cherry Orchard* rests on the heart and that is one of the reasons why I love it—the heart which, as Trofimov says, contains ninety-five senses which go beyond the mind and beyond the five senses which have officially been put at our disposal. It is the heart which puts us in a state of tears when we look back upon our past, and which also pulses on and therefore compels us to face the present and the future. It is the heart which matters, for it is superior to the head which only produces ideas, or to the senses which only produce covetousness; the heart is above all revelation, vision and why not say the word—love, that is to say true knowledge, for as Claudel wisely said, to know is to be born with, or at the same time as, the thing that one knows.

In Search of *Pour Lucrèce*[1]

THE MANUSCRIPT

While I was studying *Pour Lucrèce* of Jean Giraudoux, I often happened to meet people who said to me: 'Ah, yes, the play which was unfinished.'—'How do you know that it was unfinished?'—'Well I don't quite know, but some people say that it is so.' I found this kind of commentary irritating and worrying, and I feel that there are enough reliable witnesses to put an end to it. There is for example Edwige Feuillère to whom Giraudoux read his play in 1943 while she was playing in *Sodome et Gomorrhe*.[2] She remembered clearly the two versions and she remembers a sentence from one of them, which says: 'Here is the unicorn, see that when she leaves she is a doe', and which is not to be found in the other version. There is also Marie-Louise Bousquet to whom Giraudoux had given a fully detailed account of his play. Still, the best thing we could do was to study the manuscript. Thanks to Madame Suzanne Giraudoux and to her son, Jean-Pierre, we have been able to do so, and I could hardly describe a more sad and moving experience. Giraudoux's elegant handwriting seems to run across the white or blue paper; it is the writing of an inspired man. The first manuscript didn't have the names of the

---

[1] *Duel of Angels.*
[2] *Sodom and Gomorrha.*

characters; Giraudoux knows perfectly who they are and listens to them, noting down their words without wasting time to write their names at the beginning of their speeches. Once Giraudoux has completed a first draft, he does not work over it; he lays it aside, takes a sheaf of white paper and pens out another version from beginning to end, relying entirely on his amazing memory. His corrections take place on the text which he has in his mind. That is why there is more than one version of *Pour Lucrèce* in Giraudoux's handwriting. Here are some reflections prompted by the examination of this precious manuscript; the last, alas! First of all the version which we have chosen and which is also the one that Jouvet had adopted is contained in a manuscript of white paper written over in pale blue ink:

Act I comprises forty-one pages, ten scenes and it ends with the words, 'Take this handkerchief, my little one. That's it, hold it tight; it is your Ariadne's handkerchief; it will lead you unfailingly to calamity!'

Act II, stretching over thirty-five pages, comprises four scenes and ends with a short monologue by Paola in which we find the phrase: 'since she is already practising with muff and toque in the death of the living' . . . In this second act we find that the fourth and last scene of five pages has a variant of eight pages which begins with the words: 'This is a painful moment, but here is a friend . . .' ending with Paola's words once Lucile has walked out: 'Yes, my girl, yes!' This is the variant that we have adopted, while retaining at the same time two excellent ideas from the original version: the idea of the wake, and the idea of 'the trot of the duel' which justifies the long waiting. These two versions end with the words: 'the curtain falls'.

Act III, thirty-two pages, comprising eight scenes, which end with Barbette's monologue and its final words: 'To avenge you, my little angel, and to lead them straight to eternal damnation: Amen!' And once more Giraudoux has written: 'the curtain falls'. Such is what can be called the final version of *Pour Lucrèce*. Besides this version, there are numerous pages in Giraudoux's handwriting, in fact complete acts; here is a list:

Act I. (1) A complete version of thirty-four pages ending in the same way as the final version but beginning very differently: 'A Café, the same as before (probably suggested by the Café des Deux-Garçons which is on the "Cours Mirabeau", at Aix-en-

Provence) and a dialogue between a waiter and a non-commissioned officer.'

(2) An unfinished version of twenty-one pages which begins with a conversation between a town-crier and a waiter and which ends in the middle of the great scene between Paola and Lucile. It is obviously a working text written hurriedly without the names of the characters and likely to be one of the first drafts.

Act II. Nothing but the version which we chose including the variant which we adopted.

Act III. Two complete versions on blue paper. One runs into thirty-five pages and comprises six scenes, the other runs into thirty-one pages and comprises five scenes. In both versions Lucile's death is followed by a short scene with the Public Prosecutor, which is a kind of monologue which we decided to discard; both versions contain a final monologue in Giraudoux's handwriting which is practically the same in the two cases and which ends with the words: 'To avenge you, my little one, and to lead them straight to eternal damnation . . . Amen.' Then the words: 'the curtain falls'. In both versions the Public Prosecutor asks in the first page for 'the report of the Thomasse affair'; in the version which we chose he asks for 'the interrogation records of the Thomasse affair'.

Thus there are altogether three versions of Act III with three final monologues in Giraudoux's handwriting, and in fact in the numerous pages which still exist one can discover a fourth version of this final monologue, and once more the words: 'the curtain falls'. I don't see how after all this evidence, anybody could suggest that the play had not been fully completed by Giraudoux himself.

Besides these manuscripts, we have also found typed texts including Act III. Act II and its variant are corrected in his own handwriting. We could not find Act I, but it is bound to exist, for on the first page, for instance, Joseph's second answer as given by the manuscript: 'I have never had the means of learning that, Monsieur le Comte,' has become in Jouvet's text given to me by his son, Jean-Paul: 'I left school too early, Monsieur le Comte.' The typed script of the first act with Giraudoux's corrections is perhaps among Jouvet's papers. Still, this is not important; what matters is the fact that the manuscript of *Pour Lucrèce* is entirely in Giraudoux's handwriting and that there are at least two complete manuscripts. There could of course never be any doubt as to authorship; anybody who reads the play knows at once that it is by Giraudoux, and in producing *Pour Lucrèce* it is him we are serving, and with deep and affectionate admiration.

THE WORK ITSELF

Everybody knows that in order to interpret a character one must be able to identify oneself with him; it is exactly the same for the dramatic work which one wishes to produce. A dramatic work or a character stands in front of oneself as a true being. One cannot identify oneself with a being except by loving him, with all his qualities and his defects. In order to love, one must know, and in order to know one must get acquainted, and for that, analyses and objective observations are not enough. One must penetrate the being one tries to know, bearing in mind that finally everything is sensation. The problem therefore is to open the being one wishes to know, to penetrate him, to turn around, to converse, argue with him, and even to take his mechanism to pieces as if it were parts of a clock, but above all one must observe more with one's heart than with one's head. It is best not to think too much, and not to be in a hurry so as to become slowly pervaded by the substance of the other. The thing to remember is that all means are good so long as they remain means, the aim being to reach sensations. At the end of this tussle, in order to get acquainted, the means used fall to the ground like useless weapons, while our skin remains covered with little grains of powder, and other traces which are the beginning of knowing and of identifying oneself in love with the object with which we have been grappling. This is a happy moment, it is a moment when one has the physical sensation that the point reached could not be otherwise; it is also a very dangerous moment for if one has taken the wrong road one cannot go back, for one has become blind to anything that is not what one has discovered. When one comes to grips with a character or with a work which one has to produce, everything rests on the chancy way in which one makes the first contacts. What anxiety when one is confronted with a work which is not yet known! What panic, what cold sweat and tragic nervousness, when one knows that so much depends on this first contact when a great love is at stake. 'The experience of the beautiful is a duel in which the artist

shrieks with fear before being vanquished,' said Baudelaire.
Grappling with a work of art resembles a duel or love.

After these brief remarks let us set off in search of Giraudoux's
Lucrèce, without Giraudoux, alas! A literary work is locked up in
the manuscript like an unborn child in his mother's womb.
Giraudoux's sensibility is both poetic and extremely sharp. Restraint inclines him to secrecy, and sharpness towards the rare. If he
were not properly understood this inclination towards the rare might
easily look like preciosity. Restraint taken too literally and too faithfully respected might hide violence and the authentic temperament
of the poet. For Giraudoux is without doubt a dramatic poet. He
oscillates between Racine and Marivaux, though *Pour Lucrèce* is
nearer Racine than Marivaux. *Pour Lucrèce* is a tragedy. It is not
the verbal shape which makes a tragedy, it is the way the characters
behave; when these characters do not hesitate to go beyond their
instinct of self-preservation there is tragedy; in other words,
tragedy begins at the point where the instinct of self-preservation
disappears. This is the case with the characters of *Pour Lucrèce*
who, carried away by their passions, reach a stage of self-intoxica-
tion where the only thing that is left to them is to destroy themselves; the wording of the advertising bills could very well be:
'Fight to the death.' It is therefore a fight to the finish, in the
course of which Giraudoux nevertheless keeps a firm control and
avoids pathos; *Pour Lucrèce* is a tragedy because of its action
and not because of its expression. What will be its style?

Pour Lucrèce belongs to the family of tragedies because it is
placed under the sign of justice. It is not for nothing that Lucile's
husband is the Imperial Public Prosecutor. The play takes place
in an atmosphere of assizes, but out of restraint, Giraudoux places
his assizes in a café or pastry-shop on the Cours Mirabeau, in
Aix-en-Provence. But in spite of the honeyed atmosphere which
surrounds the town of Aix, all the laws of tragedy are respected;
they are: settlement of accounts, questions of rights, and characters
with passions so disproportionate that they are the cause of their
death. Lucile (who is Lucretia in the Second Empire style) is the
heroine of purity, but like Hamlet or Lear, she is afflicted with an
inordinate passion which is a kind of horror and disgust for life
unable to rid itself of its impurities. *Pour Lucrèce* is the tragedy
of purity, and it takes place at a level which excludes sympathy.

Though the characters are sympathetic and antipathetic in turn, the main question for each is to justify himself, to prove that he is right. The characters have each their individual reasons, which they explain and use as weapons, but in the end, life will be the judge which will show the usefulness of their sacrifice. Although the action of the play takes place in an atmosphere of bitterness and disappointment, the final dénouement produces a kind of profound satisfaction and unfathomable resonance. Some works move in a circle and, like snakes, bite their tails; others have a direction, and this is the case with *Pour Lucrèce*. *Pour Lucrèce* is a great subject, that is evident since it is the famous Roman subject of the *Rape of Lucrece*; it is obvious that Giraudoux is aiming high. In order to free himself from any traces of Roman solemnity, he removes it from its normal settings and transports it to the heart of Provence in the world of our grandmothers; but one must not forget that Aix has a Roman nobility and Cézanne's and Manet's characters obey the laws of the Empire: Aix therefore is not Rome but it is Roman, and Napoleon III is not a Roman emperor, but he is nevertheless an emperor. In the time of Lucretia, Rome was ruled by kings and not by emperors; still, that does not matter; let us continue. Giraudoux avoids conventions without of course falling into preciosity and affectation. Although Napoleon III style has been extremely fashionable during these past years, we would be unwise to insist on this aspect; in fact we shall serve Giraudoux best by avoiding fashions and we can best help him by avoiding modernity.

Pour Lucrèce is a kind of Racinian tragedy with moving characters and an extremely controlled structure. The action begins round about 4 p.m. and ends the following morning. The unity of time is strictly respected. The theme of *Pour Lucrèce*, like that of many other plays, is very close to the news item; it contains the ingredients of a kind of melodrama in the Eugène Sue manner: narcotic seduction scenes, poison and death. But then *Bajazet* and *Partage de Midi* are also close to the news item, but the point is that Racine, Claudel and Giraudoux are poets. Besides that, this tragedy of purity has another point in common with Racinian tragedy; it begins in a state of crisis, and it is the state of crisis which justifies the verbal excitement which translates itself into tirades and recitatives, and causes hallucinations, incantations and the extra-lucidity of the tense situation. One cannot move through this play without having prepared oneself for this state of crisis. To sum up, intoxication, state of crisis, Roman grandeur, transmuted news items, settlement of accounts, assizes, fight to the death, all the ingredients of tragedy handled with restraint, subtle sensibility and here and there a few drops of wit, in the magic atmosphere of Provence. Such is the first impression of *Pour Lucrèce*. All along the text, flights of poetry alternate with realistic passages; the play is a mixture of both; what style will finally emerge? Should we follow Giraudoux's style so splendidly interpreted by Jouvet; should we try to follow Jouvet, or should we on the contrary try to extract something new from this author who is always new? Jouvet's influence on Giraudoux is profound, and Giraudoux himself is no longer present to guide us, therefore we must rediscover him by ourselves.

First of all it is clear that the staging must be as controlled as the construction of the play. Light will convey to us the colour of Aix, and the indirect lightings and the transparency effects will convey the aquarium-like quality of the Cours Mirabeau; the costumes and the various accessories will convey to us the drama of the characters and the attractive aspects of the play. A blend of concrete fact and imprecisions will represent the climate of reality and dream which is that of the play. The sun and the heat will be reflected by shutters which seem somehow to try to hold it back. The best way of rendering the passionate intoxication of the play and its fundamental state of crisis seems to be by being faithful to the musical rhythm of the play. Like Racine, Giraudoux is a musician and the action of his play follows a symphonic pattern while his poetic inspiration finds its authentic expression in music. I think I have said enough; let the work have its say. The way the play takes shape on the stage will dictate to us its conditions; the characters are waiting, let us not miss our appointment with them, let us go and meet them.

IN QUEST OF THE CHARACTERS

The first character to make his appearance in the play is a waiter; Giraudoux had done the same thing in *Le Cantique des Cantiques*.[1] This waiter resembles the actor Fernand Ledoux when

[1] *The Song of Songs.*

T.J.B.—I

he was playing that part at the Comédie Française in the setting
by Vuillard. Giraudoux's waiters are charming. This one is called
Joseph; he is naïve, likeable, sensitive, quick and with a certain
innocence. Like many well-trained waiters, he has a good deal of
admiration and respect for the nobility: 'M. de la Badonnière is
related to the Lesseps!' . . . That is important. He loves his wife.
He is the first to mention the aroma of love which emanates from
Aix, a very humble and simple love indeed, but probably the only
true and profound love. Aix before the arrival of the Public
Prosecutor and his wife Lucile was the town of love; everything
in Aix was pervaded with the fragrance of love, and Joseph
himself belongs to this world of voluptuous love adventures.
Joseph's first words set the tone, fix up the setting and tell us that
this is a play about love; he is perfectly at ease in the maze of love
intrigues which cover the good warm town of Aix. We are at the
29 June, 1868, it is tea-time, and in Aix this is the time for ice-
cream; the plane trees sift through the intricacies of their leaves
and branches the long rays of honeyed light which here and there
tinges with gold the Cours Mirabeau bathing in the kind of
glimmering light of an aquarium. The scene is set at the Café des
Deux Garçons, the dream café of Giraudoux, a café situated in the
middle of the Cours Mirabeau and surrounded by pastry shops
for which Aix is famous. All the guest-characters of the play
come to this café; and they are a kind of chorus which represents
the town of Aix, the town of love. 'Let Marseilles have the plague,
here we have love,' says one of the characters. First to come on
the scene is the flower girl. Her name is Gillette; she is only
16 years old, and although she is pure she is like all children who
have had a tough childhood (her mother is in prison because of
some love-story), she knows life; she reminds one of those 10- or
12-year-old mountain shepherds who in their pastures watch with
the utmost candour bulls covering cows. Then comes the seducer,
Count Marcellus. He is the seducer who represents vice, therefore
evil, he is the Don Juan of the town. Don Juan is rather an impre-
cise character, who ranges from the devil to the young sweetheart
in films. The closer Don Juan is to vice and evil the further he is
from the good-looking young lead. The seducer in the play is
nearer Baudelaire's dandy than Beau Brummel. He is the dark
pole of the play and he has known all sorts of women, courtesans,
liars, rakes; he has tried everything that is low and vulgar, and

when he meets with the wife of the Public Prosecutor who is a woman who is pure, frank and noble, he must have her. From then on he cannot think of anything else and he is all the more determined to have her in that the Public Prosecutor has attacked him publicly. In the end, however, one cannot but wonder whether this seducer with his professional charm who has never been in love, has not truly fallen desperately in love for the first time in his life. He whom people point out as being only fit to be spat on, is very near redemption, and in fact did not the gratuitous way in which he offered his life redeem him?

Paola is the feminine counterpart of Marcellus, she is married to Armand; she has had many lovers, including Marcellus, but she takes them one at a time, and thinks that she really loves her husband. Her opinion of men is something quite personal which, unfortunately for men, is not too remote from the truth. According to her, man does not know feelings, he merely mimes them. 'Man', she says, 'is only good, beautiful, powerful when he is engrossed in the fictitious and domineering type of life which, in his eyes, makes him master of the world and which delivers him weak and blind into our hands.' She belongs to the 'maffia of women' and cannot tolerate the fact that Lucile refuses to belong to it. She is very beautiful and in spite of her destructiveness, she is truly attractive. When she is attacked, she fights back to the end and in her struggle with Lucile she very often has the upper hand. She represents feminine passion, and as such she is true to what she stands for and she fights with the weapons which are those of a wild animal. Like wild animals, she has a kind of acrid, bitter, but very attractive flavour; she is strong, she does not provoke, but if attacked, she is ruthless. If she had been living in the age of Lucretia, she would have been a follower of Epicurus; she stands for pagan Giraudoux. To this dark couple composed of Paola and Marcellus, Giraudoux has opposed the couple Lucile–Armand which stands for light. Armand is a faithful husband in love and happy with his wife Paola who is everything to him. He loves life only through her; it is he who has made Paola and that in spite of her unfaithfulness. Although he is faithful and she unfaithful, happiness was quite within their reach and capacity. Armand is the confident husband, and husband-lover, a delightful character whose misfortune draws our sympathy. He is the one who is least prepared for misfortune and he is the one who is more severely hurt than anybody else. He is a good talker, he can handle the noble style, he has been an actor in the past, and he has a deep sensibility. He is the most moving of the male characters, and the unfolding of his misfortune, which is of capital importance, is extremely difficult to handle. He will end like a cornered beast overwhelmed by his sorrows, and like a scorpion he poisons himself; he ends in a state of hypnosis, knocked out, and deprived of reflexes. After having been physically destroyed by Lucile, he rejoins her and he is throughout moving and sympathetic.

Lucile, the heroine of the play, is a very complex character. One can only know her through a kind of osmosis; she is virtue and she is not virtue, justice and not justice! She is purity but not a dreamer . . . in the end, I think she contains altogether, virtue, purity and the cruel justice of light, for light is cruel like truth. Lucile is afflicted with the double desire of light and truth, and attracted by light like night insects, she will burn herself and she will be consumed by truth. Lucile has moments of strange torpor, then she suddenly becomes a statue with a luminous look of light which condemns and executes. This strange gift is something beyond her will; she cannot fail to obey it; whenever she meets an impure person she automatically freezes and closes up and not as a judge or a saint but simply as the symbol of health. She cannot help her reactions, but there is pride and even contempt in her; yet this strange gift of hers must surely cause her suffering. One cannot possibly endeavour to give back to a town its awareness of 'original sin' without feeling the great weight of one's own responsibility. Her gift takes her to the verge of the abnormal and she will be its first and most moving victim. She is the opposite of the conventional tragic character, and at the same time she carries in herself the very essence of tragedy in the sense that she has been entrusted with a mission in which she cannot fail and which will lead her to death. She lives in a world of her own; there is something supernatural in her and she is the only character in the play who is in direct contact with God. The other characters seem to be completely unaware of God and therefore of sin. Aix enjoys the bliss of voluptuous amorality, though not without a certain bitter taste in the mouth and a nostalgia for the lost past. This nostalgia which Lucile truly reveals is the nostalgia of purity which brings back with it original sin and its consequences. In brief, two metaphysical concepts of life are in conflict; the pagan and the

Christian, and the problem is well set. Lucile, who has been entrusted with a divine mission, knows the 'strange' loneliness of heroes. She had hoped that in spite of her being afflicted with the disease of purity she would be able to live side by side with her husband; she soon realizes that he too is a stranger to her. She is utterly alone, and all she can do is to accept her heroic condition: 'the heroes are those who magnify a life which they can no longer bear.' Lucile does not look quite like that in the eyes of the others. For Paola she is a woman who loves men and who does not love her husband, and there lies indeed the weakness which will lead her to her doom. What kind of a man is her husband?

Lionel Blanchard, the Imperial Public Prosecutor, has been living in Aix for a few years. He originally came from Limousin, the province which, according to Giraudoux, has supplied the greatest number of popes, and the smallest number of lovers. Nevertheless Lionel loves Lucile in the style of the late nineteenth-century husbands, that is to say he respects her more than he loves her. He would never indulge in the coarse idea of treating her as a mistress; he will of course regret all that in the end in a moment of painful indignation. It seems impossible to decide through what Lionel gives her, whether Lucile loves or despises men. One might well wonder whether she has ever really been in love, and whether her respectful husband has ever revealed her to herself. According to the text we cannot but doubt; she only succeeds in revealing herself to herself in a dream, with Marcellus as an imaginary partner, and . . . thanks to the expert support of Barbette. There lies the profound and unavoidable drama; the notion of seduction is part of herself and is in herself. Was she not guilty of indulging unknowingly in her taste for men? She will not be able to get rid of that taste except by submitting to it and by sacrificing herself to her purity. But let us come back to Lionel, the magistrate-husband whom Lucile loves. He is like a solicitor who has acquired new chambers; he is ambitious and he displays his zeal; hence the noisy way in which he attacks the seducer; he wants to deal with striking cases; he wants to get on; and his desire to succeed stimulates his self-pride to the utmost and renders him ruthless in adversity. But he is by no means an old fogey; he is on the contrary distinguished-looking, a good talker, cultured, and probably of the same generation as Armand and Marcellus. If it were not so it would keep the play in a lower key. On the contrary, the fact that he is as young as his rivals brings out the slightly comic aspect of the character which Giraudoux has given him, for although he is elegant and intelligent, he is a bourgeois and, as such, he is a compound of prejudices and conventions from which he suffers and which contribute to the drama.

Thus, all the characters of this play are like true characters of tragedy; they each have a 'fissure', or a crack in their character which will cause their doom. Marcellus's crack is his dissolute ways, Paola's is pagan love, Lionel's is bourgeois conventions, Armand's is trust, and Lucile's is purity and the love of light which kills. There is only one character in the play who looks properly equilibrated and that is Lucile's friend Eugénie. This young woman, who radiates easy-goingness and equilibrium, is to Lucile what Philinte is to Alceste, and it is very likely that, like Philinte, she represents some of the most attractive aspects of the author's character. Like the author, she sets the play in motion, then as soon as it is started, she retires discreetly, knowing that dramatic mechanics and fate will do the rest. Eugénie is the good genius of Aix, and the only free woman in the play. She has no complexes, and like Giraudoux, no awareness of original sin; she represents life with its liberties, its loves, its indulgences and smiles. She has wit, quick repartees and she loves life and happiness and accepts readily all human foibles and weaknesses. While Lucile kills with truth, Eugénie reassures with frankness and in the end one wonders whether she could not have discreetly solved the problem involved without catastrophe! . . . I find her extremely attractive, I have a real weakness for her, and I should have loved to close with her these few notes on *Pour Lucrèce*, but someone is protesting; it is Barbette, the procuress. She looks like fate, she is the witch of the play, and she obviously knows the infernal means which can make moustaches grow on young women. Nevertheless she too has her revelation. The night which she spent with Lucile has profoundly impressed her, and at the end of the play she no longer is what she was at the beginning. She too has evolved. She has had a revelation of what authentic purity is, and it is she who gives the precious information which we hear and which is that Lucile was Lucretia. She is entrusted with the morality of the play, and we realize that it must have taken an extraordinary revelation to make this toothless procuress say while the curtain falls: 'Purity does not belong to this world, yet every ten years there is a flash of its light. This flash of purity will reveal to women their little games and turpitudes; they will remain motionless and surprised as if a photographer was taking them. Thanks to you, for weeks I shall see them when they come to me, clinging to the chest of drawers, and shutting their eyes to see the flash.' *Pour Lucrèce*, or the tragedy of purity.

Case of Conscience of Kafka

It will soon be twenty years since I began frequenting and enduring Kafka. I remember those evenings at Lyons-la-Forêt, in the little house which André Masson had rented; I can see Masson consumed by his own words, Rose Masson hypnotized by 'her man' and her two growing children Diego and Luis. The latter is now acting in *The Castle*. I can see one or two faithful friends, the disorder of the table, the wine which quenched our thirst and the revelation of Kafka, at least as far as I was concerned. In the world at large, Hitler was spreading fear a bit like the corpse invented by Ionesco in his play: *Comment s'en débarrasser*;[1] the Spanish revolution torn by totalitarian tendencies was in the end defeated; as for the democracies, they were sinking lower and lower in administrative impotence, apathy and suicide, all portents of the coming eclipse of the individual. Kafka was our temporary comfort, I say temporary, for we were becoming more and more aware that free man would soon be unable to live in the social structure which modern societies were about to offer us. Kafka announced, or rather denounced, the advent of the modern world. That was in 1937. Every free and independent being who intended to keep his freedom, while claiming the right to live, felt hounded by Fascist dictatorships, by totalitarian socialism, or betrayed by corrupt democracies; if he did not feel hunted, he felt rejected and forsaken. He felt desperately alone, guilty of wanting to remain free, therefore not innocent. And all free men, with their qualities and defects, all brothers of Joseph K., rejected by the inaccessible walls of *The Castle* or by the well organized cells of the village, felt hopelessly caught and condemned; Kafka alone consoled us.

Ten years later, in 1947, after so many world-shattering events,

[1] *Amedée, or How to Get Rid of It.*

we might have been induced to think that everything had changed and that after so many atrocities, so much cynicism, words would have regained their true meaning, values their true worth, that a new world with a new social structure capable of enduring broad daylight had been born, and that Kafka was therefore only the inspired denouncer of a period of transition which was something like a cloudy day before spring. But it was not so at all; Kafka appeared more and more as the true prophet of our times. Everything was becoming false; words were changing their meaning, imposture was becoming widespread. Who, for instance, could clearly define expressions like: 'national independence' or its opposite: 'protection of the people', without bringing in, in either case, the word 'oil'? Truth seemed to have been turned upside down; things were losing their individuality, and the snares, the cobwebs and subtle ploys of the Middle Ages were thickening and multiplying around us. The ordinary man who was supposed to be free had less and less freedom in his city: every man was fundamentally guilty. Kafka alone dared to question justice, and in a world fully organized for the systematic reduction of man to the animal level, he dared to consider man in his own freedom and as a compound of matter and spirit, natural and supernatural, realistic and surrealistic. Man stood accused, but accused of what in front of men and in front of God, or rather not in front of God but in front of churches, that is to say in front of what men extract from the gods? Kafka uttered the cry which we did not dare to utter, and he did so with exemplary scruples; his hero Joseph K. is no saint, he is somebody like any one of us and he presents him to us in his true reality. God gave us defects so that we might remain men, said Shakespeare.

That is why, in 1947, first encouraged and then helped by Gide, I decided to bring Kafka into the theatre: in fact Gide had asked me to do something as early as 1942. I had asked him to see what he could do with *The Trial*, but I had not convinced him; he had the feeling that the cinema would be a better medium than the theatre for this novel. I spent the following summer establishing a working text by writing out dialogue drawn from the excellent translation of Kafka by Vialatte. Then once this was ready we agreed upon a date, and one winter afternoon, I read him what we used to call the 'monster'. We were in his small bedroom, no bigger than a cell, and heated by gas. I can still see him all wrapped up and listening to my adaptation. I had just uttered the last words of my work which are 'like a dog', when the chandelier suddenly fell from the ceiling and remained suspended in the air by the electric wire which held the bulb. 'That's it,' said Gide, 'Kafka approves; henceforth we shall work under this chandelier'; and so it was that for a year, we met regularly under this unsteady chandelier. Gide's enthusiasm for this project went beyond all my hopes; I can still see him arriving unexpectedly at my house with Roger Martin du Gard in order to bring me the first three typed pages of *The Trial*. Then came the day of the official reading of *The Trial* in front of our company and friends. The opinions were divided, some were enthusiastic, others very reserved; altogether it was rather worrying and all the more so that I could not help having a bad conscience about Kafka. The fact is that nobody in the world can avoid having a bad conscience about Kafka, in varying degrees of course, and the reason for that is simple: Kafka wanted his works to be burnt, he did not want to have them published. If his wish had been obeyed, Kafka for us would not have existed, not a word of his would have reached us, and this exceptional being who died of tuberculosis at the age of 40 would have been known to only a few intimate friends.

Kafka's strange adventure begins with his betrayal by his best friend, Max Brod, and yet never was there a more justified betrayal than this one. Max Brod decided, in spite of his friend's will, to gather together his manuscripts and to publish them. We all owe a profound debt of gratitude to him. As far as Max Brod is concerned, his decision was right, yet we shall never know what Kafka would have thought of this collective indiscretion. There was nobody more sincere, less given to affectation than Kafka, and therefore it is reasonable to believe that if he expressed the wish that this work should be burnt, he truly meant it. Nevertheless Max Brod and a few intimate friends of Kafka decided to ignore his wish and to deliver his work into the hands of his fellow-beings. Since then they have become the prey of men and the sources of discussion. Specialists disagree about the order of the chapters and about their interpretation and special meaning. Every Kafka expert sees himself as the proprietor of Kafka; he is now discussed throughout the whole world, and it is clear that if we assembled everything that has been said about him to date, we should probably compose the best collection of stupidities of the century. That would certainly prove that Kafka's fears were justified; for he who felt too weak to stand up to the life that was proposed to him, he who could not bring himself to force any door which remained closed to him and spent his time hiding behind his work, now sees his work laid bare, and himself not only laid bare, but also masqueraded and distorted by commentators and torn to bits by philologists. To make matters worse, the rush for spoils is affecting not only writers, poets and philosophers, but also the men of the theatre, the last people who should dare to lay hands on Kafka. So Kafka is thrown to the dogs; it was not so bad as far as *The Trial* was concerned, for in this case only Gide and the theatre people were to blame; but what can one say about his most secret work—*The Castle*, which has now been brought to the stage by Max Brod himself! Oh, heresy, shame, sacrilege!

I have previously said that for a long time I have loved Kafka like an elder brother; Joseph K.'s indignation, his cunning or failings, his candour and obstinacy for individual freedom found echoes in myself. I feel very guilty about taking part in this vast indiscretion which involves the world in a lack of respect towards a dead man. I feel much closer to those who add nothing to Kafka than to those who try to give him the meaning which suits them. I am most aware of the great danger and of the risks of destruction that are part of the attempt to adapt novels for the stage, particularly Kafka's novels, yet ten years after *The Trial*, I again brought Kafka to the stage, with *The Castle*. Why? Because I love a gamble, and here the gamble rests on a profound and serious basis. I have lately spent a few exciting moments with a specialist on Kafka, one of the people best qualified to talk about him, and somebody who not only can talk with extraordinary lucidity, but who is very scrupulous and honest and who shares with all true lovers of Kafka the feeling that the editing of his works was an act of treason. Nevertheless, my feelings are that since the crime has been committed it is better to return to the scene of the crime and to spend half of one's life serving the works and the glory of Kafka. As far as this specialist on Kafka is concerned, every interpretation, every study of the work is valid; the only thing which is not so is the attempt to put Kafka on the stage. Since everything in Kafka is a theatrical representation of life, how can one stage it, since this has already been done in the novel? Every character, every thing, is a projection of what Joseph K. sees or imagines that he sees; if he disappears, nothing remains.

This gives rise to insuperable difficulties. In *The Castle*, for instance, the two assistants look exactly alike, at least Joseph K. cannot distinguish one from the other, yet one never confuses one with the other. Barnabé resembles Olga whom he confuses with Amalia, and Barnabé has the same physical appearance as the assistants who resemble K. Consequently, one might think that all these characters, projections of Joseph K., are really a kind of polarization of Kafka. All these various aspects which look light and easy to grasp when reading, could look heavy and over-symbolical on the stage. It is the same with the peasants of 'The Bridge Inn', or with the servants of 'The Gentlemen's Hotel'. The first are all endowed with the same flat cranium; does this mean that they are all alike? In truth there are moments when they resemble one another and in these moments, for K., they are all alike, even though they are different. That means that if one considers certain given aspects of human behaviour, such as the hospitality of the peasants or the rut of the servants, men resemble one another, irrespective of their peculiarities which disappear when they are considered under these aspects. They all resemble one another in their behaviour, and all the more so that they belong to the same village and also in a way to the same castle. Is this kind of ambiguity which one encounters in the very first pages of Kafka's works, an obstacle which renders the transfer of these works to the theatre impossible, or is it on the contrary one of the profound reasons which justify their transfer to the theatre? The specialist whom I previously mentioned asserted that this ambiguity was the proof that Kafka's novels were incompatible with the theatre, particularly *The Trial* and *The Castle* in which the ambiguity is pushed to the maximum. According to him, only one work could be adapted for the theatre, and that is *America* which is one of his early works in which the characters are as clear as if they had been filmed. In the theatre, the characters must all be clearly seen from the same angle; in Kafka, on the contrary, the characters are seen simultaneously by the narrator and by the hero of the work and their angle of vision is different. Thus it is the narrator who says that there is a castle in the village, and when Joseph K. is awakened he looks surprised when this castle is mentioned. As the reader has instinctively merged narrator and hero into one person, confusion ensues, and when the play is staged one is faced with the question: How will it be possible to know without Joseph K. knowing it too that the village has a castle, since no character exists without him? In order to answer this point made by this rather 'upsetting' specialist, one would have to deal with the subject: 'The theatre, the art of ambiguity'; we shall come to this problem in a moment; but first let us return to the difficulties of *The Castle*. Barnabé, the messenger, never enters the castle; he stands in front of it like a will o' the wisp. In the theatre one must see people entering what they are meant to enter, or one must use the means used for the supernatural: apparitions, darkness, traps, etc., and there is nothing like that in Kafka who places his poetry in a kind of strange realism. Then there is the question of the style which one should adopt for the staging of these plays. When one reads Kafka, one has the impression of being confronted, not by a continuous movement but by a series of stills; what is stressed is the attitudes not the incidents, and one could best embody the novel not so much in a film as in a series of photographs. The problem therefore consists in how to convey this authentic impression without falling into artificiality. Besides this, we must remember that even these attitudes are ambiguous; the innkeeper, for instance, is supposed to stand in front of K. in a way which makes it impossible to decide whether he is listening or having a snooze; it is the same with the other characters. Ambiguity is the true word.

Well, in spite of all these important obstacles, and others too, which bar the way to anybody who tries to bring Kafka on the stage, I could not resist the urge to try to do so. First of all, I must confess that my urge is a kind of love. Theatrical work is a kind of marriage, and once I had married *The Trial* I wanted to marry *The Castle*; I wanted to visit it and to wrap myself in it; above all, I wanted to share my great admiration for Kafka with as large a number of people as possible, and I attempted to do so with all the more good faith that I look upon the theatre as the very art of ambiguity. The theatre is the art of man and his double, and a theatrical performance is in some ways essentially ambiguous. Both actors and spectators have a dual behaviour. There is the actor and the character, and as far as the spectator is concerned, there is in him the person who looks and the one who receives. The spectators who form an audience are both active and passive. They receive

and they send back, they take and they are taken; the actors do
the same, they send out and they receive, and a theatrical performance is a kind of collective mêlée on the physical as well as on the
spiritual plane, from which emerges a kind of androgynous creation. The spectator is like Kafka's innkeeper, and one cannot know
whether he is asleep or follows with the closest attention; 'they
look and listen as if they were asleep', said Claudel. As for the
actor, he can only control his emotions because he has cultivated
the art of dividing his frailties, and the actor wrapped up in his
character is the very symbol of ambiguity. More than that, the
stage is the ideal field of ambiguity, it is the place where reality
and dreams, god and men can mingle; and what can one say about
this art, that is to say, about the dreams which we absorb not only
through the eyes and the ears, but through the ninety-five other
senses which come under the mysterious label of the sense of
touch? This is truly magic. What is this character who, born from
the marriage of true imagination—that of the actor and that of the
spectator—has nevertheless the life of a being of flesh and blood? Is
not such a creation something essentially ambiguous? Is not the
life of the theatre continuously lived on two planes, the real and
the unreal, the natural and the supernatural; and is not one continuously aware of 'the two sides of the book', the temporal and
the religious? There is no need of symbolism in the theatre, for
everything is naturally symbolic.

In *The Trial*, the public easily understood that all the characters
were personal projections of the hero, and that of course is exactly
what happens in life. Does the idea you have of your janitor correspond to your janitor himself? No, it does not, it corresponds to the
personal notion that you have of your janitor. Every human being
has his own theatre, and, like Kafka's hero, Joseph K., is continuously surrounded by characters who gravitate around his life. Thus
when Joseph K. enters the stage, it is as if every member of the
audience entered with him. To produce a work by Kafka really
means to try to offer to each spectator a personal vision of the world
which surrounds us. This vision, which rests on the ambiguity of life
which is both logical and absurd, tragic and burlesque, hostile and
friendly, is essentially theatrical. I must confess that the problem
of staging Kafka presents many difficulties, but they are exciting,
and as they are all related to questions of ambiguity, there is
no incompatibility between Kafka and the theatre. Drama is a

social art and that is what makes it essentially ambiguous; one man's drama must become the drama of a collectivity; the particular case is turned into a collective case. The characters on the stage are both individuals and also the collectivity, while the spectator in the audience is alone and part of the rest of the audience. The first dramatic problem of the theatre is that of man as the prey of society or collectivity. Man fears solitude, which breeds anxiety; there is comfort in the presence of other human beings, and men want to live in society, but most of the time the price of admission into society is the loss of liberty. Every individual who wishes to remain free will remain alone, and society in order to protect itself from this strange being called the free individual, has built a perfect system of self-protection, symbolized at its best by the administration. So the individual who wishes to be free remains free, but he is forsaken. Liberty brings despair; the wider the space surrounding the free man, the more stifling it is. This is the human aspect of *The Castle*; one suffocates and one longs to be allowed to share in the secluded and comforting life of the others, without however becoming completely tame. The same fear of solitude prevails on the religious plane. It is the anguish of the void; we would love to be admitted up there in the luminous world which some people call the world of grace; we would love to be admitted on the earth and above the earth; such is Joseph K.'s problem; such is the most important problem for us all. *The Trial* dealt with the opposite problem—that of claustrophobia. Guilty from the start, Joseph K. was stifling in his prison of culpability, and he was trying in vain to get out of it. His was the drama of powerless innocence caught in the vast patterns of human and divine justice. *The Castle* is the drama of liberty in solitude. Joseph K. batters in vain on the impassable door behind which shelter men and gods; he would love to be admitted among them but his efforts are of no avail. His is the fundamental drama of every human being, every spectator; therefore Kafka's description of this drama could not fail to be appropriate to the theatre. One has only to realize that this is a simple subject and that it is not at all necessary to be an intellectual addicted to mental sophistication, in order to discover that life is full of ambiguities. Shakespeare had the kind of genius which could discover such ambiguities, and in the plane of modern life, Kafka has also this kind of genius.

V

With Jean Racine

ATTEMPT AT A PORTRAIT

Mon Dieu, quelle guerre cruelle!
Je trouve deux hommes en moi.[1]

Can I imagine Racine, and shall I be able to depict him without distorting the picture? I fear it may be impossible to know what Racine was truly like. There is no doubt that he combined in himself the best and the worst; he had a multiple heart, and if, as Lautréamont says, it is more difficult to plumb the depth of the human heart than the deepest abyss of the ocean, how can one hope to fathom and to judge Racine? He had his dreams, he laid his heart bare, and there one is reminded of the words of another poet very close to him, Baudelaire, who also bared his heart and said, 'Il y a dans tout homme, à toute heure, deux postulations simultanées, l'une vers Dieu, l'autre vers Satan. L'invocation à Dieu, ou spiritualité, est un désir de monter en grade; celle de Satan, ou animalité, est une joie de descendre.'[2]

> Je trouve deux hommes en moi:
> L'un veut que plein d'amour pour toi
> Mon coeur te soit toujours fidèle.
> L'autre à tes volontés rebelles
> Me révolte contre ta loi.[3]
>
> —*Cantiques Spirituels*, III

[1] God, what a cruel war!
I find two men in myself.

[2] Every man is always torn between two strong pulls—one towards God, the other towards Satan. The call for God or for spirituality is a longing for ascent, the call for Satan or animality is the joy of sinking lower and lower.

[3] I find two men in myself:
One insists that my heart, full of love for you,
Should always be faithful to you;
The other, rebellious against your will,
Is in revolt against your rule.

Racine seems to have had a similar heart. This heart whose first beats began at La Ferté-Milon in the poet's house which belonged to his maternal grandfather, Pierre Sconin, on the 22 December 1639, beat for fifty-nine years and four months until it flickered out between three and four in the morning, on the 21 April 1699, in Racine's house, rue des Marais in Paris. It flickered out! But before doing so it produced a blaze and a music which is the most striking that France has ever produced in dramatic poetry. Although Racine had reached serenity before dying, his whole life had been an uninterrupted and sad succession of flights of faithfulness followed by revolts, of irritations soon replaced by repentance and of moments of extreme insolence followed by the most amazing modesty. It is in fact his final control of his seething violence at the cost of much suffering, that makes of him one of the most typical examples of our classical genius.

RACINE AND PORT-ROYAL

The first image one has of Racine is that of a beautiful and pure boy with an angelic soul, gambolling joyfully in the picturesque setting of the Abbey of Port-Royal-des-Champs. Racine is at first Eliacin, the beloved child of Port-Royal, honouring God in his pure soul:

Dont la bonté s'étend sur toute la nature.[1]

How can one fail to imagine him 'clad in white linen', ethereal, full of divine love in the midst of the 'inimitable nature where he lived'? He meditates on 'the solitude of the woods', he melts into tenderness before these 'charming plains' and he is terrified by 'sad sights' and by 'the fights of angered bulls'. He wanders about entranced by the mirrors of pools.

> Là l'hirondelle voltigeante,
> Rasant les flots clairs et polis,
> Y vient, avec cent petits cris,
> Baiser son image naissante.
> Là mille autres petits oiseaux
> Peignent encore dans les eaux
>   Leur éclatant plumage:
> L'oeil ne peut juger au dehors

[1] Whose goodness embraces all nature.

Qui vole ou bien qui nage
De leurs ombres et de leurs corps. [1]

He was then 16 years old; throughout his whole life, in spite of his
rebellious nature, Racine never forgot the influence of Port-Royal.
His family had long and close ties there. In 1638 when Racine
was not yet born, the Abbey had already endured persecutions
and the arrest of St Cyran. Many of its members like Lancelot, Antoine le Maître, etc., had sought refuge at La Ferté-Milon,
and had been welcomed by the Vitart family, relations of the
Racines. Already one of his aunts, 'Suzanne', had retired to Port-
Royal; later on his grandmother, who brought him up, also
rejoined Port-Royal, and finally his Aunt Agnes, the famous
Sainte-Thècle became the Abbess. If one wishes to understand
Racine, one must bear in mind the numerous bonds which bound
him inextricably to Port-Royal, bonds which are all the stronger
when Port-Royal is persecuted. The obstinate hatred of its
members by the Jesuits acted as a cement which kept them all
together. The more they were persecuted the more they helped
one another. Port-Royal in the course of its long struggles against
persecution had developed in all its members a spirit of resistance
and a powerful urge to rally to the defence of the community.
Racine himself was accused of the crime of rallying; the fact
is that there was a Port-Royal 'network'. Racine was born in it,
and he never left it. Port-Royal taught Racine two things: first
the infinite love of God which he never forgot; secondly a strong
hypersensitivity to the spirit of persecution. Besides Racine's
strong ties with Port-Royal, it is important to know that he was an
orphan; he lost his mother when he was 13 months old and
his father when he was 4 years old; that gave him the wilting
look of innocence. Racine was brought up by his grandmother,
Marie des Moulins of the Vitart family who were the confidential
agents of Port-Royal. It was thanks to Port-Royal that Racine went

---

[1] There the vaulting swallow
Skims the smooth, shining waves
In which, with a hundred shrieks,
She kisses her rising image.
There a thousand small birds
Paint their colourful plumage on the waters;
The eye cannot distinguish
Between their shadows and their bodies,
Between what flies and what swims.

first to the Collège de Beauvais and then to the Ecole des Granges where he learnt his humanities with the masters of Port-Royal; Lancelot taught him Greek, Hamon law, and Antoine le Maître acted as his 'father' and wrote to him: 'Always love your father as he loves you.' He therefore took his first steps in life in an atmosphere of holiness among the nuns of Port-Royal who were 'earthly angels'. His aunt the Abbess Sainte-Thècle watched over him and it is in this atmosphere of profound piety that he had his first revelation of Nature. He was so marked by his environment that his first poetic writings, his first odes, could really have been written by Eliacin himself. When the Abbey was persecuted, Racine, like Esther, prayed God to protect these virgins and these innocents in such lines as those of the wonderful *ad Christum*: 'My God, you are the only hope of our unhappy house. . . . Turn your gaze towards the virginal company which inhabits the cloister.' Joad, Mardochée, Josabeth protected the childhood of Racine who began his life in the same way as he was to finish it, that is to say by playing *Esther* and *Athalie*. [1]

But fate stood on guard at the gates of Port-Royal. Racine had no idea of the long detour he would have to make before he could return to this solitary and holy place, on the day when he left to study philosophy at the Collège d'Harcourt in Paris on the 1 October 1658. This is the famous detour to which we owe the most accomplished masterpieces of our dramatic literature. The first baptism of young Racine, transplanted from Port-Royal to Paris in his nineteenth year, takes place under the auspices of 'wit', and once more it is his Uncle Vitart who is God's instrument. There is no doubt that after Boileau it was certainly Vitart who was closest to Racine. It was thanks to him that Racine had been adopted by Port-Royal, and it was thanks to him that he was introduced into the elegant society of Paris. Although he was a very pious and learned man, Nicolas Vitart was also a man of wit, with broad ideas, wealthy and with an extremely good position in society. He was a Jansenist and was the confidential agent of the Duc de Luynes. He watched over Racine, protected him and behaved towards him as Jannart behaved towards La Fontaine. As he loved literature and wit, he encouraged his nephew in that direction. It might very well have been he who gave to Chapelain the ode to the *Nymphes de la Seine* by young Racine. Vitart had been for Racine the man

[1] *Athaliah.*

of Port-Royal, for two or three years he would be the man of Paris.

The young poet soon showed great gifts as a courtier. His guides were no longer Nicole, Hamon or Lancelot but the charming Abbot Levasseur, the attractive and idle La Fontaine and the dashing captain of dragoons, Poignant. The secluded walks of Port-Royal were now replaced by cafés which were visited at least 'two or three times a day'. Our poet was not without adventures; he composed topical verses and odes to the King and he tried to please and to win over Chapelain and Perrault who were then very influential. La Fontaine, who was eighteen years his senior, must have had a great influence on him, at least one likes to think so, and he might have imparted to him a kind of daemonic effect, and the daemon is precious to the arts. In brief, our poet shook off his former ties, 'hunted with the wolves' and moved away from the Jansenists: 'I was ready to consult an old servant (that of the Duke of Luynes) when I realized that, like his master, he was a Jansenist'. He began to take up arms against 'hypocrites and devout ones', admired what was forbidden, and wrote about Retz: 'it is feared in Paris that there might be something stronger, something like "an interdict" '. To 'solid' things he preferred trifles and the pursuit of petticoats; Venus began to preoccupy him, and he began to talk about 14-year-old darlings and to assert that 'Love is the God who knows best the way to Parnassus'. Besides the poetic competitions in which he took part in order to attract attention, Racine began to think of the theatre and particularly of actresses. He had a real weakness for actresses. One of them called Mademoiselle Roste was greatly interested in one of his plays entitled *Amasie*; later it was an actress called Beauchâteau who supervised the *Art of Love of Ovid*. Racine, in short, plunged into life with excitement and enjoyed the blaze of his youth. His temptations were all the more strong in that he had just spent three years in the austere seclusion of Port-Royal. His childhood had been pure, pious and chaste, his youth was about to unfold in the artificial atmosphere of literature and in the enchanting world of the court.

THE HUNT FOR POSTS

One fine day Racine set off for Uzès. Still under the contradictory influences of Port-Royal on one hand and of Paris on the other, he would spend two years trying to assimilate them in that remote little town of Languedoc. One might call his stay in Uzès his period of incubation. He described his journey south in his charming letters; and he tells us that he went to Lyons on horseback, and he says that 'he never fails to gallop every night in front of the others so as to book his bed'. He confesses that he does not understand the language, a mixture of Spanish and Italian, which caused him some strange adventures. One night, for instance, having asked a maid for a bedchamber, she produced a small stove which she stuck under his bed; 'You can well imagine what can happen when a sleepy man tries to use such an instrument in the middle of the night', he says in one of his letters. From Lyons to Vienna and Valence he travelled by boat. The journey took him two days. The aim of his stay in Uzès was to enable him to occupy a priory or a vicarship; but that proved to be very difficult even in spite of the help, the tenacity and goodwill of his uncle the Rev. F. Sconin who welcomed him. It is known that he submitted to the tonsure, but he did not enter religion, 'although he had me dressed in black from top to toe'. He is sometimes described as Abbot Racine but one doubts whether he ever deserved such a title; anyway, whether he was Abbot or not, he was first and foremost poet, more than ever a poet. His reputation spread and people came to ask for his advice. Uzès offered Racine opportunities for meditation and concentration. He wanted to learn how to control himself, and he returned to serious living. No more adventures; he had one single temptation which was 'a kind of tender idea, something approaching an inclination'. He lived reasonably and he refused to be carried away by 'all sorts of objects'. In fact he felt in need 'of getting rid of some kind of incipient anxiety'.

> J'irai parmi les oliviers,
> Les chênes verts et les figuiers
> Chercher quelque remède à mon inquiétude
> Je chercherai la solitude, etc. . . .[1]

On one hand he disliked the ecclesiastical world around him; he was irritated by monks, by their laziness and their stupidity; he writes to his great confidant Vitart 'I have conceived a kind of

---

[1] I shall go through the olive groves,
Ilexes and fig trees,
In search of solace for my restlessness,
I shall look for solitude, etc. . . .

horror which I could not hide, for the lazy life of monks'. On the other hand, the country where he lived was a great source of poetic inspiration; he discussed this point with his great accomplice La Fontaine: 'Might it be possible' he said 'that the muses might hold greater sway in this country than on the banks of the Seine?' This indeed was a country where passions were strong, love was exciting, and, above all, the climate and the ancient beauty of nature made a deep impression on the scholarly hellenist that Racine was.

'Et nous avons des nuits plus belles que vos jours.' And so it was that our young tonsured Abbot, rather irked by the bad state of his affairs and by the petty difficulties which beset the acquisition of a post, found greater satisfaction and sincerity in composing the *Stances à Parthénice* [1] and in searching for subjects for plays such as *Théagène et Chariclée*,[2] or perhaps *La Thébaïde*.[3] Living in a country which was the true country of Cythera, he found it very rewarding to dip in 'les Bains de Vénus':

> Vous savez bien que les déesses
> Ne sont pas toutes des Vénus.[4]

It was probably in the semi-seclusion of Uzès that his poetic vocation gained the upper hand against his other strong temptation to remain faithful to God. The young and pure child, the innocent and sensitive orphan of Port-Royal whose heart used to melt when he listened to the hymns of the Breviary which he set about translating, began to follow the influence of Venus and to become fully awakened to the Mediterranean sun; he talked about 'anemones which resemble those which surge from Venus's blood'. In fact it is clear that this Eliacin of the Ile de France consecrated to the holy Virgin could well have become in this Provençal world, so similar to that of Greece, a Hippolyte consecrated to Diana; but our Hippolyte was in love! Port-Royal had given birth to a young Racine whom we christened Eliacin; Paris at the time of Racine's studies at the Collège d'Harcourt had given birth to another being, a kind of worldly poet albeit passionate and wild and who was the opposite of the first. It was the latter who

---

[1] *Stanzas to the Parthenon.*
[2] *Theagenes and Charicleia.*
[3] *The Thebaïd.*
[4] You know very well that not all goddesses are Venuses.

triumphed at Uzès. God did not seem to wish to hold back young Racine, and in fact if he had allowed the birth of these two opposite tendencies in the same man it was probably because he wanted them to devour each other, so that they might accomplish their mission. Be that as it may, when Racine returned to Paris in 1663, the 'growing monster' was ready to write *Les frères ennemis*. That very same year his dear grandmother Marie des Moulins died; that was one bond less with Port-Royal; God seemed to loosen his control over him still more. This was also the year when he met Boileau whom he described at the end of his life as 'the best friend and the best man in the world'. Boileau was going, from then on, to replace Uncle Vitart; he would be the chosen friend, the best adviser, and the most precious of men: 'a true friendship is the sweetest thing in the world'. With Boileau it was Pylades who entered the stage of Racine's life, and few men have been closer friends than Racine and Boileau: 'and then I meet again such a faithful friend. . . .'

> Les héros de l'Antiquité pleuraient bien . . .
> Eh bien, dit Acante, nous pleurerons![1]
>   —LA FONTAINE

By November Racine was already fully immersed in the excitement of the profane life of Paris. We soon find him present at the King's morning rising; he began to frequent new cafés like 'Le Mouton Blanc', 'La Pomme de Pin', and 'La Croix de Lorraine', taking part in battles of epigrams. He had found his friends again, and he took part in all sorts of mischief. This is what La Fontaine says: 'Four friends formed a kind of society which should have been called an academy, had there been more of them, and had its members been as devoted to the Muses as they were to pleasure. The first thing they did was to decide to avoid set conversations which involve protracted discussions on the same subject, and to pass, on the contrary, from one subject to another like bees moving from flower to flower in search of their food.' The four friends were Boileau, La Fontaine, Molière and Racine whom La Fontaine describes under the name of Acante: 'Acante loved gardens, flowers and shady woods. Poliphile (La Fontaine) resembled him in that respect . . . the passions which filled their hearts with

---

[1] After all, the heroes of the ancient world used to cry . . .
Well, said Acante, we shall cry!

tenderness overflowed in their writings . . . they both inclined
towards lyricism, with the difference that Acante's lyricism was
more touching while Poliphile's was more adorned;' and further:
'the heroes of antiquity did sometimes cry . . . well, said Acante,
we too shall cry!' Racine loved to cry.

Racine detached himself more and more from Port-Royal which
was more and more threatened; the signature of a new convention
left him unmoved and even drew from him a mild touch of cynicism:

> Contre Jansénius, j'ai la plume à la main.
> Je suis prêt à signer tout ce qu'on me demande
> Qu'il soit hérétique ou Romain
> Je veux conserver ma prébende.[1]

All his efforts and attentions were now focused on the theatre and
on actresses. Molière, who was seventeen years older than he,
helped him and produced his first play, *La Thébaïde*. Racine's
choice was now made, the daemon of poetry had won and Port-
Royal was definitely rejected. Consequently his aunt, Sainte-
Thècle, the Abbess, was very upset and she banned him from
Port-Royal. 'I have learnt with sorrow that you now frequent more
and more people whose names are rightly hated by any pious person,
for many are forbidden to enter churches and many are separated
from the faithful even in death. . . . In what kind of abyss have
you thrown yourself? . . . If you are unfortunate enough to keep
up connexions which dishonour you in the face of God and men,
you need not think of coming to see us . . . for I could never
speak to you knowing that you are in such a state which is so
deplorable and so contrary to Christianity.' At this juncture, it is
interesting to watch the slow emergence of his tragic characters
from life. We have seen that earlier the fathers of Port-Royal had
supplied the texture of Joad, Mardochée and Josabeth; later on
Boileau supplied that of Pylades, and seen from Paris Aunt Sainte-
Thècle resembles Agrippine like a twin; at least so it seems! The
fatal storm which would temporarily separate Racine from Port-
Royal was about to break out. Was it because he was becoming
more and more aware of the coming conflict and also of the fact

---

[1] I have taken up my pen against Jansen
And I am ready to sign whatever is asked
Of me, whether it is heretical or orthodox,
I wish to preserve my stipend.

that he must obey the irresistible call of his vocation? The fact
was that Racine became more and more irascible, fierce, insolent,
cruel and without scruple. The man who could start the rehearsals
of his second play *Alexandre* in two theatres at the same time, in
Molière's theatre and in the Hôtel de Bourgogne, and finally end in
giving the play to the latter, is an example of black ingratitude
towards Molière who had guided his first steps on the stage. After
three centuries we still find it difficult to forgive him for this kind
of betrayal. But the fact is that the wild animal that lurked in
Racine had reached its full growth, and was about to rebel:

Mon innocence enfin commence à me peser [1]

and this rebellion was provoked by his former master Nicole.

In 1666, Racine was 27 years of age. Nicole at that time published a book entitled *Les Visionnaires* in which he condemned the
theatre with the utmost severity, and described dramatists as
'poisoners of the public'. Racine, stung by his attack upon what
mattered most to him—poetry and drama—rose at once to the
defence of these subjects and published two letters addressed to
the author of *Les Visionnaires*, which even now cannot be read
without a shudder. They could not have been more insolent.
Bearing in mind the time when he wrote them, the fact that Racine
had been brought up by Port-Royal which was now persecuted,
and the dire consequences of his action on this persecuted community, one realizes the violence of Racine's revolt and the
extraordinary temper which lay behind it: 'What have novels and
plays to do with Jansenism? Why should you say that these pro-
ducts of the mind are the fruits of rather dishonourable labours,
and as such, are horrible to God? . . . You have enough enemies,
why look for new ones? Do you expect people to take your word
for what you say? No, sir, one does not believe you as easily as all
that. For twenty years you have been repeating day in and day out
that the five famous propositions were not to be found in Jansen; yet nobody believes you! [2] We know the austerity of your
ethics; we do not find it strange that you should condemn poets!
You have condemned other people too. . . . Well, sir, do devote
your time to assigning ranks in the other world, but don't try to

[1] At last my innocence begins to weigh upon me.
[2] This is a fearful perfidy; for the five propositions were precisely the
basis of all the persecutions against the Jansenists. That Racine should
make use of such an argument is tantamount to treason.

order the rewards of this one. . . . Concentrate on serious matters, they obviously befit you. Everyone must follow his own vocation.'

THE SEASON IN HELL OF ELIACIN

'What can a rat caught in a trap do except eat the bacon?' said Hobbes; and Gide in *Saul* said: 'With whom or with what can man console himself for his decadence except with its cause?' Is it not possible that Racine might have shared Gide's feeling when in *Andromaque*, he makes Orestes say:

> Méritons leur courroux, justifions leur haine
> Et que le fruit du crime en précède la peine.[1]

Caught in a trap, Racine decided to 'eat the bacon'. Wonderful decision! How did he proceed? First of all by going to war against the innocent Eliacin of his youth, for what is indeed *Andromaque*'s subject except a child's life staked against passion? Eliacin in this case is Astyanax, the door behind which Astyanax-Eliacin is locked up is the crux of *Andromaque*. The following year the same subject reappeared under the name of *Britannicus* and it still concerned a sacrifice of an innocent child to fierce passions. One would think in fact that Racine was trying to get rid of his other self or of his double.

> Tant qu'il respirera, je ne vis qu'à demi.[2]

Let us try as a pastime to cast the people who surrounded Racine at Port-Royal as the characters of *Britannicus*:

Britannicus: Young Racine as he was at Port-Royal.
Nero: Racine the author of *Les Lettres aux Imaginaires*.
Burrhus: Any one of his former masters—Lancelot, Antoine le Maître, Hamon.
Narcisse: The Abbot Levasseur.
Agrippine: The Abbess Sainte-Thècle.
Junie: The memory of some Lucretia from *Parthénice*.
In the wings, Pallas: Nicole.

We can easily imagine the Abbess Sainte-Thècle, clad in the diabolical clothes of Agrippine, declaiming:

[1] Let us deserve their wrath, and justify their hatred,
   Let the outcome of the crime precede the penalty.
[2] As long as he breathes I am only half alive.

Du fruit de tant de soins à peine jouissant
En avez-vous six mois paru reconnaissant
Que, lassé d'un respect qui vous gênait peut-être
Vous avez affecté de ne plus me connaître . . .

Et lorsque vos mépris excitant mes murmures
Je vous ai demandé raison de tant d'injures
(Seul recours d'un ingrat qui se voit confondu)
Par de nouveaux affronts vous m'avez répondu . . .[1]

With *Andromaque* and *Britannicus* Racine had plunged into waters from which he would only emerge ten years later. The famous actress Duparc, whom he had taken away without scruple from Molière, died and left him 'half dead with sorrow'. He seemed to have brought back from the Mediterranean world the urge to push passions to their extremes. Paris, unchanging, always ready for rumours, accused him of having poisoned his mistress; in fact she died in childbirth or from a miscarriage. The insoluble problem remained. Who was responsible for her condition? Racine continued his descent. One night at a performance of *Andromaque*, he saw a young actress playing the part of Hermione in place of the usual actress—Mademoiselle des Œillets. He was completely bowled over; this young actress was La Champmeslé. Racine offered her the creation of the part of Berenice, and then continued his descent towards phosphorescent depths; he started a liaison with La Champmeslé which lasted until *Phèdre*. La Champmeslé was a masterly woman, married to a complacent husband who did not wish to lose the source of his income and who therefore continued to work with the Hôtel de Bourgogne. La Champmeslé became the official mistress of Racine, who every now and then had to share her with others. She must certainly have been an extraordinary combination of charm and stubbornness. Nevertheless, since he paid the bills, Racine was the official master of the house. La Fontaine was very often a guest at dinner, and when

---

[1] You had barely enjoyed the fruit of all my cares
And for six months showed gratefulness,
Than, tired by a respect which perhaps bored you,
You pretended that you no longer knew me.

And when your contempt prompted my protests
And I asked you the cause of so many insults,
You took the only course open to an ungrateful son
Who sees himself confounded—you answered me with new obloquies.

later, another master took Racine's place, La Fontaine continued to be a guest at dinner.

Racine had become by then the effective head of the theatre of the Hôtel de Bourgogne, whose fortunes he guided for ten years. The first thing he did was to rejuvenate the company. The average age of the company which created *Andromaque* was 60; among them there was Montfleury who had a paunch so big that he had to wear a steel corset.[1] The average age of the company which created *Phèdre*, ten years later, was approximately 30.[2] Racine was both an excellent reader and a good producer. He revived the art of declamation, doing for tragedy what Debussy was to do for song at the time when he produced *Pelléas*. His private life was involved to the full in the profane life of the theatre; it was described by him later in his will as 'the scandals of his past life'. He then continued his journey downwards and he reached rock bottom with *Bajazet* which is more a modern drama than a tragedy. In it sadism reaches its zenith; it is the only one of his plays specifically written for an actress—La Champmeslé. In this play the fierce cruelty of the wild animal is at its worst, yet the strange thing is that it is the woman who is the wild animal. Bajazet herself is a kind of Macbeth, half victim, half wild animal. Does this mean that woman begins to get the better of the untamed Racine, does it mean that he, the glorious author and official protector of the great actress, is really beginning to wear out his teeth on her? Whatever its profound causes may be, *Bajazet* marks the lowest point reached by Racine in search of darkness; the year of *Bajazet* was also the year of his entry to the French Academy. He was then 34 years old and from then on the swimmer would move slowly from the depths towards the surface. Soon we have a first miracle, for up to this point the wild animals of his plays had always devoured their victims, but from then on the victims will get the better of the wild animals, from then on it is the latter who die and the 'lambs' are miraculously saved: it is Mithridate who dies, and not Monique or Xipharès; it is Eriphile, who sacrifices herself to Iphigénie, who is divinely protected. While God is not yet present, the gods begin to intervene and to loom larger in his world. The swimmer begins to

---

[1] Floridor who played Pyrrhus was 61 years old. Montfleury who played Orestes was 67. Des Œillets who played Hermione was 47.
[2] La Champmeslé who played Phèdre was 30. Baron who played Hippolyte was 23. D'Ennebaut who played Aricie was about 30.

see on the surface a kind of fluorescent light which heralds another world and could very well be the light of Grace; indeed, is it not some kind of grace which rescues Iphigénie from death? The years pass and the academician becomes more and more a public figure. It is probable that one gets tired even of 'hell'.

We are in 1676; Boileau, 'who is serious without being boring' and always full of good advice, tries to bring about an atmosphere of reconciliation between Racine and Port-Royal. So the shadow of the dear Abbey begins to reappear in Racine's life, and what is all the more ominous is the fact that Racine's passions begin to cool down and that the fashionable Paris which, up till now, has been constantly at his heels begins to get tiring and tired of him. Strange worries begin to assail Racine, and he begins to feel an overwhelming urge to reconcile his conflicting selves and to re-create his own unity.

> O grâce, O Rayon salutaire
> Viens me mettre, avec moi, d'accord
>
> Et domptant par un doux effort
> Cet homme qui t'est si contraire,
> Fais ton esclave volontaire.[1]

His reconciliation with Port-Royal would really mean the reconciliation of the two brother enemies which form the personality of Racine, and what a triumph it would be if this reconciliation could be effected through the theatre and through poetry! It would mean that passion had reconciled itself at last with love, and that was obviously Racine's intention as stated in his preface to *Phèdre*. 'The theatre is a school where virtue is as highly thought of as in schools of philosophy. . . . If authors followed the true aim of tragedy, which is as much concerned with instructing as with amusing their audiences, they would probably find in this approach a means of reconciling tragedy with many people famous for their piety and who, having lately condemned it, would take a more lenient view.' If *Phèdre* could reach this goal, it would be the victory of a lifetime: all his hopes were on this play. As soon

---

[1] O Divine Grace, O healing light,
Come and restore my distraught self

And by a gentle effort tame this man
Who is so opposed to you, and make of him
Your willing slave.

as it was published Boileau read it to the great Arnaud who admired it. All hopes seemed possible. The only remark made by Arnaud was the remark which shows his extraordinary perspicacity—'Why did he have to make Hippolyte fall in love?' Love was indeed the main motive of Racine's drama, and Arnaud was right, this new Christian—Hippolyte—was in love. Who could describe Racine's sorrows in the course of these past years, for there is no doubt that if he had always loved God, he had loved poetry and tragedy with equal strength. One cannot forget the fact that it was in the Abbey of Port-Royal-des-Champs that he received his first poetic impressions. He loved God and he loved nature—God's creation, and he could neither separate one from the other nor renounce either. Perhaps he did think that one can always come to terms with God, that there is always time, while the problem is different with the burning pit of passion which was in the middle of himself and which made him writhe with pain. He had first to get rid of that; it was an irresistible vocation and he had to submit to it. Thence his dive of ten years' duration in waters which were intended to cool his blood; and now after these ten years, thanks to *Phèdre*, reconciliation was in sight at last. What a joy it could have been!

Phèdre was produced on the 1 January 1677. Everybody knows the conspiracy which ruined this presentation. Three days later Pradon's *Phèdre* was produced, and the Duchesse de Bouillon, having bought up the two rival theatres for the same evening, packed her friends in the theatre which was giving Pradon's *Phèdre*, compelling Racine's company to play to an empty house. Racine was struck down by despair; his attempts to reconcile himself with Port-Royal had not been quite successful; his play which carried all his hopes had failed; something in him snapped, and the 'season of illuminations' came to an end, after ten years. He renounced the theatre for ever; he was then only 37 years of age.

> Je veux et n'accomplis jamais
> Je veux, mais, ô misère extrême,
> Je ne fais pas le bien que j'aime,
> Et je fais le mal que je haïs.[1]

---

[1] I am willing, yet never accomplish anything,
I am willing, but O extreme sorrow!
I do not perform the good which I like,
I perform the wrong which I hate.

Six months elapsed between the *première* of *Phèdre*, and his wedding on the 1 June 1677; six very important months marked by his official renunciation of poetry and of the theatre and his acceptance of the post of historiographer royal. Boileau went with him; they decided together. Much has been written as to the possible cause of Racine's renunciation of the theatre. No doubt the plot which caused *Phèdre* to fail affected him all the more that it certainly influenced his relations with Port-Royal. He himself said: 'Although I have been much flattered by the applause which I have received, the slightest criticism has always caused me sorrows which far outweighed the pleasure caused by praise.' There is no doubt therefore that he was deeply wounded and disappointed; ten years later, his hatred for Pradon was still as strong. It seems an obvious fact (and here we can vouch for it ourselves) that the atmosphere generated by certain elements in Paris can be so unbearable, so laden with hatred, meanness and futility that one can easily understand how the cabal of *Phèdre* could have led Racine to renounce the theatre. But there were certainly other reasons; it was probably the last drop which caused the pail to overflow; besides it is quite possible that the wild animal which inhabited Racine had by then uttered its last cry. This was also the moment when La Champmeslé preferred, perhaps too much and too openly, the Duc de Clermont-Tonnerre to him; she may have been compelled to reserve some kind of exclusiveness for the duke. In the papers of the time, as gossipy as those of today, one can read the following rather biting quatrain:

> A la plus tendre amour elle fut destinée
> Qui prit longtemps Racine dans son coeur,
> Mais pour un insigne malheur
> Le Tonnerre est venu, qui l'a dé-Racinée.[1]

But the most important reason for his renunciation of the theatre is probably connected with Port-Royal. His former friends had not been placated by his attempt at reconciliation through tragedy, however noble the play may have been. They therefore seized upon this opportunity to force Racine's hand and to compel him to a

---

[1] She was meant for the tenderest love
Which was rooted for a long time in Racine's heart,
But by striking misfortune the thunder
Came and uprooted it.

more sensational gesture. His aunt, Sainte-Thècle, must have done her best to bring 'this child' back to God. We know from Racine that 'she taught him how to know God in his childhood, and that it was also through her that God saved him from the aberrations and the misery in which he had lived for fifteen years'. There is no doubt that Port-Royal urged him to accept the post of historiographer royal, for they were thus killing two birds with one stone.

Firstly, in order to occupy such a post both Boileau and Racine had to renounce poetry; they had to have no other occupation except that of attending on the King.

Secondly, by occupying this post Racine would be near the King and could therefore act as a buffer between the King and Port-Royal.

It was in fact a splendid victory for Port-Royal which had succeeded in having one of its members, and one who had repented at last, as the King's historiographer. It is also possible that Racine's loving nature felt the need for a change. Up to the age of 20 he had loved God and his creation; from 20 to 37, he had loved poetry, the theatre, the world and women; after that he concentrated all his urge to love on the King, his wife and his children. He truly loved Louis XIV who was about his own age and whose example he had followed for the past twenty years.

A sudden disgust with the futile hatreds of Paris; the disgust of certain degrading love affairs, the desire for penance, the love for his King, the urge for a home, the loss of youth, all these motives may have caused his renunciation of the theatre. He had failed to find his unity; it was therefore time to renounce, forget and begin anew; and what road this time? The road of noble and simple modesty!

THESE GENTLEMEN OF THE SUBLIME

Racine and Boileau were attached to Louis XIV in order to glorify his reign and therefore followed him to his wars. The sight of these two poets living soldiers' lives must have been quite amazing. Whether at the siege of Mons, at the camp of Namur, or against the Germans, their ignorance and their fright were the delight of their friends; they were described as 'these Gentlemen of the Sublime'. As far as we know they do not seem to have been fascinated by the epic life; the only weapons they had taken with them were fieldglasses. 'I could see the whole attack fully at ease', says Racine.

'In truth I was a little far away, but I had excellent field-glasses, and my heart was so excited at the sight of so many brave men in danger that I could hardly keep still'. . . . And further on: 'I was so tired that I wished with all my heart that all the men I saw might all have been in their cottages or houses with their wives and children, and I in Rue des Maçons with my family . . . we are encamped along the Trouille, etc.' It was reported that 'they were no longer amazed at the bravery of the soldiers' and that 'they felt that they were quite right to want to be killed in order to put an end to such a frightful type of existence.' It was obvious that Racine was no hero, for the day after his death the King said to Boileau:

'Despréaux, you and I have sustained a great loss in the death of Racine.'

'What consoles me', replied Boileau, 'is that my friend, in spite of the fact that he was very afraid of death, has made a very Christian end.'

'I know,' said the King with a smile, 'and that surprised me, for I remember that at the siege of Gand, you were the braver of the two.'

It is nevertheless a very great pity that the history of the reign of Louis XIV, on which Boileau and Racine worked for eighteen years, should have been destroyed in 1726 in Valincourt. It is a pity and there is something strange about it. How can one explain the fact that eleven years after Louis XIV's death, twenty-seven years after Racine's and fifteen years after Boileau's, there had not been a single edition of the enormous labour of the two poets? Strange certainly, but let us go back to Racine.

Although Paris's hatred seems to have taken as a target 'his devotion' and his so-called hypocrisy, Racine now seemed happy and relaxed; his letters are amusing and witty and he still knows how to bite and to joke. He never fails to have a laugh at each of Pradon's new plays:

Un chacun bâille, ou s'endort, ou s'en va.[1]

He writes epigrams on plays which are booed or are flops:

Quand à Paris commença la méthode
De ces sifflets qui sont tant à la mode . . .

[1] Everybody yawns, falls asleep, or walks out.

Quand les pièces représentées
De Boyer sont peu fréquentées
Chagrin qu'il est d'y voir peu d'assistants
Voici comme il tourne la chose:
Vendredi la pluie en est la cause
Et le dimanche le beau temps.[1]

Racine shows no signs of frustration when he deals with the theatre; he takes an interest in the actors and their compulsory removals and their poverty. He prepares for his own pleasure the plan of an *Iphigénie en Tauride*;[2] he thinks of a play on the subject of *Alcestis*, and he corrects the collected edition of his works. A metamorphosis seems to have taken place; from the chrysalis to the butterfly, that is all. The letter which he wrote to his elder son about novels and plays could easily have been signed by his Aunt Sainte-Thècle. 'Be sure that the day when you can talk about novels and comedies, you will not be much more advanced in the world, and you will not be more esteemed for that either. . . . If I knew that these kinds of books had inspired you with disgust for more useful reading, particularly those concerning piety and morality, I should be inconsolable. Your conscience and religion compel you to these readings . . . and with the exception of my salvation there is nothing which worries me more.' When one thinks of the letter which he once addressed to Nicole, one wonders if one is not in a dream, and one understands how those who did not love him as we do, were unable to forgive such a change and such a denial of his former self. Racine surrounded by 'his small and agreeable family' was now happy; his wife was a holy woman, who, thank God, had not much of an education. She knew that her husband had written some plays but she had never read any. He had seven children, and his elder son, Jean-Baptiste, gave him

[1] When Paris inaugurated the habit of whistling
Which has now become so fashionable . . .

When Boyer's plays are produced
And are badly attended,
Sad as it is that there are so few spectators,
He explains the whole thing by saying
That Friday's poor attendance
Was caused by the rain and Sunday's
By fine weather.

[2] *Iphygenia in Tauris.*

T.J.B.—L

every satisfaction; four of his five daughters were in holy orders, only the elder, Marie-Catherine, did not follow the tradition. Each time one of his daughters took the veil was an occasion for him to cry. Apparently 'Monsieur Racine loved to cry'; he had obviously kept up this trait which he had when he was called Acante. His daughters had charming names; they were Nanette, Babet, Fanchon and Madelon. At the age of 53 he was proud to see the birth of his last son Lionval who was no other than Louis Racine, the author of priceless memoirs about his father.

For twelve years Racine 'simmered' quietly in a kind of convalescent state; the two halves of his personality came closer, looked at each other cautiously, recognized each other, and finally fused into one; the healing period was over, 'Viens me mettre, avec moi, d'accord'; and in 1669, divine grace gave the reward that he desired. The circumstances in which he composed *Esther* are well known; it was intended for the young ladies of Saint-Cyr, an orphanage run by Madame de Maintenon. At last he was given a chance to work for the theatre while performing an act of devotion at the same time; that was an old and cherished idea, it was also an opportunity to do something for his old friends of Port-Royal who were now more persecuted than ever. The Jesuits had closed in on their prey and the Archbishop of Paris, M. de Harlay, had planted his teeth in the Abbey and would not let go. Once more one cannot fail to draw a comparison between the situation in which Racine was and that of the main character of his play *Esther*. Esther's task consists in defeating the influence of the cruel Aman, and in persuading the just king Assuérus to pay tribute to Mardochée who was under sentence, and to obtain the rescindment of the sentence which ordered the persecution of all these Jewish virgins. In reality, Racine's task consisted in defeating the influence of the bad Archbishop of Paris and his Jesuits and in persuading the just King Louis XIV to rehabilitate the great Arnaud, exiled in Flanders, and to stop the persecution of the holy virgins of Port-Royal. In order to achieve his aim, Racine chose a woman, in the hope that Madame de Maintenon might agree to plead his cause with the King. Here again we could do once more what we did for *Britannicus*, and should have no difficulty in casting Racine's friends in the various parts of *Esther*. In fact, at that time, Madame de Maintenon was described as 'the new Esther'. But it must be said that with *Esther*, Racine was still first and foremost the man of Port-Royal. *Athalie* enabled him to find himself in his entirety and is a personal triumph, and a glorious conclusion to the adventures which began in 1666 when Racine left the boat of his youth to dive into the strong waters of poetry and the theatre. Now he reappears at last carrying in his arms what he has rediscovered—the young child of Port-Royal—Eliacin, the pure young king once full of promise who had been piously protected by old Joad—the true genius of Port-Royal. Eliacin is the infinite love of God, the young orphan, Jean Racine when he was at Port-Royal, and also the pure soul of Port-Royal. *Athalie* marks Racine's crowning hour on earth; he had walked the path which God had laid out for him, he had lost himself in the maze, and at last he had found himself again; he rediscovered the young Eliacin of the first odes who had been betrayed by his inimical brother—Racine's other half. The circle was now closed. *Esther* and *Athalie* completed his work and Racine had won his battle on earth. What was left of the long years which covered his revolt against Nicole and his other masters of Port-Royal? The triumph of Port-Royal, which was now dearer than ever to him, and together with it there was the true faithful friend of his life—his brother by choice Pylades-Abner; whose real name is Boileau. His long struggles had left their mark on his liver, and a tumour, which could easily be given its proper name, brought about his end. In spite of a long period of disfavour which obviously did no good to his health, he died with serenity and Christian resignation. As always Boileau was by his side and it was to him that Racine addressed his last alexandrine:

C'est un bonheur pour moi de mourir avant vous.[1]

His last wish was a final gesture in favour of Port-Royal. It was a bold gesture which showed that he was not 'currying favours' from Louis XIV; he asked to be buried at Port-Royal-des-Champs at the feet of his master Hamon. That decision gave rise to one flash of wit so typical of the inexhaustible humour of Paris: 'Il ne s'y serait pas fait enterrer de son vivant.'[2] The last bite as a form of leave-taking, but as Saint-Simon remarked, 'A dead man does not care much about such things'.

---

[1] It is joy for me to die before you.
[2] He would not have got himself buried there when he was alive.

THE SYMPHONIC MOVEMENTS OF *PHÈDRE*

Racine is the most musical of all French dramatists, and *Phèdre*, which was the play which he preferred to all the others, remains, in spite of *Bérénice*, the most musical of his plays. We shall try for our own pleasure to make a brief study of *Phèdre* from the point of view of rhythm. From the symphonic point of view, the five acts of *Phèdre* could be divided into four movements which would be the following:

1st Movement—Act I
2nd Movement—Act II
3rd Movement—Act III and Act IV
4th Movement—Act V

The two movements which are most difficult to direct are without doubt the first and third movements. The first is difficult because it has to be firmly controlled throughout, and because it contains the seeds of all the themes which will reappear in the other movements. The third movement is difficult for reasons which are in part the opposite of the first; in it violence is let loose and it calls for the full power of the orchestra; it is the longest and the most important movement and it is also the most difficult to play. The play follows the rules of the ideal dramatic circle; the first act sets the action in motion and suggests the pattern of the whole work; the second act contains all the agitation which is going to bring the action to a head; the greater part of the third act is a kind of jumping board; the fourth act describes the falling graph of a long recitative; the fifth act closes the circle by passing again through a final period of agitation. The play follows a perfect geometrical construction which is repeated inside each scene. One could therefore draw the exact geometrical representation of *Phèdre* in the same way as one analyses the compositions of Poussin or of da Vinci in ellipses and triangles.

The first movement of the play must be conducted with the maximum of attention and control. It comprises only two brief explosions which precede and follow Phèdre's confession; it is placed under the sign of mystery. The second movement, which must on no account encroach on the orchestral volume of the movement which follows, must be conducted with all the more restraint that it is under the sign of desire. The third movement must be run with the best scientific technique, if not the actors are in danger of being left behind by the work, in the same way as cyclists who race behind motor-cycles can suddenly be left on their own; it is under the sign of 'delirium', that is to say under the sign of extra-lucidity. The fourth movement must swish quickly like a taffeta dress when its wearer walks, like the crackling of a spreading fire, like the hissing of rain, or like the continuous tremolo of the double-bass. This background music is broken twice, symmetrically by a kind of organ music, the first break is in order to celebrate the spiritual marriage of Hippolyte and Aricie, the second to describe Hippolyte's funeral. The fourth movement is under the sign of combustion. All that remains of this tragedy on the stage is a small mound of ashes representing the dead body of Phèdre, and further, on the feet of 'these ancient tombs', the shapeless remains of Hippolyte.

FIRST MOVEMENT (ACT I)

Just as for a concert the conductor stands on the platform, and waits with his outstretched arms until silence has fully descended upon the audience, in the same way, Hippolyte does not strike the first note until the theatre is absolutely silent. In fact it is wise to let a short while elapse, between the three knocks which precede the rise of the curtain, and the extremely important first bars of Hippolyte's music. The gap of time is filled by the raising of the curtain which fades in the dark and by the slow rise of a blue dawn which is traversed by the first golden ray of the sun and by the slow emergence of Hippolyte's silhouette from the misty air. The first movement of the concert starts just at the moment when the first ray of the sun illumines Hippolyte's face. This first movement comprises two exactly symmetrical parts, separated by the fateful turmoil which generally precedes Phèdre's appearances, and which in this case is represented by Oenone's short but powerful scene. The orchestra while playing the two symmetrical parts is divided into two groups so as to represent the internal cleavage of the characters torn between two opposite forces. Hippolyte wishes to run away, to free himself; this is the first motive, yet he is constantly brought back to his starting-point by the second motive which torments him and which is his love for Aricie. In the same way Phèdre also wants to flee away into another world; that is her first motive, but she is constantly brought back by the beast which lurks in her and which is her love. These two parts are the negative and positive aspects of the same photograph, while Hippolyte wants to flee away towards life, Phèdre agrees to flee towards death; while Hippolyte tries to summon white forces, Phèdre has made a pact with black forces. Each of these two parts is a kind of circumference. Hippolyte starts with the wind instruments which are blocked or with silencers on, and with the wood instruments:

Le dessein en est pris, je pars cher Théramène. [1]

Then he drops the rhythm which Théramène takes up sonorously; they do that many times until they reach the point where Hippolyte, pressed by Théramène, confesses:

Si je la haïssais, je ne la fuirais pas. [2]

After this confession there is a slight pause (the first). After this first musical phase which has been conducted by Théramène, we have a phase of agitation and high level of tension, that is to say a recitative, then a fall and finally the closing of the circle:

Théramène, je pars et vais chercher mon père. [3]

That is the first part; after a good pause between lines 152 and 153, Phèdre appears on the stage and shows us in succession the five main aspects of her character. First, we have the mournful, dying note of one single violin which is meant to announce a *dying woman*. Then we have a passage of grating and sharp sounds which represent a woman whose *nerves* have been torn to shreds; that is followed by the deep and moving music of violas and cellos which are Phèdre's *farewell to the sun*. This is followed by the theme of the *lover* followed by the theme of *shame* which is like a bitter shudder rippling over the orchestra which fades away with a last sigh. The movement is taken up by Oenone, who proceeds exactly as Théramène had done previously and who after a pause following the words 'Tu le veux' [4] succeeds in making Phèdre confess:

Hippolyte, grands dieux!
C'est toi qui l'as nommé. [5]

[1] My decision is taken, I am leaving dear Théramène.
[2] If I hated her I should not run away from her.
[3] Théramène, I am leaving, I am going to look for my father.
[4] You insist.
[5] Hypolitus, ye Gods!
It is you who have uttered such a name!

This is followed by exactly the same pattern as the one at the end of the first part: agitation, high level of agitation, recitative, a fall and finally the closing of the circle. The fateful turmoil caused by the bird of bad omen—Oenone—is counterbalanced by the funerary message of Panope; here the moving music of the brass instruments is punctuated by the very significant silence of Phèdre. The symmetrical confessions of Hippolyte and Phèdre, broken by the whirlwind interventions of Oenone and Panope, have been played in an atmosphere of mystery only lit up by the two flashes from Phèdre and Oenone which encompass Phèdre's confession like the two brackets of a parenthesis. The finale of the first movement dissipates the internal and external opacity of the preceding motives. The false news of Thésée's death liberates both Hippolyte and Phèdre and disperses the fog which was stifling these two people; while hope begins to take root in them, the sun rises and lights up the palace. Passion will be able to have its say; the lively rhythm of the last four lines prepares us for the allegro which starts the second movement.

SECOND MOVEMENT (ACT II)

There is only a slight pause between the first and the second movements. The sun is at its zenith and the passions of the play are at their zenith too; the temperature is burning hot; a kind of heat haze scintillates in the dazzling light, like slate roofs in the summer sun. One can hear a steady buzz which is very much like the buzzing of a fevered head. The second movement is subdivided into an overture and two parts. The overture is fast and joyful, the acting light and lively; the entry on the stage of the two young women, Aricie and Ismène, follows a very precise rhythm. Instead of avoiding the object of her love, Aricie rushes to meet him, being nevertheless torn apart by the same contradictory motives which affected Hippolyte and Phèdre in the first movement; her hopes are indeed very fragile.

> Hippolyte demande à me voir en ce lieu?
> . . . .
> . . . Tu vois depuis quels temps il évite nos pas
> Et cherche tous les lieux où nous ne sommes pas![1]

---

[1] Does Hippolytus wish to see me in this place?
. . . .
You know for how long he has been avoiding us
And hunting places where he knew we would not be.

That is why after excitement and hope she is assailed by doubts and the movement is allowed to drop, to be revived by Ismène who proceeds with her in the same way as did Théramène and Oenone with Hippolyte and Phèdre; and so we have exactly the same variations which we noted before; agitation, high level of tension, a fall and the closing of the circle with the words:

> Hippolyte aimerait? Par quel bonheur extrême . . .[1]

This first circle constitutes the overture of the second movement. The allegro is over and it is followed by two perfect diptychs which comprise Hippolyte's declaration on one side, and that of Phèdre on the other. A short and whirling phase sweeps over the orchestra and takes away with it all traces of allegro:

> Vous l'entendrez vous-même.
> Il vient à vous. [2]

Thus the conductor with a swift twist of his wrist stops all vibrations from the orchestra. Then a long pause, and total motionlessness of characters and orchestra; the players wait, keyed up for the start; one single battery of drums marks with a slow rising tempo the arrival of Hippolyte who is the theme; his arrival is followed by a new pause more pregnant with anxiety than the preceding one; everything is motionless except the drums which seem to imitate the excited beats of the two young people's hearts. Then follow again the same conflicting motives as in the first movement. First we have the reasons of state which Hippolyte manages to explain with great difficulty; that is followed by an explanation of his father's policy, the cause of his death, and the historical background of his attitude to the dynasty of the Pallantides, followed by a statement of Hippolyte's political views and his conclusion:

> L'Attique est votre bien. [3]

But all these rational explanations are opposed at an increasing pace by Hippolyte's rising passion which gnaws him and tears him apart with its desperate urge to reach the light. This second motive which grows stronger and stronger nearly overwhelms Hippolyte who nevertheless manages to say:

[1] Could Hippolytus be in love? By what strange good fortune . . .
[2] You will hear him yourself,
He is coming in just now.
[3] Attica is your kingdom.

Je vous laisse aussi libre et plus libre que moi, [1]

then having said as much as he dares to say he takes leave of Aricie
with the words:

> Je pars et vais pour vous
> Réunir tous les voeux partagés entre nous. [2]

At this moment the orchestra holds itself tightly under control as
if to avoid letting itself go. A melodic motive from Aricie slowly
opens it up. After a rapid scale on the violin's highest notes, there
rises the most piercing and moving melody which strikes at the
heart of Hippolyte. The orchestra, transfixed, stretches its limbs
like a wounded stag and plunges into flight with the recitative of
Hippolyte's passionate love:

> Mon arc, mes javelots, mon char, tout m'importune
> Je ne me souviens plus des leçons de Neptune
> Mes seuls gémissements font retentir les bois
> Et mes coursiers oisifs ont oublié ma voix! [3]

This is music as fluid as the best of Mozart. The recitative ends in
a period of agitation which marks the end of the first part. The
second part which begins with Phèdre's entry is preceded by the
whirlwind appearance of Théramène, in a very short scene:

> Seigneur, la Reine vient et je l'ai devancée. [4]

Hippolyte caught in this whirlwind is like a half-stunned sleep-
walker. The orchestra seems to have got out of control; waves of
sound seem to sweep over the instruments and to bend them in all
directions:

> Cependant vous sortez. Et je pars. Et j'ignore . . . [5]

Out of this confusion caused by Phèdre's arrival, and in reply to
Hippolyte's declaration, Aricie's avowal rises like a song. She too
loves; she says so and then disappears, leaving behind her silence
and the only moment of true joy in the play. Hippolyte remains

---

[1] I leave you as free and even more free than I am.
[2] I am leaving, and I shall try to bring about for you
    All the things which you and I share.
[3] My bow, my spears, my chariot, all bore me;
    I no longer remember Neptune's lessons,
    My groans alone disturb the woods,
    And my idle steeds have forgotten my voice.
[4] My Lord, the Queen is coming, I am preceding her.
[5] Yet you are leaving, and I also am leaving, and I do not know . . .

surprised, then whirls round tense with joy and says to Théramène:

Ami, tout est-il prêt? [1]

This is the moment of light of the tragedy; will happiness be possible?

Mais la Reine s'avance. [2]

Just as on some stormy days the sun sometimes manages to break through the dark clouds and then disappears not to be seen again for the whole day, in the same way this brief glimmer of happiness only lasts for a few seconds. Hippolyte's reply ends with a disquieting background of double-bass music; Théramène leaves speedily, while Hippolyte manages to retain control of himself. Another pause, and the second part begins; Phèdre leaning on her 'evil fate' slowly enters; silence. The orchestra is in a state of suspense as before, but this time the drums instead of rhythming the throbs of two hearts moving one towards the other, emphasize on the contrary the throbs of a lonely heart which moves feverishly towards a wall without echo. Phèdre's declaration is exactly symmetrical with that of Hippolyte. We have once more the two contending motives; the motive of the reason of state which is slowly overwhelmed by passion. Hippolyte has dealt with the theme of the father, Phèdre deals with that of the son, the difference between the two is that Phèdre is much less successful than Hippolyte in controlling her passion; she is all the more unsuccessful since Hippolyte, who was first indifferent, tries to sympathize with her sorrows and is therefore all the more charming. In fact the more he misunderstands Phèdre's behaviour, the more attractive he becomes, and the harder it is for her to resist. Owing to this temporary misunderstanding the two motives, Hippolyte-Phèdre, which ought to have struggled one against the other, fuse for a brief moment into one, as if to sing a duet which is followed by the strange voluptuous and indecent passage which begins:

Oui, Prince, je languis, je brûle pour Thésée [3]

which Hippolyte interrupts three times. This passage is full of strange sonorities, perverse refinements, and extreme sensuality which verges on indecency. It is perhaps the passage which is the

[1] Friend, is everything ready?
[2] But the Queen is coming.
[3] Yes, Prince, I am longing for—I am burning for Theseus.

most difficult to render; for one moment it seems to fly out of reality, but Hippolyte brings it back to earth with the words:

Dieux! Qu'est-ce que j'entends? [1]

Phèdre, who had been carried away, returns to reality with a strange phrase whispered on the violas:

Et sur quoi jugez-vous que j'en perds la mémoire, Prince? [2]

We are right in the middle of a high level of tension; the recitative is not far off, and it bursts out with the words:

Ah! Cruel, tu m'as trop entendue. [3]

Henceforth, the rhythm increases its tempo until the end of the movement, and the passionate recitative unfolds some of the themes which haunt this tormented woman; we have the theme of the passionate lover, that of the queen, daughter of the sun, that of the sensual woman, that of the shameful woman, and finally the theme of the longing for death. The tempo becomes faster and faster until with the fall of the curtain Hippolyte is horrified, Phèdre is completely out of control; Oenone is mad with fear, Hippolyte's sword is brandished, the Queen is seized and carried away and Théramène arrives very excited. Meanwhile everybody is trying to recollect what really happened, and the audience has witnessed it all without having the time to realize its implications. The tempest is let loose, the fire has started, the third movement can come, the second movement is now ended. With the exception of the overture it is exactly symmetrical with the first, the tempo has been slightly increased, and the tone slightly raised by desire which has now revealed itself.

THIRD MOVEMENT (ACTS III AND IV)

Thus each movement ends with a rhythm which prepares the start of the next movement. We have seen that during the two previous movements, with the exception of Hippolyte's and Phèdre's declaration, the orchestra had succeeded in mastering itself at the cost of great efforts. But towards the end of the second movement, the orchestra lets itself go. Phèdre's declaration has gone through it like a knife; the boat has caught fire, the flames nuzzle up to the cabins, water comes in from all sides, the boat

[1] O Gods! what do I hear?
[2] What makes you think that I have forgotten about him, Prince?
[3] O heartless man, I have already told you too much.

begins to sink; we are at the crucial point of the tragedy, the point of equilibrium when the characters tire of repressing their passions, confess them and are prepared to fight for them, we are at the summit about to pass on to the other side of the mountain.

On the plane of rhythm the third movement comprises three big waves followed by eddies and then by the triumphant return of Thésée interrupted by the piteous departure of Phèdre. The eddies, the return of Thésée and Phèdre's departure, constitute one single period which is the period of agitation; then comes a high level of tension astride the third and fourth acts and followed by the recitative composed of a diptych of maledictions—Thésée cursing Hippolyte and Phèdre cursing Oenone; finally a phrase which connects the third with the fourth and last movement.

The third movement offers us a perspective different from the previous one. There has been a kind of enlargement, we have come nearer the characters and we look at them in close-ups. This change in the rhythm, which we mentioned in a previous chapter, enables us to examine in detail the behaviour of the characters which have now been enlarged. Phèdre and Oenone come in with a wide-embracing movement which forms the first big wave which sweeps in with full force and slowly dies down at the pause:

Je ne le puis quitter, [1]

Then the second wave swells up and sweeps in to die down at the second pause:

Oenone, il peut quitter cet orgueil qui te blesse [2]

Then the rhythm changes with the return of Oenone; it becomes feverish and as agitated as a net full of glittering fish; it rises up to meet Thésée's arrival:

Dans le trouble où je suis, je ne puis rien pour moi. [3]

After this eddy we have trumpets and bugles which mark the return of Thésée, interrupted quite suddenly and replaced by the faint sounds of violins representing exhausted Phèdre, and coming to a halt when she leaves the stage. We wait anxiously for what might happen next; the tension mounts with this slowly rising storm; the rhythm changes into a kind of ominous rumble of fear and forebodings broken here and there by the deep voice of Thésée.

[1] I cannot leave him.
[2] Oenone, he could forsake the pride that hurts you.
[3] In the confusion in which I am, I can do nothing for myself.

Hippolyte shyly presents his request to Thésée who mumbles in his beard and goes out without saying anything. Hippolyte decides to opt for his love, and so transformed he goes out. The curtain falls on the third act and it looks as if the incomplete third movement was about to come to an end when the brass suddenly roar out from afar the great:

Ah!

which starts the fourth act; the third movement was therefore not finished and it will only end with the fourth act. The curtain has risen again; the 'Ah!' has changed the atmosphere like a sharp crack of thunder on a sultry day, the storm breaks with Thésée cautiously followed by Oenone who is watching for the effect of the poison with which she has injected him. The rhythm goes diminuendo and the theme of calumny is soon replaced by the noble theme of the return of a transformed Hippolyte who comes to his father carrying his head high and determined to tell the whole truth. His first words, clear as light, only draw angry grunts from his father; these words and grunts mark the end of the level run; the recitative takes flight and will perform its bouncing curve without a single break:

Perfide! Oses-tu bien te montrer devant moi. [1]

From now on, we have a series of explosions, the rhythm changes and the tempo and the noise are stunning; the highlights of this passage are: 'Perfide', 'Fuis', 'Fuis, dis-je', 'Cesse, cesse', [2] and finally:

Ah! que ton impudence excite mon courroux, [3]

which is the highest pitch reached by Thésée, followed by Hippolyte's question:

Vous me parlez toujours d'inceste et d'adultère? [4]

In the midst of this turmoil of conflicting passions, there seems to be a brief moment of respite, which is an island over which the rhythm remains for a few seconds in suspense, and which is the moment of Hippolyte's confession in answer to the question:

Tu l'aimes? [5]

[1] Traitor! How dare you show yourself to me.
[2] Traitor! Away, away, I say. Cease, cease.
[3] How your impudence angers me!
[4] You keep on talking about incest and adultery?
[5] Do you love her?

An important pause here hints fleetingly at a possible reconciliation; but it is too late and hope is quickly dispelled by the brass
which redouble their fierceness, while the movement regains it
ascending tempo:

Et quoi! de votre erreur . . . [1]

Hippolyte leaves, pursued by Thésée who must not allow the
movement to fall away from the line when he says:

Je t'aimais (line 1161) etc. . . . [2]

which is an aside. Thésée must at all costs keep in the movement.
Phèdre comes in and throws herself at his feet and echoes with her
moans the violence of the preceding outburst.

Sauvez-moi de l'horreur de l'entendre crier. [3]

Thésée helps her to get up, gathers strength and anger in her
presence, then goes out, carried upon the surge of a movement
which, with the exception of the slight pause during Hippolyte's
confession, has never ceased to rise in tempo from the moment it
burst forth with the word 'Perfide'. But before leaving, Thésée
has unknowingly divulged the final, fateful piece of news that
Hippolyte and Aricie love each other. The tempo of the movement and the staggering last piece of news have upset the orchestra
which, like Phèdre, stumbles. The various instruments are more
or less out of tune and every one has each its say. The bassoon
laughs at the violin; 'Too much sorrow laughs' said William
Blake; the sudden break out of the jealousy theme which Racine
had carefully prepared for this moment of total disarray makes the
whole thing wellnigh unbearable. One enters a new world where
sonorities achieve an hallucinating effect. One is plunged into a
kind of dream world in which the rhythm has nothing in common
with reality, and one has the same effect as if one were watching a
slow-motion film. Phèdre breaks into this world at a slant; she
might even laugh, but her laughter grates terribly; Oenone, who
has followed her stealthily, has caught up with her and Phèdre
keeps up for a brief while the pretence of irony, then suddenly
crumbles down,

Ah, Douleur non encore éprouvée. [4]

[1] Well what! your error . . .
[2] I loved you . . .
[3] Spare me the horror of hearing him cry out.
[4] Ah, grief as yet unfelt.

and utters the most sorrowful solo of the whole play:

> Les a-t-on vus souvent se parler, se chercher?
> Dans le fond des forêts allaient-ils se cacher?
> Hélas! Ils se voyaient avec pleine licence.
> Le ciel de leurs soupirs approuvait l'innocence;
> Ils suivaient sans remords leur penchant amoureux;
> Tous les jours se levaient clairs et sereins pour eux. [1]

That is followed once more by a deeper probing of Phèdre's main
themes which are: Phèdre the capricious, the noble daughter of
the sun, the scrupulous woman, the remorse of the unrequited
lover, etc., to which is added the most harrowing theme—that of
the jealous woman. Oenone's sepulchral voice increases the atmosphere of unreality and nightmare which borders on outright madness.

> Quel conseil ose-t-on me donner? [2]

The orchestra bursts into a wide and shrieking flight, then stops
suddenly after Phèdre's drunken disappearance. Once more the
third movement seems to be ended, but there is yet something
more to come. For the first time the organ intervenes, and it does
so with a very simple and brief phrase in order to suggest Oenone's
tragic punishment and to prepare the coming of the fourth and
final movement. The phrase flows 'sforzando' while the curtain
very slowly falls.

FOURTH MOVEMENT (ACT V)

The fourth movement comprises two main rhythms which correspond respectively to the carrying out by Neptune of Thésée's
evil vow, that is to say the preparation for Hippolyte's death, and
to the slow death of Phèdre. These symmetrical rhythms each have
an orchestral pattern superimposed upon them which on the one
hand corresponds to the ritual of Aricie's and Hippolyte's wedding
ceremony:

> Aux portes de Trézène et parmi ses tombeaux . . . [3]

---

[1] Were they often seen speaking to each other, seeking each other?
Did they go and hide in the depths of forests?
Alas! They saw each other in full freedom.
Heaven approved the innocence of their love,
They followed without remorse the call of their feelings,
And every day which rose was for them bright and serene.
[2] What advice dare they give me?
[3] At the gates of Trezena and amongst its tombs . . .

and on the other to the ritual of Hippolyte's funeral:

A peine nous sortions des portes de Trézène . . .[1]

The rhythm of the first part of this movement must have great urgency, for Neptune's chariot is moving fast. The organ is heard again stating Aricie's and Hippolyte's pledge which sounds like a litany.

Nous prendrons à témoin le dieu qu'on y révère;
Nous le prierons tous deux de nous servir de père.
Des dieux les plus sacrés, j'attesterai le nom.
Et la chaste Diane, et l'auguste Junon.[2]

But Neptune is implacable, the rhythm becomes more pressing and Hippolyte disappears never to be seen again. Reaction of Aricie and panic of Thésée followed by the fateful whirlwind arrival of Panope who always precedes Phèdre's arrivals. Thésée is thrown into the most complete confusion; the rhythm of the movement continues to rise until it suddenly stops in a syncopated clatter of drums with the arrival of Théramène:

O soins tardifs et superflus!
Inutile tendresse! Hippolyte n'est plus.[3]

For the third and, this time, the last occasion, the organ music fills once more the nave of the theatre and sings of the courage, the innocence and the glory of Hippolyte. Théramène's monologue like a church psalm is the hinge between the two parts of this last movement. All the orchestra has to do now is to suggest Phèdre's slow arrival, to whisper her confession and to accompany her slowly to her end which is the finale of a classical symphony and also the finale of the tragedy.

Allons, de mon erreur, hélas! trop éclaircis.[4]

Phèdre's body, burnt out by passion, is cruelly abandoned by Thésée who has no longer any other concern except his children—

---

[1] We had scarcely left the gates of Trezena.
[2] We shall take as witness the God who is worshipped there;
We shall both beg him to act as our father.
I shall invoke the names of the most holy of the gods,
And chaste Diana, and august Juno.
[3] O too long delayed and useless attentions!
Wasted tenderness! Hippolytus is no more.
[4] Let us go, alas, and having learnt all too well the extent of my errors.

his son Hippolyte and his daughter Aricie. The tragedy of Phèdre and Hippolyte is finished. In *Mon coeur mis à nu*,[1] Baudelaire says: 'What I always liked best in a theatre in my childhood, and even now, is the chandelier, a beautiful object, luminous, crystalline, complicated, circular and symmetrical . . .' The chandelier of a theatre does indeed comprise the five principal qualities which a masterpiece must possess; it must be:

Luminous
Crystalline
Complicated
Circular and
Symmetrical

In the temple of dramatic art it is *Phèdre* which occupies the place of the chandelier.

[1] My heart laid bare.

VI

Paul Claudel

(Notes for intimate memoirs)

Connaissance
Le Soulier de Satin
Partage de Midi

Un drame parfait doit présenter le caractère d'une composition logique, où les rôles de chaque personnage sont strictement dépendants les uns des autres et ne s'expliquent que par la conclusion. Il faut que tout concoure à l'ensemble et chaque partie à chacune des autres. Il y a là une rigueur sévère qui exclut le lyrisme creux. Ce qui se rapproche le plus de cet idéal austère est *Britannicus*. [1]

—PAUL CLAUDEL, 1948

These notes are not intended to be a profound study of Paul Claudel, they are simply some personal reflections on a dramatist whom I loved. I only hope that they may interest those who feel as I do about him. My earliest memory of Claudel's work brings me back to l'Atelier and to the bare and comfortless room of the school where Madame Dullin, who had a predilection for Claudel, was teaching us *L'Annonce faite à Marie*. [2] I can still hear the melodious, sing-song voices of the pupils saying 'O ma fiancée à travers les branches en fleurs, salut—Bonjour Jâââcques—Oui, Violai . . . ne.' These words generally pronounced with eyes

---

[1] Perfect drama must have the shape of a logical construction in which each character's behaviour is rigorously bound to that of the others and is only explained by the conclusion. Everything in it must be part of the whole and every part must be made to connect with the others. There is in drama a kind of compelling rigour which leaves no room for hollow lyricism. The work which comes nearest to this austere ideal is *Britannicus* by Racine.—PAUL CLAUDEL, 1948.

[2] *The Tidings brought to Mary.*

turned upwards as if overwhelmed by poetic ecstasy always reminded me of: 'Bonjour Cousin, j'ai cru m'apercevoir à tort ou à raison que vous me quittiez tristement ce matin . . . je vous ai refusé un baiser, le voici . . . asseyons-nous là et causons' from *On ne badine pas avec l'amour*.[1] These were the usual worn-out tags repeated generation after generation by the pupils of the Conservatoire.

At l'Atelier we worshipped Claudel. To us he was the standard-bearer of what was beautiful in the modern theatre, and we contrasted him with everything that was mean, humdrum, bogged down. We knew that he prevented Clément Vautel from sleeping and we were delighted. We looked upon him as an undisputed master, yet, alas, a distant master, distant in space, and also spiritually; indeed, on the one hand, he was an ambassador, somewhere in America, and we couldn't help thinking that instead of occupying the post of ambassador, which made him waste time which he could have devoted to his dramatic work, we should have much preferred to see him appear as inspector of education at l'Atelier in order to find out what we were doing and to tell us what to do. On the other hand, although we were overwhelmed by this 'green sea of poetry' as Thibaudet put it, we could not be too sure of understanding him. We knew that only genius could create what he had created but our ideas about the shape and content of his work were anything but clear. These verses, which sometimes stretched into the next line and beyond, had a rhythm of breathing which did not quite correspond to ours. Besides that, we wondered whether the miracle of the resurrection through a leprous woman was meant to be real, purely imaginary or simply symbolical—whether we had really succeeded in extracting the drama from the lyrical garments in which it was wrapped up. Still we saw that it was beautiful; we were delighted and fully carried away by it, and we were prepared to declare war upon any who dared to attack it in front of us! What contempt, what scorn would have been ours! Only one man had the right to criticize Claudel because he seemed to us to be worthy of the task, it was our resident poet—Antonin Artaud, who had the undeniable advantage over Claudel of not being an ambassador. He was more

---

[1] Rightly or wrongly, I thought you were rather sad on leaving me this morning. . . . I have refused you a kiss, here it is now, let us sit down and talk.

fragile, less powerful, but certainly purer. These two poets were probably both bleeding; the great difference was that we could see Artaud's blood. That is why when following our playing of the first act of *Partage de Midi* at the Alfred Jarry Theatre, Artaud said: 'the act of *Partage de Midi* which you have just seen is by Paul Claudel, poet, ambassador and traitor', we all indulged in an excited laughter which did not take anything away from our admiration for Claudel. This kind of joke was typical of Artaud, and Claudel's standing was totally unaffected by it. After all, it was *Partage de Midi* that Artaud the pure had chosen for his theatre and it was this same Artaud who had made typescript copies of *Partage de Midi* and given us a text which we devoured with as much eagerness as if it had been the forbidden fruit.

Claudel then had a great reputation in the surrealist *milieu* which we frequented. Neither his conversion, nor his opinions or his position could possibly please this atheistic, leftist *milieu*, but they all admired the poet. I still remember my great friend Desnos's answer to a journalist who was asking him who was the greatest living French poet: 'It's Claudel, by God!' The great friends of l'Atelier numbered among them a close collaborator of Claudel, Darius Milhaud. I could not describe my debt to Milhaud and his wife for the kindness they showed me when I was at l'Atelier and later in the army; they were both full of generosity and love for young people. I remember we used to question them a great deal about this legendary distant genius called Claudel. Time went by and I had just produced my first show, *As I Lay Dying*, which contained everything I already loved, namely aspects of the infinite resources of the human body. Milhaud, probably in order to encourage me, used to tell me that Claudel would have loved the production of this play; 'unfortunately he wasn't due to arrive until a little later which was too late for the show'. Anyway would he have come if we had invited him, and if he had come wouldn't we all have died, or wouldn't the curtain have fallen on our heads? In fact, Claudel was due to be in Paris round about that time, and one day Milhaud told me: 'He is giving a lecture in a hall' (the name of which I cannot remember), 'join me there and I shall try to introduce you to him.' What a prospect! What flights of imagination were suddenly suggested to me! I went, and true enough he was there, on the platform at the other end of the hall, all round in his sturdy frame. The steady flow of his words hammered on my chest and I felt the increasing rise of a red wave of shyness. The hall was full to capacity. There were a lot of ladies, and that annoyed me. What had Claudel to do with these ladies! Would I ever be able to make my way through those barricades of hats? The lecture was over; a thunder of applause, and the chosen few darted forward to congratulate him; I plunged forward in the wake of Darius Milhaud. . . . I could see a compact group progressing towards us and in the middle of it, Claudel walking with a steady diplomatic step, neither too fast so as to remain approachable, nor too slow so as to get the whole business over; in short the true gait of a professional. He advanced towards us, the crowd closed in on him with a babel of noises reminding me of an aviary. Claudel's answers to questions vaguely reached me like the faint notes of a bassoon; he passed by; my eyes must have tried to flash some sign, some youthful S.O.S. which he did not see; he disappeared; it was over. Darius Milhaud had not managed to introduce me, and even if he had, would he have seen me in this swaying crowd? Sledge-hammer for hatted ladies! I returned to the Atelier in a rage; I had to turn into rage what was truly sadness. . . . I had to wait two years before I could meet Claudel, thanks to the play *Numantia*.

Once more Darius Milhaud had done his best, and Claudel had agreed to come to the dress rehearsal. We learnt that he had been delighted, and that must have been true for he reserved a box for an indefinite period so as to offer it to his friends. So every evening there was someone in Claudel's box. We were very proud, and soon the great day came; he said he would like to meet me, at least that is what I was told, and of course I believed it. Was it one of my friends' kind attentions towards me? I went to his house in the Rue Jean-Goujon and introduced myself to him. For me it was a memorable encounter, in the course of which, to use his language, we became acquainted or rather, we recognized each other. Talking about *Numantia*, we fully agreed about the importance of the gesture, the resources of the body, the beauty of words, the importance of consonants, the danger of lengthening vowels too much, the prosody of speech, long and short syllables, the anapest, the iamb, and the art of breathing. Then he spoke about the Japanese Theatre and he went so far as to say to me: 'What a pity we did not meet forty years earlier!' I went away brimming over with excitement; he had given me the biggest boost up I ever had. Through my shyness, soon dispelled, I had discovered a man who was simple, who could talk about the theatre as a true crafts-man; in short a dissatisfied fellow-artist, engrossed as I was in fascinating problems and prepared to share his discoveries, his observations, and his ideas. Here was a man genuinely devoted to art; he was 69 years old, I was 27. This immediate communion between us filled me with wonder and I felt like saying 'thank you' to everything; to God, to life and to the first passer-by I met. I learnt later that at that time he had been very ill, practically at death's door, and since then, I have kept on thinking that he might have disappeared then, and of the kind of subtraction this would have meant for me. It was probably when he was very ill at that time that he received a telegram from a friend saying 'When you are in heaven don't forget me in your prayers' to which, once he had recovered, he answered: 'I shan't fail to do so, I shall make a knot in my shroud.'

Two years passed; we were now playing *Hamlet* in Laforgue's translation, and *Hunger* by Knut Hamsun. Claudel came and went, and right through these performances, he had a seat reserved for the Sunday matinées. We therefore had a regular and important spectator. What an encouragement for us, and how inspiring! At last he wrote me a first letter, which I showed to whoever wanted to see it, and which I kept constantly in my wallet during the first year of the war which followed. I kept it as a relic, and today I still have with me its dirty and creased remains. We were in 1939. My mother's death compelled me to give up the performance of *Hunger*. I rejoined Madeleine Renaud in Vichy. After the waters we went for a cure of pure air in the Alps. We went to the Col de la Madeleine (of course) and there we paid our first visit to Brangues. The Comédie Française had decided to give a new production of *L'Annonce faite à Marie* [1] and Claudel wished to discuss with Madeleine Renaud the character of Violaine. We had for the first time the chance of visiting this beautiful centuries-old castle surrounded by majestic plane trees and venerable lime trees. Claudel and his wife were waiting for us on the steps of the splendid Louis XV façade. We were very shy, and although our conversation was lively we were, Madeleine Renaud and I, very much on our guard. After that Madeleine Renaud went into Claudel's study, I nearly said his confessional, to discuss Violaine;

[1] *The Tidings brought to Mary.*

I remained with Madame Claudel. Not far from us, I could see a very young woman with a rather wild look which delighted me; her casual style of hair and clothes put me at ease; I felt in my element, and wondered whether she was Mara or Louis Laine? It was my good friend Renée, the youngest of Claudel's daughters. The confession about Violaine being over, we explored our numerous agreements about many aspects of his writings, particularly *l'Art poétique*[1] and *Positions et Prepositions*. After that, once we were well warmed up, I couldn't resist offering my services to Claudel, and I asked him for three plays: *Tête d'Or, Partage de Midi, Le Soulier de Satin*.

'Why such a choice?' said he.

'Because *Tête d'Or* is your sap, *Partage* your trial, and *Le Soulier* your synthesis.'

'My dear friend,' he went on, 'this will be difficult; *Tête d'Or* has become practically unreadable to me; it is an incomprehensible jargon which will only cause laughter. I shall never give permission to perform *Partage de Midi*; as for *Le Soulier de Satin*, I should like to see it performed, but it must be the whole of it, without cuts, and that does seem quite impossible. Why not begin by producing the fourth play entitled *Sous le Vent des Iles Baléares*?[2] It is a full play in itself, and I began with it; the other three days of *Le Soulier de Satin* were added much later.'

I left him slightly disconcerted, but nevertheless very pleased with these conversations which had brought us nearer. I was desperately anxious to get to grips with his work, and I was determined to tackle this problem again! But the war came and with it mobilization, the exodus and my entry into the Comédie Française thanks to Jacques Copeau. In 1941 I approached Claudel for I wanted more than ever to serve him. He was living at Brangues in the unoccupied zone. As I had not heard anything further about *L'Annonce faite à Marie*, I renewed my proposals of 1939, and this was Claudel's answer: 'What a joy, and how I should love to work with you! *Tête d'Or* still frightens me—*Le Soulier de Satin* would be splendid, but what a lot of work it entails! Don't you think we could begin with something easier? I thought of *Christophe Colomb* without music, but with tremendous animation. This would prepare the way for *Le Soulier de Satin*. In this connection

[1] Poetic Art.
[2] In the wind of the Balearic Islands.

I had this morning a series of ideas, one more amusing than the others. I shall tell you when I see you in Paris. Yours ever . . .'
Thus the project to produce *Christophe Colomb* dates from 1941, but as for being more easily produced than *Le Soulier de Satin*, that was another problem. From then on we never stopped writing to each other until the end. I have just reread his numerous and enriching letters, and they are all pervaded with enthusiasm, youthful vigour, or better still, the undiminished freshness of childhood. They are packed with exclamations of happiness, cajoleries, flights of imagination, moments of indignation or brutal reactions, judgments without compromise and over-generous compliments. They are obviously the work of a passionate young man, a young man attached to his art, and as full of enthusiasm as when he wrote *Connaissance de l'Est*. I believe that in order to understand Claudel one must consider not Claudel the great man, genial poet, wise patriarch presiding over a large and splendid family, but a young colt, whinnying, gambolling around, rolling itself on the grass and suddenly coming to hang its halter upon the foot of the altar in order to find some peace and calm. Some people are surprised by Claudel's fits of violence. They would of course find these fits of violence tolerable in a young man whom they would excuse with the words 'What arrogance!' and with the hope that they will pass. Well, with Claudel they have not passed; he has kept his youth in spite of the years, and of course those who have aged and mellowed with the years do not forgive him. Claudel in *Tête d'Or* still continues to describe *L'Arbre*:

> Comme tu tètes, vieillard, la terre
> Enfonçant, écartant de tous côtés tes racines fortes et subtiles!
> Et le Ciel, comme tu y tiens!
> Comme tu te bandes tout entier
> A son aspiration dans une feuille immense, Forme de Feu.[1]

I read *Christophe Colomb*, but the play which truly haunted me was *Le Soulier de Satin*. The productions which I had directed until then had never had a completely satisfying text. I wished to apply myself to a great text, a concept of theatre which would give the

---

[1] How you suck the earth, old man,
How you sink and spread on all sides your roots,
And how you long for the sky,
How you tense yourself under its attraction
Like a large leaf, Shape of Fire.

actor the opportunity of expressing himself fully. One of the scenes of *Le Soulier de Satin* which excited me most was that in which Dona Sept Epées and La Bouchère swim together and the latter gets drowned. Today this scene would be very easily staged, but to attempt to do so fifteen years ago on the stage of the Comédie Française was sheer madness. Besides that the blackout regulations and other transport restrictions during the occupation compelled us to shorten *Le Soulier de Satin* considerably; a large slice which contains this scene was left out, but I did not give up hope and I succeeded in putting it on in the course of a matinée devoted to poetry. Julien Bertheau played the part of La Bouchère, and I that of Dona Sept Epées; the public were delighted, and the 'child Claudel' was even more so—the next day he wrote to me with his customary enthusiasm: 'stunning with gaiety and lyricism! The hall seemed to be splashed all over with briny foam; the public were enchanted; in fact they always are with you if one knows how to deal with them!' I am convinced that what the public love is to rediscover with us, their own childhood.

The drowning scene of *Le Soulier de Satin* was only one of its numerous problems, each more exciting than the other. It seems to me that the more one knows about one's art the more one is attracted by problems of form, for a satisfying form carries with it the content and the very soul of the work. Besides one must remember Valéry's words: 'Il n'y a pas un temps pour la forme et un temps pour le fond,' and I loved *Le Soulier de Satin* in its totality. I always thought that its theme was superior to that of *Tristan und Iseult* and I wanted to love this play as one loves a woman. Therefore it is not surprising that desire could be set alight by the smallest details. A great love sometimes begins with the love of a detail—a certain smile, the grace of a neck, the perfect shape of an arm or the shell of a delicate ear! My love for *Le Soulier de Satin* began with the charming and faithful La Bouchère. Wherever I went I had the text of *Le Soulier de Satin* with me and I worked on it all the time, even when I was camping. I can still see the stains of butter and sausage which dotted my first notes on the play. My idea was to adapt it for two performances lasting three hours each. The full length of the play would require nine hours; I therefore thought that it would be acceptable to Claudel. So, one day in June 1942 with the connivance of Jean-Louis Vaudoyer, director of the Comédie Française whose

patience, courage and tenacity made possible the staging of *Le
Soulier de Satin*, I passed the line of demarcation and made for
Brangues. I reached Lyons where I was due to spend the night and
I looked for my good friend Salacrou who had sought refuge in
this part of unoccupied France and with whom I was hoping to
stay. The problem was how to find him. I thought that the theatre
would be the most likely place. There Roussin, Ducreux and
Mercure were giving the *Barber of Seville* to a full and very lively
house. At long last I discovered Salacrou in the Taverne du
Théâtre des Célestins which was packed with people and thick
with smoke as if it were market day; Salacrou was having dinner
with a gentleman, M. Massigli. In spite of my travelling attire
and my rather tousled hair I decided to walk in. . . . These were
tense exciting times when what truly mattered were the tragic
moments through which France and the world were passing.

The next day at dawn I took the train for Morestel. Alighting
there I set off full of hopes and apprehensions on a three-mile march,
my inseparable rucksack on my shoulders. I tramped gaily along a
pleasant road which wound its way through rows of poplars, fields
of young oats and grass. Walking stimulated my mind, so I found
myself talking aloud, laughing, and my eyes full of tears at the
joy of life which was filling me and surrounding me. An unreal
Soulier de Satin kept on fluttering around me like a sea-gull
following a boat, 'un bateau ivre' and 'je devins un opéra fabu-
leux'. [1] At last I saw at the end of a little path, the railings, and
behind them, framed by a nave of plane trees, the big castle and
inside it, the Master. I spent the two or three days which followed
reading him my adaptation which he accepted. After that we went
through it scene by scene. Claudel was interested not only in his
text, but also in the smallest gestures about which he had all sorts
of suggestions to make. He had said in one of his letters: 'How I
should love to discuss with you the rather neglected art of gesture
and attitude', and now that the opportunity had arisen we were
enjoying ourselves.

After that we tackled the problem of the scenery and we agreed
about the main lines of each set; there were thirty-five of them. We
produced sketches which only the two of us could understand, and
finally we produced a series of pictures which could be used for
designing the costumes. Looking at an illustrated page of the

[1] . . . a drunken boat, and I became a fabulous opera.

twentieth-century *Larousse* he would say: 'Don't you think that this brimless hat with feathers is really dashing?' He continued to attach great importance to the costumes, as his correspondence proves; here is an extract from it: 'As for the Negro woman, I should like to see the sketch of your new costume, that which is worn at present in Bahia—silk skirt with large flowers, and many starched petticoats, white blouse, madras, bracelets, necklaces and coral earrings. All this in the dance scene, held in a ray of moonlight, and she practically jumps into them, as in children's cardboard games.' The whole letter deserves in fact to be quoted and here are some more extracts: 'As for the decorative poem, this is impossible for the moment; my head is just crammed full with all sorts of problems and there is no room for anything else at this stage. I am most sorry, for the disappearance of great craftsmen is regrettable. How often have I not heard Rodin complain about this! Do you know the idea which obsesses me and which I can't shake off at this moment? It is the project for a light comedy entitled the *Affair of the tricolour pig*! I have been thinking about it for ten years and I have tried in vain to get rid of it. Now, I have completed the scenario, but I should need a collaborator. What a pity that Georges Feydeau is dead.' In fact in the course of our lively, searching conversations he often spoke to me of his *Affair of the tricolour pig*, and he even went as far as to inquire: 'Who is this Prévert? I am told that he is a great chap; would he agree to work with me?' I thought it wise not to pursue this project for Prévert. This dear friend and child-poet ran the risk of not hitting it off absolutely with Claudel. Even though they had both kept their childlike freshness, there are children who fight among themselves. But I must add that Claudel's love of farce is something real and genuine. 'Farce', he said, 'is the exacerbated form of lyricism and a heroic way of expressing the joy of living, and life has never been more heroic than now.' But let us come back to *Le Soulier de Satin*.

From the costumes we passed to the music of the play, and we used to hum tunes beating the rhythm on the table with all sorts of utensils; we thoroughly enjoyed ourselves, like two young friends in their teens, yet I am glad that Honegger dealt with this problem of music in a more professional fashion. These exciting sessions were only interrupted for the meals presided over by the wise and very kind Madame Claudel. The meals were full of life and noise, for Claudel's household tended to speak very loud—another thing which delights children. It was probably in the course of one of these meals that he said to me with a wink full of humour: 'My life is rather strange; I have managed to cram four careers into it—a diplomatic career, a business man's career, a religious career, and now a dramatist's career.' I was filled with wonder by this powerful man, this kind of baroque cathedral which had successfully housed four contradictory characters, like those of his play *L'Echange*; they were a wild young man, a ruthless business man purely concerned with doing, a pathetic and heroic daughter of the Church, and a half-crazy, fascinating actress; all that must have caused quite a hullabaloo inside Claudel.

After the meal came coffee, the news and the radio which made Claudel sombre and gruff. He could not hide his hatred of the occupation and his disgust with the Vichy Government. He had said about Marshal Pétain: 'How can we, anarchists, get on with this man who has learnt how to read from the Infantry regulations book?' Claudel, his eyes fixed on the radio set, listened attentively while we drank our coffee in the middle of a strange cacophony. All sorts of nightmarish noises used to break through, and every now and then Madame Claudel's sweet voice rose above the noise: 'What are they saying, Paul?' Claudel heard only the good news, if it was bad he had not heard it. After that we returned to work. One morning he said to me: 'Don't you go to church, Barrault?' Slightly put off I replied: 'No, Maître.' He continued: 'I feel the need for it every morning' and after a while: 'It soothes me.' At last we reached the last sentence of *Le Soulier de Satin*: 'Délivrance aux âmes captives.' [1]

I returned to Paris with Claudel's full agreement duly confirmed by a letter which I carried like a treasure. When I reached the demarcation line, the Germans tore my letter to bits; I gathered them up and reconstructed the letter on a sheet of cellophane. I submitted the new version of *Le Soulier de Satin* to the reading Committee. The play covered two performances. I offered to give a reading in order to convince my audience. So for the first time we deserted the reading room with the famous nineteenth-century painting representing the brothers Mounet, Claretie, Le Bargy and others holding their bearded chins in pensive poses, and we went to the green room. There I slipped off my jacket and I duly

[1] Freedom for the captive souls.

sweated off the first part of *Le Soulier* which was acclaimed and supported by all with the exception of one dissenter. Mary Marquet offered to play the guardian angel; it was an excellent omen; I then read the second part for the second performance. This time no success, the Committee refused to support it. Everything had to be begun over again; the actors did not want to give two performances; for them one was enough, and I felt neither the inclination nor the strength to compress the two parts into one single performance. After a long debate, I proposed to approach Claudel again to see if I could persuade him to accept the compression of the play in one single performance on condition that the Committee would agree to stretch the performance beyond the normal duration, in fact to accept a performance of five hours. This new project was accepted. I therefore prepared a new version and went once more to Brangues, where I submitted it to Claudel who accepted it.

It only remained to proceed with the casting which was easy, thanks to the admirable company of the Comédie Française, and to write a few additional lines here and there. Claudel loved fiddling with his plays, and once he started he sometimes rewrote whole plays. In this case he even asked me to write one or two connecting sentences, which I did with pleasure. Claudel is not like some writers who refuse to alter a comma or a preposition in his writings; he is only interested in the spirit and he never hesitates to sacrifice what he has done. Like all creators who had a great imagination, he had no superstitious respect for what he had written. Then came the problem of a stage designer. Claudel wanted José-Maria Sert; I was not in agreement with him, so we looked for a painter whom we both liked. Claudel reproached painters with lack of imagination. 'Look at Cézanne,' he said, 'he has only painted apples.' I had of course my own ideas but I was biding my time; meanwhile the list of possible painters was lengthening. One day a friend of mine suggested an idea which I adopted at once; he said, 'Why not Rouault? Would this strongly religious painter not be the right blend for Claudel?' I was told that Rouault was not an easy man. Still, I wrote to Claudel proposing Rouault and with Rouault, Derain. Claudel would not hear anything of Rouault; 'as for Derain,' he said, 'no objection, but I still hope that we have not said the last word about Sert.' This was not easy. Finally, I took the plunge, and proposed as a

counter to *his* friend Sert, *my* friend Coutaud. Claudel easily understood that one can only work with a friend, for it is only in an
atmosphere of friendship and love that one can produce good
work; he therefore gave in and allowed me to have my Coutaud.
And so we were ready to get down to work.

Alas, it was not as easy as that; the actors and actresses of the
Comédie Française who are used to working fast and to passing
quickly from one subject to another had already forgotten *Le Soulier
de Satin*. It was difficult to bring them together again. We fixed up
the rehearsals, but the first three times nobody came. The first
time I found myself completely alone on the stage watched by the
highly amused stage hands and electricians. After all, I was not
even a full member of the Comédie Française and it must have
taken the administrator Jean-Louis Vaudoyer some courage to
entrust a production to a temporary member. Jean-Louis Vaudoyer
decided to give me some support and he appointed a full member
André Bacqué as supervisor. The second time I had taken with
me an orchid for Marie Bell; once more the same attitude, nobody
came, and the stage hands continued to smile; it reminded me of
Charlie Chaplin in the dance of the loaves in the *Gold Rush*. The
third time I became truly fed up and I went to see the administrator who summoned the Committee and the leading members,
so as to discuss with them what they wanted to do. The atmosphere was rather tense, but Marie Bell, Mary Marquet and
Madeleine Renaud brought back goodwill, and the dear André
Brunot produced wisdom; we all agreed to fulfil our engagements,
and we got down to work. Meanwhile Claudel was getting anxious
and he was ceaselessly writing to ask 'What is happening to *Le
Soulier de Satin*, what is the cause of this delay? Is it a matter of
censorship, everything seems to have been dropped; is there going
to be another postponement? I should like to hear from you.'
Some newspapers like *Je suis partout* began to insinuate that we
were waiting for the arrival of Eisenhower to present *Le Soulier*.
This was quite enough to stimulate us; the honour of our camp
was at stake.

Ten days before the first night Claudel came to Paris. Up till
then I had managed to persuade him not to attend rehearsals on
the ground that we sometimes used coarse language which could
not possibly tally with his vision of *Le Soulier de Satin*. Besides
that, he had given me all his instructions and his presence ran the

risk of upsetting us. He had accepted these explanations, but now he had arrived and we had to offer him a first trial run of *Le Soulier*. I was quite pleased with the first part which ran for two hours and a half without a break, but the second part which lasted one hour and forty-five minutes was not so satisfactory. There was what we call in theatrical jargon 'a bone'. We could not get over a certain point. Marie Bell, who was admirable throughout, could not get over this scene. I tried everything I knew and could not improve it, even my memory failed me and I was at a loss and very worried. Claudel arrived as usual, earlier than required, and as soon as he came in a kind of cathedral silence filled the hall. While waiting for the latecomers I imparted my worries to Claudel who simply said 'We shall see'; followed by a very heavy silence. I stammered a few words which I have now forgotten; this was a tough examination; when Claudel concentrates his thoughts he seems to rejoin the mineral world. The rehearsal started at last, Claudel and the administrator were the only two people in the empty hall. For two hours and a half Claudel followed his text silently; then the break came and we all waited for his comments. I went up to him and he said, 'Well they will get their money's worth!' 'What else would you say?' and Claudel replied, 'It is quite all right, let us continue!' So we proceeded with the second part. All went well until we reached the famous scene where we stumbled and stopped. I suggested a cut, and Claudel suggested that we should skip this part and continue to the end. At the end of the performance, Claudel agreed that this was a bad patch. 'I did not quite understand what you told me about cuts before,' he said, 'but let us try to attend to the tooth before pulling it out.' We went over the mechanics of the action, and we agreed that the Jesuit Father who starts the action going and who reappears on the second day with the shipwreck, could very well reappear in the second part; why not? Claudel agreed and rushed away. The next morning Madame Claudel telephoned me very early to say: 'The Master has been working the whole night, he would like to see you; where will you be?'

'At the theatre at 8 a.m.'

'He will come, but would like to be alone with you.'

'Agreed.'

I went to the theatre and waited for Claudel, who for the first time was late. He arrived at last, looking upset, his eyes red with tears. He had just lost his fair copy in the subway and had had to go back home to fetch the original draft which he gave to me with the words: 'It's wonderful, it was dictated to me last night; it does not belong to me; I give it to you!' His tears began to flow and he told me the story of this drama. The previous day's re-hearsal had enabled him to grasp the true meaning of *Le Soulier*. He understood it that night, and that was typically inspiration.

'Are we alone?' he said. 'Will you please lock the door? I'll read you the whole thing,' and with a certain amount of snivelling and snapping of the jaws, Claudel read in his old and emotional voice the beautiful song of this inconsolable lover. This rough copy bears no trace of rewriting. The whole text had flowed without inter-ruption and Claudel was still very upset. I was as moved as he was and I gazed with admiration upon this genial 76-year-old poet consumed by love in the middle of his tears. I shall always see Claudel as a young man with white hair. The afternoon was quite enough for Marie Bell to learn her part. After that, the production flowed as if by itself. *Le Soulier de Satin* had finally given its consent. The last rehearsals took place at an increasing tempo, Claudel was both a judge and an attentive partner. He endeavoured to perfect the slightest details in diction and in acting. He never addressed the actors directly. He sent in tactful and detailed notes. On the opposite page, as an example of his way of working, begins a note on diction.

In every dramatic production there is always a moment which is as dangerous and critical as the line of surf or the tidal wave which bars the entrance to a harbour. This moment generally coincides with the arrival of the décor and the costumes, the first tests of the machinery and lighting and the hullabaloo of the orchestra rehearsal. All these things falling at the same time on the actors who have not yet got a firm hold of their parts generally unnerve them and make them run the risk of letting their characters slip away from them. As these kinds of calamities generally take place just a few days before the dress rehearsal, everybody gets into a panic. With its thirty-three tableaux, its ninety different types of lightings, its one hundred costumes, eighteen musicians and the various changes of scenery, *Le Soulier de Satin* gave rise to a unique tussle in the course of which Claudel and I had a great deal of trouble to save what we cared for. In fact, in the course of this Homeric battle we only lost the scene of the double shadow

La diction des œuvres, sans doute, est bien perfec-
tionnée. Pourtant j'ai des observations à faire à X........
et à Y........, q. se remettent de tempo en tempo à Rome.

X........

Flamboyante dans le souffle du Saint Esprit

                            unis et non allongés

Non ! non ! non !

D'un seul trait accentué par une fuoi vertical dodenahas en une
seule volonté ogenoisonnel accentué par les points des doigts

<u>Fl</u>amboyants dans le <u>souffle</u> du Saint Esprit

Sont l'élan donné par le Fl initial encore accentué par le vent,
le expo en rõmo depuis les reins et les journées participent

Une étoile

     <u>Et</u> l'embrayante...
               au contraire

Dans <u>souffle</u>, c'est-à-d. g. donne la force (curieux !)

Pt d'Esprit important.

A obtenir

La mère

Ces 2 valeurs ne sont pas
du tout le même !

Au revoir, sœur chérie, dans la lumière d'éternelle
Grosse, grosse faute !
Au revoir, cœur chéri

j'aurais voulu mais le *fa*; doit être dire la place pour l'expression au
ch tendre, caressant

Dans la lumière d'éternelle
l'élan, la force, l'enthousiasme est donné par l'*fa* initial
être est important mais *fa* *sol* est dure à l'*fa* répété donne d'ex-null
demi-soupir après *mi* et *la*

Sur ta ligne dure et légèrement à la voix qui mène sur null
la mélodie est trop délicate pourtant sur un rythme amorçât f. le
e, le 2 e ouverte de ré et ton n'étant pas trop à fait la même
Ce qui il y a de bien curieux, c'est q. c'est la même q. donne le
timbre de la voyelle !

Mais que   ne m'affole pas de ce subtilité. L'important est l'élan.

donner voir l'il à la lumière

<u>Q. Y.</u> .... maintenant

——— Je ne puis entrer dans le détail, la musique m'y oppose géné;
mais j'oserais insister qu'il ne faut pas dire avec une enfilade de valeurs
homophones (à la Mounet Sully)

... vers moi, le grand Apôtre du Firmament g. sais le dans
cet état de transport

Quelle soit-l'idée principale, soulignée par le orateur, g. g. m-
logue des récitant?

¡Mmoi] <u>le grand Apôtre du Firmament</u>
C'est-là le point fort. Le P. mis présente communication avec la
bass. Firmament: une obliditè dilatante et indestructible
affirmé par le P. et confirmé par les 2 syllabes homophones;
Mmmon. Donc beaucoup d'autorité:

Qui serait donc cet état de transport
est très mystérieux malgré le coup d'éclairage (un) de la syllabe final.
Qu'est-ce q. cela veut dire?

C'est le même que je celle exprimé par le Préparés :

Ce qu'il voyage en moi-même de ceci sur le train, j'avais
la jambe et trouvais dans l'œil.

Je gagne sur une espèce d'enghien remontant je te remonte
les choses d'un monde à l'autre, de la terre au ciel, du fait au vrai.
C'est pourquoi le train et [5 avec 2 et 3 nous 6!]
j'avais dans cet état de transports.

Je faut sur dire – en absolument la voir ayant finnam
et en oyllabisant

Qui croit dans cet état de trans prêt !
Le va-t-il rend prend alors un éclat ne qui figure pour
finni, comme une étoile !

En va-t-elle générale tout ce cœur du 2h. Fr. doit redemander :
Qui aurait fait Monneirs sully à ma place ? (vont trom

prés amment magnifique pourtant !)

Et ne vous le faire !

which we both regretted and for which we have not yet consoled ourselves.[1]

The music was so loud that we couldn't hear the text; wrong lightings suddenly placed the actors in darkness; it was total chaos; we were all running around in circles and I shouted: 'Don't try to snatch what you can all at the same time; have some patience!' Jean-Louis Vaudoyer who was in the auditorium made a very quiet remark which I have now forgotten but I remember that I looked at him in anger and said something very harsh and completely out of place. Madeleine who was behind him was ready to plead for me, to defend me or to excuse my insolence, but the dear man simply said with a smile: 'Oh, as long as he doesn't beat me, all is well!' The dress rehearsal took place in the afternoon, Claudel loved disorder on condition that it was perfectly organized. The play was due to open with Honegger's overture, soon interrupted by a loud-speaker which in those days was also used to give out instructions in case of air raids. The élite of Parisian society was present; Valéry was sitting in the front row and Claudel was just behind him. The curtain rose, the music began and at the very moment when the loud-speaker was due to come into play, the air-raid warning siren was sounded; at once the lights went out and people began to get up. Claudel, who had not heard the siren and who simply thought that it was the loud-speaker announcement which was part of the play, stood up with arms outstretched and kept on saying: 'Sit down, sit down, this is part of the play, don't worry.' It took all Valéry's patience and persuasion to make Claudel understand that a true alert was actually in progress.

I have loved the *Soulier de Satin* as if it were a living being, and it has given me sublime moments such as when we produced it at the Théâtre de la Monnaie in Brussels, immediately after the liberation. The public were so enthusiastic about this play by Claudel, who had previously been ambassador in Belgium, that they went completely mad, breaking seats and windows and singing the Marseillaise and the Brabançonne. We also had painful moments as when we were playing in a temperature of two degrees

---

[1] A child never consoles himself for the loss of a dear thing. As early as June 1943 Claudel had written to me to say 'I am very preoccupied by the double shadow, real characters seem to be rather heavy, the cinema could give us the necessary poetry.'

below zero, and Marie Bell in a light and low-necked dress had to struggle hard to avoid fainting. We had funny moments as when the little girl who was playing Dona Sept Epées for the first time, refused to go on the stage in company with the two huge Negroes who were to accompany her, so that when Marie Bell said with outstretched arms: 'Here is the child which I have made with my heart so full of you', there appeared, instead of the child, a huge and rather discomfited Negro. Then there was of course the most sad moment of all, the one when I left the Comédie Française, leaving behind my dear *Soulier de Satin*. Once we were established at the Marigny, I renewed my offers to Claudel. I asked him for *Partage de Midi*, *Tête d'Or*, *Christophe Colomb*, and I added *Le Père humilié*.[1] But Claudel wanted me to produce *L'Annonce faite à Marie*. He wrote to me: 'The first play *Partage* is forbidden. As for *Tête d'Or* I have already told you my objections. The play does not lack sincerity; it has too much, but it is precisely this crude, misplaced and frightfully naïve sincerity which makes me shudder. It is as if I were compelled to face the public not only without my shirt, but skinless. In fact I can't bear to read this play; the mere thought of seeing it on the stage sends shudders down my spine. 'One is not afraid of anything when one is only 20 years old!' *Christophe Colomb* is what tempts me most. . . . The Comédie Française will have to decide about *L'Annonce*. My idea has always been to keep *L'Annonce* for you as a basis for your future theatre. If it is well produced it is something like *Cyrano de Bergerac*. You won't find a better stock play, I say nothing of the possibilities for films. What a pity I am not younger! My wife and I regret that you have not been able to come to Brangues, which once it has lost the happy young world which fills it now will soon return to austere solitude.'

Louis Jouvet, who had just returned from a tour in South America, had just produced *L'Annonce*. I knew his extreme sensibility and therefore I felt that I could not attempt to produce this play. Claudel bore me a slight grudge over it, and we had an interview which was quite dramatic, a scene of jealousy, the breaking up of a love affair, and pain on both sides. His nerves were at breaking point and my heart was in bits. He had offered me *L'Annonce* so often. A few days earlier he had written: 'In my eightieth year, I should like at last to see this play well pro-

---

[1] The humiliated father.

duced': and a little further, 'this virgin has made a martyr of me'.
Yet in spite of all that, I could do nothing for I loved Jouvet. I
stuck to *Partage de Midi* and Claudel stuck to his position. At that
moment I was working with Gide on *The Trial* by Kafka. He never
questioned me about Gide, he seemed to ignore him. All he did
was to stick in his scrapbook, which he kept up to date, a photograph of Gide taken from some magazine. Gide on the contrary
was very curious about Claudel, and he questioned me, of course,
without the slightest animosity. He used to say with his charming
smile: 'If Claudel met me, he would make the sign of the Cross.'
Concurrently with *The Trial* which I prepared with Gide, I
worked secretly on *Partage de Midi*. I knew that it was Gide who
had corrected the proofs for his friend Claudel, then Consul in
China, when the play had been published in the *Revue de l'Occident*
fifty years before. Working with them both, and being their friend,
I could not help thinking how good it would be to reconcile them.
I was of course rather naïve. At a certain moment I felt that Gide
was not opposed to it; indeed he had never said a word against his
friend of earlier days. We therefore decided to invite them both to
a reception which we gave at the Marigny. They both came, and
in the course of the party Madame Claudel, with a kindness which
filled us with hope, said: 'I should like to say hello to Gide.' Gide
was then talking to Madeleine Renaud, so we went up to him, and
Madame Claudel said: 'Hello, Gide.' To my great surprise and
disappointment, Gide replied coldly, 'Madam', followed by a very
embarrassed silence. Nothing more could be done, but from that
day onward I loved Madame Claudel a little more.

Claudel loved *The Trial*, and said so in the *Figaro*, in a splendid
and friendly article in which he did not say a word about Gide. He
loved *The Trial* not only because of our work, but also because of
Kafka. One day while we were talking literature and I was trying
to find out which poets and writers passed muster according to him,
he said: 'With the exception of Racine whom I consider as the
greatest, there is another in front of whom I bow, and it is Kafka.'
Was it a joke? Faithful to his habits, as was his wont Claudel
returned to see *The Trial* on a Sunday matinée. Gide happened
to be backstage; he was full of mischief and high spirits, and probably in order to revenge himself for the fact that Claudel had not
mentioned him in his article, as soon as the curtain went down, he
made for Claudel in the auditorium, and stretching out his hand

said: 'Thank you, Claudel, for the splendid article you have written for *The Trial*.' Later on, Claudel, who had barely recovered from his surprise, said: 'I suddenly saw a very wrinkled face make for me, and I was so taken aback that I could do nothing but give him my hand!' This joke had immensely amused Gide who laughed and showed all his good teeth. Claudel also laughed, but he laughed with all his body, shaking like Jove or God!

While I was thus playing the part of Scapin between these two brother enemies, my work on *Partage de Midi* was proceeding, and as soon as I had finished *The Trial*, my urge to produce *Partage de Midi* increased. My work was complete and the only thing to do now was to convince Claudel. I wrote to him to make an appointment, and went to see him; it was a decisive meeting. We had known each other for ten years, and now we could put our cards frankly on the table, and so we did; this is roughly what we said:

CLAUDEL: You know that I have always been against the idea of staging *Partage de Midi*; indeed, I have withdrawn from circulation all the copies of the first edition. *Partage de Midi* was an experience of youth which cost me such suffering; it has lasted throughout my whole life; the wound is still open today. It is not because I am afraid of hurting certain people that I do not wish to have it staged. Time takes care of that and blunts all things; it is simply because I still have feelings which haunt me ceaselessly. I am held back by a certain form of reticence: there are certain cries which men must not utter; *Partage de Midi* is such a cry. I should be as embarrassed to see it staged as if I were walking about naked.

MYSELF: Your present sorrow is of no importance. *Partage de Midi* is the very heart of your message and the key to your work. However interesting its reading might be, it will never be as potent as if it were staged. Even if it is a sacrifice to you, you must offer *Partage de Midi* as a nourishment to those who love you and follow you, and this nourishment can only reach its full value through the stage. The struggle between flesh and spirit which it embodies will only be apprehended physically through the nerves, hearts and gestures of human beings. We shall only understand the authentic and harrowing drama which you have endured for fifty years, if we ourselves live through this trial caused by sin. Remember what you said in *Le Soulier de Satin*: 'Sin also serves.' Rodrigue and Prouhèze only reach their state of sublimation through desire and the moral acceptance of sin. I grant you that they make for evil with a rather lame foot, for the Holy Virgin Mother and Protector of their House impedes their progress with all sorts of mysterious obstacles; yet if they prefer to deny each other in order to find each other in heaven in the shape of a noble star instead of uttering the sacramental 'yes' of marriage, it is because they have felt in their souls the urge to sin, and because they have benefited from your experience and Mésa's. You began writing *Le Soulier de Satin* with its last part, *Sous le Vent des Iles Baléares*, and from that end you have moved backward, right through the life of the Conquistador and that of Prouhèze; yet all that was not quite your life, so let us go back still further in time. I have lived you in Rodrigue, I want to relive you in Mésa. I want to walk back the way which led you to trial by fire. *Partage de Midi* is the kiln in which you and your work have been baked and in which you have taken your true colour; it is the central piece of your metamorphosis. Everything which preceded it converges towards it, and everything which came after, flows from it. What do you fear on the moral plane, since in the struggle between flesh and spirit which the play shows, it is the spirit which triumphs 'in the transfiguration of noon'?

CLAUDEL: Whatever I decide, I could not stand the erotic frenzy of the second act which now makes me shudder.

MYSELF: This erotic frenzy no longer belongs to you; it is a cry which you have uttered, and which you cannot stifle since it lives beyond you.

CLAUDEL: Ah, you think that it doesn't belong to me, and that at my age, I don't feel its torture?

MYSELF: Some day you will consent to have the play produced and it will not be I who will have such a joy, or rather who will have the advantage of enjoying its true life. I have lived with *Le Soulier de Satin*, which is the best blossom of your poetic life, I want now to live through the documentary part of your life; you owe that to our generation.

CLAUDEL: You are shaking my convictions; come back and see me in three days.

I did so, and as soon as he saw me, he said, 'Ah, there you are, tempter, you have won, I give you *Partage de Midi*.' I was stunned, and remained speechless, while he added: 'I must say that you owe my decision to a Dominican monk, whom I love and who is my guide. I have consulted him and he advised me to let you produce the play, for according to him, it is the play which has caused the greatest number of conversions.' I asked for the telephone number of this Dominican Father and I immediately thanked him for pleading so well the cause of *Partage de Midi* and mine. A few months after, while *Partage de Midi* was on, Claudel sent me a letter with these words: 'My dear Barrault, read the enclosed letter, I think it will please you as much as it pleased me. Cordially, see you soon.' The letter he sent me came from a young man who had gone back to God after having seen *Partage de Midi* at the Marigny.

The fewer the number of characters in a play, the more tricky the casting; nevertheless we were lucky with *Partage de Midi*; without hesitation, I took the rôle of Mésa myself, without caring too much about the fact that I was not as thick-set as I should have been for the part. Pierre Brasseur, who seemed to have been made for the part of Amalric, agreed to play it. The most important rôle of course was that of Ysé, centre of the drama, and God's instrument; for *Partage de Midi* has truly five and not four characters. The characters are: a gorgeous, frustrated and unmarried woman, a complacent husband, an adventurer ready for anything, a 'little priest' all dried up in his spiritual miserliness and egoism, and there is God. It is God's presence which transforms this common everyday subject into one of the most important subjects ever put on the stage in our time. Edwige Feuillère seemed the ideal choice for Ysé, and luckily she was prepared to play the part. I made arrangements to introduce her to Claudel and when he saw her he looked at her from all sides as a good trainer examines a thoroughbred, and in the end he seemed bowled over: 'Edwige really looked like the model he had in mind'. I gave the part of De Ciz to Dacqmine whose authority I much admired in spite of his youth. Claudel thought he was too good-looking: 'De Ciz', he said to me, 'is the male insect with a sickly appearance yet quite able to deal sexually with the gorgeous woman who is his wife. He does not need to be a good actor, his physical appearance is what matters most.' Dacqmine had no difficulty in getting into the part. My friend Labisse was chosen to be the stage designer and Christian Bérard the costume designer. We got down to work.

First Claudel and I had to reach agreement about the final text, for Claudel had no sooner made fresh contacts with his work than he relived it and found that the original experience was as alive and as cruelly moving as when it first occurred. We plunged into a very lively correspondence. Claudel saw this experience of his youth with a fresh vision and a new heart, and he was anxious to put *Partage de Midi* again in the melting pot. So he began plying me with notes; new scenes, new versions, endless changes with explanations such as 'the present version of *Partage de Midi* is the result of forty years' maturation', or 'my intermediate version was only a progress, a kind of flickering light with dazzling flashes, but not a peaceful, sustained and convincing light'. Claudel's creative machine had again been set in motion. I, who like the rest of my generation had been fed on the *Partage de Midi* of 1905, felt the need to defend this version, and therefore resented the changes. Claudel on the other hand had been compelled to relive the major drama of his existence and he said: 'This concerns my life, the meaning of which I can now grasp. It is something more important than literature. If I manage to transfer from my heart to yours and that of Edwige Feuillère all I feel, the whole audience will be in tears. . . . If you can't come couldn't you at least send me Feuillère? I need so much to transfer my soul into her! This is not a play like the others. . . . I have written it with my blood. . . .' 'Harrowing night,' Rimbaud used to say, 'the dried up blood steams up from my face.' . . . 'If nothing else can be done,' he added with sorrow, 'I shall endeavour to explain what I mean by letter, but it won't be easy; for I shall have to explain my whole life!' I was in a panic, wondering whether I should manage to save this work which had enthralled my young days and those of my contemporaries; at the same time I kept asking myself whether I was right to oppose the direction which Claudel was now taking. Claudel not only rethought his work, but as a man of the theatre he could detect slight difficulties or imperfections, and with great skill corrected them. I accepted them whole-heartedly and we kept on working concurrently on both the technical and the spiritual plane. Just as this work partakes of the real and the unreal, the metaphysical and the physical, in the same way we kept on working on two planes of the play—that of the mechanism of the play and that of its deep meaning. Claudel found the end too literary and the lyricism too hollow. He used to say, 'Five words ought to characterize the dénouement and they are: logic, simplicity, suavity, intensity, mystery.' If in 1900 he had been inspired by Wagner and Dostoevski, now he had moved away from them, and he used to say that having studied Beethoven in the past, he had learnt a good deal from him from the point of view of composition. I did not know what to do; I loved *Partage de Midi* in its first version, and yet could not help finding Claudel's alterations attractive and stimulating. The final result was that the version which we used for performances was, in spite of Claudel, very close to the original version, with the exception of a few technical alterations. The version which was published six months after the *première* of the play was very different from it.

The situation for the various versions of *Partage de Midi* is therefore the following. There is *Partage de Midi* published in 1905; there is the second version of *Partage de Midi*, published by Gallimard in 1949, and there is our acting version which has just been published by Gallimard in the complete works of Claudel edited by Robert Mallet. On the 8 February, when we had already been playing *Partage de Midi* for three months, Claudel wrote to me to say: 'I ask you to read this new manuscript of the play from beginning to end and with a mind completely free from the previous versions, in fact as if it were a new work.' I read it and we gave a performance on the radio with the same cast as in the Marigny production; Claudel was delighted. I could not help preferring the version which we had staged which seems to me the one which is faithful to Claudel as a young man and to Claudel as an old man. I have a strong partiality for *Partage de Midi* 1905, but I must confess that the new conclusion reached by Claudel after his deep explorations seems to me of great beauty and is in fact a new key to the understanding of his work. Making use of some of his notes it could be summed up in the following way: 'Spirit . . . yes, but also egoism, greed, hardness and pride which is the thing which God detests most. . . . Flesh? yes, that is true, it is the need for the other, the slavery to the other, and also the awareness that it is impossible to reach the other which truly resembles hell. Above the flesh there is something which goes beyond it, there is the heart which is also flesh and which is much wiser than we know. God placed it in our breast only in order that it might echo in the breast of another.'

Claudel was quite right to try to get rid of the lyrical drapery which choked the end of the first version and 'which did not quite fit the extremes of passion', but he has tried to replace it by 'a flat, simple and naïve language, something shorn of elevation and rather childish and coarse'. These are merely different types of beauty, and we, as his servants, cannot judge. While we were exchanging these various versions which he examined with patience, the rehearsals started. They were most exciting. If I were asked to say which of my productions absorbed me most, I should say the first act of *Partage de Midi*, which is a masterpiece of the art of the theatre. Edwige Feuillère and Pierre Brasseur were working with exemplary discipline. There were only four of us and the atmosphere was just the opposite of that of *Le Soulier de Satin*. If the atmosphere of this cosmic fresco had something of the pomp of the great ceremonies of St Peter's in Rome, that of *Partage de Midi* was more monastic. Whatever we did, we did with monastic intensity, and God's presence hovered constantly above us like a humming of stars, for as Claudel had remarked, 'if one looks at a starry sky with sufficient attention, one notes that stars make a noise'. Claudel followed the rehearsals with great regularity. He winced at the erotic scenes, but I stuck to my beliefs: we had made a bargain, I had told him 'you give me the second act, and I give you the end of the third act'. His greatest happiness was when God's presence was clearly felt in the play. Besides that Claudel was full of ideas. I spent all the time I could spare from rehearsals in widening my knowledge of Claudel. I went to Notre Dame on Good Friday in the afternoon and stood by the grey stone pillar where, in 1886, young Claudel had been converted to Catholicism. On that day, Claudel was sitting in the choir among the priests. I felt an extraordinary emotion at the sight of this ceremony which has been slowly perfected through twenty centuries of practice. The deeply moving ritual of the slow progressive extinction of the candles, one after the other, until the last is taken behind the altar as if to keep the light of the very soul of the world dimmed throughout Christ's death, broke my heart. At the end of the ceremony, Claudel passed by me, and I remained still and deeply upset by my emotion. When he discovered me there against that very same pillar which was 'his' we shook hands in silence as a sign of communion. Who will ever write a study on men's reticence?

These weeks of work were indeed very exciting. Nevertheless there is a time during rehearsals when tension reaches a danger- ously high level and when the actor has gone as far as he can go; that means that the moment has come to hold on to the level which one has reached, if not disintegration sets in and everything crumbles down. One could easily see that Claudel, oblivious of the approaching first night and fully immersed in reliving his story, would have gone on endlessly. I felt that I had to take myself away from his standpoint and adopt that of the performers, and that upset me and exasperated me. Claudel, unaware of these problems, continued to work on us. Exhausted, unable to bear up any more, I finally said to him: 'I can't go on under these conditions; I shall have to stop rehearsals.' This was met by a tense silence, interrupted by the sad voice of a child on whom one has inflicted a punishment: 'You are turning me out.'

'Well, no, not quite as bad as that, Master!'

'Still you want me to go.'

'Well, I should be happier if you did.' A silence and then a question.

'Is the Church of St Philippe-du-Roule far from here?'

'No, not at all, it is next door to the theatre.'

'Right, I shall go there. Will you tell my wife to come and fetch me there?' And sad and crestfallen he slowly walked away. I was as miserable as could be, for I really loved this man like a father, and I feel sure I have made this quite clear in my accounts of our meetings.

Next day it was my turn to be crestfallen. I telephoned at lunch-time and spoke to Madame Claudel:

'Is the Master annoyed with me for yesterday?'

'No, not at all; he only wonders if he could come to the theatre.'

'Of course he can come.'

'Good, he was rather afraid you might forbid him to come.'

Soon settings and costumes were ready. Christian Bérard wanted Edwige Feuillère to wear a sari; somebody remarked that the sari was worn in India, but not in China. 'Well,' said Bérard, 'she bought it in India,' and the retort, 'Yes, but the spectators do not know that.' Then Bérard adopted his usual attitude when he really wanted something very badly, he began to whisper softly: 'She will wear it, she will wear it all the same,' while continuing to drape Feuillère in a sari which suited her perfectly. The first night was a battle as usual; we won it. Claudel was of course in the auditorium, and as he was deaf he had provided himself with a splendid electrical hearing aid which he handled with impatience and roughness, so that it only lasted him a few days. Nevertheless this apparatus caused us a great deal of excitement on the first night. While Feuillère and I were playing the great love duet of the first act saying to each other: 'Say that you will not love me', followed by, 'I shall never love you, Ysé, etc.', this scene was suddenly interrupted by a strident whistle coming from the auditorium. It was Claudel's hearing aid, which Claudel was trying to work at full pressure. What a shock! We never saw that hearing aid again.

Claudel came often to hear his play, and each time when he came to see us after the first act, he was completely overwhelmed and his eyes were red from crying. I stood in front of him dressed in a white colonial suit which I had copied from a photograph of him taken in 1900; through me, Claudel looked at Mésa, and at himself fifty years younger, fifty years which had produced fruits such as: *Les Cinq grandes Odes*,[1] *La Cantate à trois voix*,[2] *L'Annonce faite à Marie, Le Pain dur*,[3] *L'Otage*,[4] *Le Père humilié, Le Soulier de Satin, Christophe Colomb* and other works bearing the imprint of eternity. *Partage de Midi* was a mirror in which Claudel looked at his life, and he talked to me about Amalric as if we had been living the story; he used to tell me how this man made him drink vermouth, told him saucy stories and sang to him, 'poor little priest', of the charms of Ysé. That's how we spent the interval. One day I said to him:

'Won't you go and see Ysé?' and he replied in a glum and grumpy tone: 'I have nothing to say to that woman!'

'What about Feuillère?' Then he suddenly awoke, 'Ah, that is different, Feuillère, yes, she is wonderful!'

Well, I had now produced *Le Soulier de Satin* and *Partage de Midi*, and thanks to Rodrigue and Mésa, Claudel's soul and mine had become homothetic. I was eager for other works.

THE REDISCOVERED LE *SOULIER DE SATIN*

A LIVING CLAUDEL

August 6, 1958. Today Claudel would be 90 years old if he had lived. For the first time I find myself in front of his work, without

[1] Five great odes.
[2] Cantata for three voices.
[3] Hard bread.
[4] The hostage.

him, completely alone. For the second time I am in front of his masterpiece: *Le Soulier de Satin*. By my side in a file, I have *Tête d'Or* waiting for its turn. Then my big adventure will have consisted of retracing Claudel's life in time: *Le Soulier de Satin, Partage de Midi, Tête d'Or*. On this anniversary day, I read the notes prepared five years ago for the inauguration of our 'cahiers'. These notes stopped with *Partage de Midi*. The very heart, or the trunk of Claudel's work, with *Le Soulier de Satin* as its shining foliage, or its leaves of fire. This takes me back to 1950. At that time, after producing *Le Soulier de Satin*—the synthesis of Claudel's work, and *Partage de Midi*—his trial, I was compelled to halt since I could not explore the roots which are contained in *Tête d'Or*. But Claudel was opposed to a production of *Tête d'Or*, and so I had to think of something else. The subconscious links between a given work and a man of the theatre are mysterious and incomprehensible. For years, I had read and reread *L'Échange* and I had always admired it, yet I always felt that it was tied up with the memory of Charles Dullin who had played Louis Laine, and with that of a top-hatted Copeau who had played Thomas Pollock Nageoire; to these two I have to add the memory of Georges and Ludmilla Pitoëff. One evening I had one more reading of *L'Échange* and then went to sleep. The next morning, I woke with the firm desire to produce *L'Échange*. It was a physical need. An attempt at analysing the play quickly showed me that the four characters of the play were polarized upon Claudel. Louis Laine was the poet without pockets, disciple of Rimbaud; Marthe was the equilibrium, the Church, the holy Virgin; Thomas Pollock was Claudel the business man, and Léchy Elbernon, Claudel the man of the theatre, hovering madness, and buffoonery. These ideas gave me the basis of my *Connaissance de Claudel*.[1] I thought that this quartet of characters would give me the chance of renewing the adventure of *Partage de Midi*; I thought of Madeleine in the part of Marthe, Jean Servais as Thomas Pollock Nageoire, myself as Louis Laine, and if she accepted, Edwige Feuillère as Léchy. I was very enthusiastic and when it came to enthusiasm, Claudel and I were always ready for it. I went to see him and told him about my project which he accepted with joy. I can still see today his face furrowed by wrinkles; his childlike blue eyes, his throbbing nostrils and his mouth half open. As soon as a project

[1] Introduction to Claudel.

took shape, he did not look at anything else, his eyes fixed on the horizon, his body like a block, his legs crossed, one could feel joy oozing out of him, while he restlessly moved the hands crossed over his tummy. He said to me: '*L'Échange* is one of my few plays which I have never touched up, it is perfect!' Alas, these views were going to be short-lived! We agreed about the casting and I set off at once to charm Feuillère who after a reading which moved us both deeply, accepted. Unfortunately in the end her other commitments prevented her from playing the part; so I asked our friend Germaine Montero to lend the curves of her body and her guttural voice to the part of Léchy Elbernon. *L'Échange* was too short to fill up an evening; we therefore needed another short play. Claudel, who had seen *Scapin* produced by Jouvet in our theatre, wanted to write a kind of Pirandellian sketch on *Scapin*—a poet's divertissement in which a Tartuffe-like Descartes played Scapin; Silvestre was a child and there were two Gérontes instead of one. I had to disappoint him, and he did not insist. On the other hand his daemon for alterations got hold of him and so he set about rewriting *L'Échange*.

We ran into a maze criss-crossed with letters filled with resistances, proposals, pleas, resigned acceptances, and occasionally stubborn reprisals. I was sometimes amazed by his discoveries and his profound knowledge of the theatre, sometimes I howled with grief and indignation at his destructive cruelty. He had no pity for his work. 'You have found me hard, violent, cruel, exacting and sometimes unjust, but did I ever spare myself?' says Rodrigue in *Le Soulier de Satin*. Page after page, he supplied me with a new version of the play; I sent him back a third which was a synthesis of the first two, and so we went on. He conceded one passage and haggled about another. I was doing my best to defend the young Claudel of 1891 against the decorated patriarch. I felt that since Claudel had taken to hobnobbing with Cardinals he seemed to be unable to recognize the young man who received his illumination standing by the third pillar of Notre Dame. Work was fraught with difficulties; certain scenes were mutilated beyond hope of recovery, others on the contrary were splendidly improved. The idea of the swing was sheer genius and burst forth from the very source of his work. The opening monologue of Marthe in the third act gives an idea of the harrowing and sacrilegious struggle which took place. In the first version Marthe stands by the sea

T.J.B.—O

and, overwhelmed with sorrow, pleads for 'Justice'; in the second
version Marthe is made to send a letter to her priest. I thought that
was a disaster, such churchiness was unacceptable. But oh! What
did this letter say? 'Do you remember once upon a time that book?
Do you remember the poor, distressed person walking up and down
the shore and shouting: "Justice, Justice!" Well, I think it would
have been better if she had wrung her hands and shouted: "Forgiveness, forgiveness!"' Claudel's whole poetic adventure is
summed up in this change of words. When he was 23 years old,
he shouted 'Justice, justice!'; when he was 83 years old, he asked
for forgiveness. What a moving thing for those who loved him!
I can't find another letter which hurt me at first deeply; it is probably because of that that I lost it. This letter said that he refused
to go on with the work and he insisted that I should produce the
second version. I think it was in this letter that he talked about
love as seen by man, the male: 'Desire, desire, is never big enough;
it is what is strongest and best. It is the only thing that matters;
fulfilment is only a break, a failure!' I managed to persuade him to
change his mind. We agreed on a mixed version which he anno-
tated with constructive and sometimes very amusing remarks like
the following: 'About "it is a shame to lie", I'll show you a bit of
acting which I have learnt from Marshal Pétain.'

J.L.B.

J'accepte votre version du Un, sauf une coupure
C'est la page 145 qui j'aime le moins,
Enfin . . .! (gros soupir)
'*Il est honteux de mentir*', je vous apprendrai un jeu de scene
que j'ai appris moi-même du Maréchal P.
À bientôt le deux.[1]

21.10.51

I decided to complete the evening by giving Musset's *On ne badine
pas avec l'amour*. It was a big mistake. The show was far too long;
the two plays did not blend to make a good evening, and besides
that, Musset is not quite my line of country. The rehearsals were

---

[1] I accept your version of the first act with the exception of the cut.
Page 145 is the one I like least, still . . . (a big sigh) 'It's shameful to
lie', I'll teach you the kind of mimicry which I have learnt from Marshal P.
Looking forward to seeing the second act soon.

21.10.51.

a great joy. Claudel was never happier than when he was at work. He was full of fun and we sometimes enjoyed ourselves immensely, as when, for instance, he mimicked for Servais the shaking knees of an old man possessed by lust. His eyes were twinkling with impishness, his mouth was watering, and his body shook with laughter while his teeth were chattering. He stood among us like a pole and we moved around him like horses tied to a tether. Nevertheless as the first night was approaching, I asked him on the night preceding it, to go and watch from the auditorium and to let us get on by ourselves. He made this disarming reply: 'Let me stay today with you, it is the last time that I shall hear it.' His deafness had become worse; we therefore installed him in the middle of the stage and, very moved, we played around him as if the play had been taking place in a salon.

The first night was frightful; it was much too much of a social event for our taste. The President of the Republic and the Queen of Belgium had agreed to come. So there was a great display of uniforms, evening dress, and beautifully groomed and bejewelled women; but all this elegance did not constitute a truly magnetic field for the simple and concentrated work that we were performing. The curtain rose late, the interval was endless; we gave *L'Échange* as the second play, from 11.30 p.m. to 1 a.m.; the spectators were obviously tired, inattentive and perhaps thinking of the supper they had missed. There were a few polite curtain calls, and nothing more; Claudel sitting in the front box was rather glum, and I was distressed and feeling very guilty. Happily, the play picked up; the other performances were a success and *L'Échange* was a victory. Still I must confess that *On ne badine pas avec l'amour* which preceded it was always a handicap, and that was my fault.

We took *L'Échange* on tour, and in order to complete the show I composed the *Connaissance de Claudel* which was published in our theatre series. I submitted my manuscript to Claudel who sent it back to me with the comment: 'I love this kind of spectacle, it moves me like a sunset; it is drama at its beginning. You have opened up a new field which could result in a style capable of tidying up many things.' We tried this spectacle in places such as Lyons, Brussels, Hamburg, Montreal, Bogota, Caracas, Port-au-Prince, where it had such a success that we had to give it twice. It is a text which shows clearly the drama of Claudel's life, and it helps to explain both it and the various characters of his plays.

Simon Agnel and Cébès of *Tête d'Or* are more easily understood when one has seen Louis Laine. *Partage de Midi* is more readily comprehended when one knows that Claudel nearly became a priest, and we rejoice to see that instead of dying like Moses on the top of the mountain he has, like Josiah, succeeded in crossing it:

> Après la longue montée, après les longues étapes dans la neige et dans la nuée
> Il est comme un homme qui commence à descendre . . .
> Et il entend derrière lui dans le brouillard le bruit de tout un peuple qui marche.
> Et voici qu'il voit le soleil levant à la hauteur de son genou comme une tache rose dans le coton.
> Et que la vapeur s'amincit et que tout à coup
> Toute la Terre Promise lui apparaît dans une lumière éclatante comme une pucelle neuve.
> Toute verte et ruisselante d'eaux comme une femme qui sort du bain![1]

Everything falls into place when one comes to the universal world of the *Soulier de Satin*, which is his great blossom.

Délivrance aux âmes captives: this is the key word of Claudel.

In Montreal, *Connaissance de Claudel* gave rise to some amusing comments on his part. In the autumn of 1952 we were touring the U.S.A. and Canada, and we had felt that we could not go to Canada without taking with us something of our most Catholic poet, Claudel. But Claudel himself was worried about *Partage de Midi*, which according to him was perhaps too daring for Canada. *L'Échange* was rather short, *Christophe Colomb* had not yet been produced and so he chose to begin with my *Connaissance* which seemed to him an excellent introduction to his work. He had written to me as follows:

---

[1] After the long climb, after the long hours in the snow and in the clouds,
He is like a man who begins to descend . . .
And in the fog he hears behind him the sound of a whole people on the march.
And while the sun which is at the level of his knees looks like a pink ball in a mass of cotton-wool,
The haze slowly scatters and suddenly
The whole Promised Land bathing in glorious light lies in front of him like a shining virgin,
Green and glistening with water like a woman stepping out of her bath!

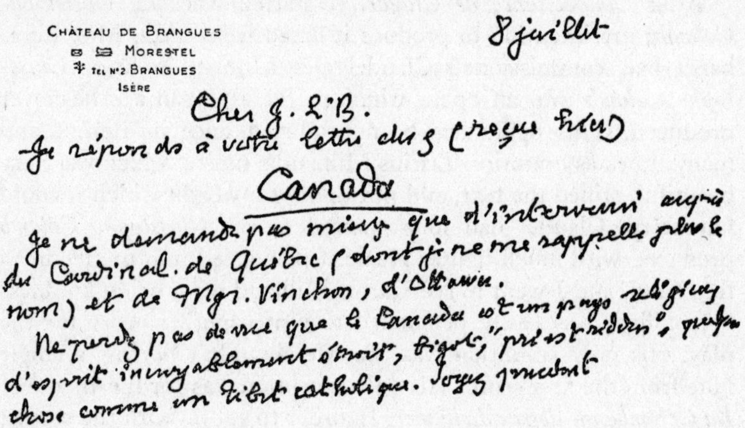

CHÂTEAU DE BRANGUES
MORESTEL
TEL N°2 BRANGUES
ISÈRE

[handwritten letter in French]

The more Claudel advanced in age the more he loved to joke. He
enjoyed a kind of relaxed humour which probably came from the
feeling that he had accomplished his duty and completed his work.

One day he was sitting side by side with Mauriac at a luncheon
given by the *Figaro Littéraire*. Mauriac was describing a doddery
old member of the *Académie* who was pretending to dial telephone
numbers on his watch and then to carry out a conversation by
telephone. After the laughter and the silence which followed one
suddenly heard Claudel say: '*I* have passed to the age of dodderi-
ness.' He was always amusing when he talked about the *Académie*.
He had named his permanent secretary Georges Lecomte the
'zouave de l'Alma'. One night we were having dinner with Claudel,
who was much preoccupied over the health of Georges Lecomte who
was ill. At that very same time, Gide was dying and I was greatly
upset, so I said to Claudel half teasingly and half to relieve my
feelings: 'Bravo, Master, your sympathy for Georges Lecomte is
the mark of a good Christian; it's excellent!' and he crossly replied
'That's true, I have from time to time some Christian impulses!'
But let us return to Montreal. As soon as I arrived there, I obtained an interview with Cardinal Léger, who was extremely kind
to me and who did us the great honour of attending the performance of *La Connaissance de Claudel*. It was the first time that the
Church attended a theatrical performance. So Claudel had been
proved wrong; the Canadian Church had evolved, and I was very
proud to bring back this piece of news to Claudel.

After *Connaissance de Claudel*, I started work on *Christophe Colomb*; my intention to produce it dated from 1942. Max Reinhardt had commissioned Claudel and Milhaud to turn *Christophe Colomb* into an opera which as far as I can see he never produced. This opera has been produced once in Berlin, and many times as oratorios. Darius Milhaud's music, which was very beautiful, stifled the text, and put upon it a weight which it could not carry. Claudel had long wanted to see *Christophe Colomb* produced with much lighter music. I persuaded him to give me a free hand, and I went to see Darius Milhaud who, being kindness personified, was easily persuaded to write another score for the play. His only condition was that we shouldn't borrow a single note from the first score. His only exception was for the theme of *La Colombe au-dessus de la mer*. In order to get on with the work I agreed to produce *Colomb* for the Bordeaux festival in May. Claudel was slightly worried and he asked me: 'Do you think you will manage it?' But once he had said that he left me full freedom. Strengthened by his permission I endeavoured to give free rein to my imagination in order to express what I felt about the theatre at that time. The great difficulty was how to cope with the numerous short scenes. I did not want too large a cast so I decided not to exceed thirty-three performers in all. Once I had worked out every detail, I began my co-operation with Milhaud. I re-enacted the whole play for him, bit by bit, and I hummed tunes at the moments when I felt that there should be music. We discussed this music very carefully and thanks to Milhaud, it fits exactly within the play like a living character. When we came to the décor, I realized that there were so many changes of scenery that I needed to discover some kind of magic object round which the whole thing would grow. The need to have a screen for the parts which had to be filmed, the constant presence of 'Colombe', a pigeon stretching its wings, the important participation of the sea, the wind, and Columbus's caravel, pointed to one single magic object: a sail. I knew that the text of *Christophe Colomb* had been admirably illustrated by Charlot in an American edition of the book. I should have loved to use these illustrations. Unfortunately this painter lived in America, and so I asked my friend Max Ingrand, a man with an extremely lively mind and who shared Claudel's Catholic faith, to help me. When the sets were ready, Milhaud entrusted Boulez with the music, and we decided to have a general reading which took place in Madame de Volterra's house at Neuilly. Boulez was sitting at the piano, with two singers by his side, Claudel and family were facing us, and together with them, our company and our hostess, I played the whole thing, helped by Boulez and his two singers. I have found that the impression left by a reading is generally very similar to the impression which the public will have of the play. This is the only moment when a play resembles what it will be on the stage, and in fact the impression caused by the reading was exactly the same as the one which it produced when it was performed. Nothing is more important than this first reading; I have noted that in connexion with *The Cherry Orchard*, *Vasco* and recently with *Numantia*. My reading of this play reminded me of the reading of the same play which I had done twenty years before. The reading of *Christophe Colomb* will remain one of the most moving memories of my life in the theatre.

Claudel was enthusiastic. He said, 'I shall remember this all my life'; he was 85 years old. It was thanks to the kindness of M. Lévy-Despas that we could prepare and rehearse *Christophe Colomb*. He offered us the use of his theatre, the Théâtre Pigalle. In fact, M. Lévy-Despas has helped us not only with *Christophe Colomb* but with two other plays—*Vasco* and the *Oresteia*. Without him we should have been lost, and our company was only able to continue its work thanks to his generosity. Some parts of the play had to be filmed and Le Théâtre Pigalle was excellent for that:

> In the beginning God created the heaven and the earth, and the earth was without form and void, and darkness was upon the face of the deep. The Spirit of God moved upon the face of the waters.

The shapeless and naked earth was fresh mud spread on a large tin tray. By pouring over it a chemical substance it fermented and produced gas which bubbled up and broke through the bubbling surface. The layers of vapour which were supposed to hover over this first surface of the earth were obtained by using tetrachlorine of titane, and the Spirit of God became the Finger of God, for which I humbly lent my hand. I can still see myself lying on a scaffolding, my arm hanging above the tray covered with mud. The fumes caused by the tetrachlorine of titane tickled my throat and every now and then 'God's Finger' was shaken by bouts of coughing which made filming impossible. While God's hand was moulding the earth, God above was shedding floods of tears as if he had been engaged in peeling onions. Once more we were enjoying ourselves like children.

The doves were objects of great excitement. We had borrowed them from a bird-fancier called M. Oedipus. When we wanted them to flap their wings so that they might be filmed, we had to submit them to all sorts of mean tricks which obviously puzzled them. We tickled them, we poked them, we shook their stands, and they looked at us, first with one eye, then with the other, completely nonplussed by the behaviour of these stupid and troublesome animals called men. We fell in love with a couple which could not be separated. The female, called Isabelle, did nothing or at least was unable to do anything; all she did was to preen herself and to lay her eggs. Her husband Christopher was a perfect performer; a good husband and a good father, he did everything; he hatched the eggs and did all the work, and it is he who is seen in the photographs. Whenever we got mixed up and took Isabelle by mistake it was a disaster; so in order to avoid that, we took the precaution of drawing a cross with lipstick on Christopher's back. He was beautiful and as proud as a Crusader. These two warm-hearted birds were rather prolific, and they produced a large family which had to be taken to their foster parent, M. Oedipus. The two birds went everywhere with us and they experienced all methods of travel; they crossed seas and oceans, they went to Brazil, Uruguay, Argentina, and they crossed the Andes by plane. On our arrival at Santiago in Chile the American pilot of the plane handed them back to us, together with an egg which Isabelle had laid when she was being flown over the mountains. Had she been upset by the whiteness of the high summits or by fear? We couldn't say. I am inclined to think that it was caused by fear. We had taken with us Simone Valère's dog Wack who was our mascot for ten years, and our own little black poodle Amie, and they were really afraid when they were in the plane. Dogs don't like to be in planes, they are more sensible than men, they look through the port-holes and see the earth far, far away, and they begin to shake. Christopher entranced Claudel who loved to hold him on his finger. So the work went on with great excitement. There was one single dark spot, I did not like Claudel's picture of Mexican gods. I loved Mexican civilization; Soustelle's book on that subject had increased my admiration, and that is in fact why I asked him to rehabilitate them in our theatrical publication. Claudel was rather surprised by my attitude and one day he said to me: 'Why spare them since they are false gods?' He never convinced me and I am glad of it, for the subsequent journey to Mexico confirmed and strengthened my respect and admiration. On the contrary Claudel's attitude consisted in saying: 'We must only respect the things that we make use of and that we need.' He may be right, but I can't help my views and I continue to respect Mexican civilization. Although I am a Christian, I respect all civilizations. That is why I like Teilhard de Chardin, but that is another story. . . .

For the masks we asked the help of a young Mexican painter and dancer called Juan Blanco. The less scenery there is, the more careful one has to be about it. The central platform which had been constructed by the Chevreux works was too high. We decided to lower it and to give it a slope. It was a mad attempt for we had no idea of the result until the whole thing was finished. In the theatre, the only thing that counts is the real thing, and there is always a big difference between a drawing and a real object. We were lucky with our platform, which once we had finished with it was exactly what was required. But we really had been worried, for if we had had to begin again we would not have been ready for the appointed opening. That kind of excitement is not good for the nerves, the liver or the heart! Claudel came from time to time but as he was witnessing a new type of work he was more curious than anxious and did not interfere with it—one would have thought that the work belonged more to me than to him. Up till now my duty had consisted in serving his text, now I was allowed to use the text as I wished, that is why I call the text a libretto. For him also this work had been a commission, and more an entertainment than a committal of his whole being. Besides that, Claudel saw in the work that we were doing the concrete realization upon the stage of his dream to seize drama at the moment of its birth. The dramatic shape of the history of Columbus was slowly emerging from the loam represented by the cast. I have always been struck by the beginning of Ravel's waltz; the pure theme rises like a spiral from the musical loam; it is, therefore, creation seized at its birth!

The moment came when we could invite Claudel to the dress rehearsal, and the best reward was that he was full of admiration. So much the worse for my modesty but I can't refrain from quoting him; when the last words of the play were uttered he exclaimed: 'This man has genius, we must kill him!' It is because of the 'we must kill him', that I quote him, and I hasten to say that life is looking after this part of Claudel's suggestion. After our elation we had to confess the fact that the end of the play contained a 'bone'. It was exactly the same with *Partage de Midi* and *Le Soulier de Satin*. What is the cause of this repetition of the same flaw? Is it because Claudel proposes dramatic endings difficult to accept, or is it because he invents solutions for life's problems? That is quite possible. Life, like death or after death, inspires us on the religious plane with imaginary conclusions. The theatre is more realistic, more implacable and it is too much concerned with justice to stop at question marks. Kafka was satisfied with questions tinged not with hope but with perseverance. The endings of Molière's plays are successful because they are artificial. They are spectacular pirouettes. Claudel wished to give a solution and the theatre, faithful to the rule of justice, could not accept his solutions. I am also convinced, for I resemble him in that respect, that Claudel was a man of desires and not of fulfilments. Fulfilment is an interruption in a rising of movement and a failure. On the contrary, the rise gives infinite pleasure and like Prometheus reaches up to the gods. Unfortunately men cannot dwell for long at that level, and they soon disintegrate into fulfilment, get into a spin and crash to the ground. Joy has also its tragedy, and it is from this tragedy that the arts are born. What is best in us is condemned to death.

Well, being stumped by the ending of *Christophe Colomb*, I went to Claudel for help, but he could not find a way out of the difficulty, and one day, while I was urging him on with the hope that the inspiration which I had seen at work ten years before might return, he said: 'Too late, Barrault, I am too old, my inner flame is burning low.' The opening night was drawing near. We set off for Bordeaux. As long as a play has not been fixed in performance in front of a public, it is slightly inchoate or soft and it can disintegrate. When we reached Bordeaux we had to start all over again. I kept the company at high pressure. The dress rehearsal lasted till 4 a.m. We were all exhausted; and some of us were lying down on the floor, others were leaning on their props like watchmen overwhelmed by sleep; the musicians' heads were swaying over their instruments, Boulez kept on swearing, the

older members of the cast had given up and gone to bed. It was
not the eve of Austerlitz but that of Agincourt. I decided to stop
everything and to go back to our hotels. I couldn't sleep and I
kept on saying to myself: 'It's not possible, you must find a solution, you must.' I was trying to relax, and I tried once more to see
the whole show. I no longer knew whether I was awake or asleep;
all I know is that at 6 a.m. I suddenly felt I had found the solution.
I sprang out of my bed shouting 'Let us rehearse!' But everybody
was asleep. 'What the hell are these asses (or something else) doing
at this time when the auditorium is filling up?' This exclamation
brought me to my senses and good temper and I simply wrote
down the solution. Then we worked the whole day, and in the
evening the company did its best and won the day; Claudel had
had his triumph. Two hours before the curtain rose I had scribbled
my last-minute impressions and here they are: '21st May, 7 p.m.,
Bordeaux, just finished, only two hours before the curtain rises;
exhausted, can't even write, yet I should like to; never worked so
long, so hard, so desperately. My opinion: I love this show; it
belongs to the "Numantia category". "Everything through man";
my dearest ideas! Yet if there is a hitch, I fear that the public
might only fasten upon this hitch and fail to see what is in the play
which contains everything I love; shall explain later.

'What I don't like: the scene in Mexico; staging is not clear
cut; until now I did not like the end of the play, but I think that I
settled this a little while ago, thanks to the lighting, and thanks to
Madeleine's veil which transforms her into a Spanish Virgin all
clad in white; thanks also to three sentences which, being spoken
with music, instead of being sung, shed their aspect of Catholic
club manifestation. What I particularly like: The sail which is the
seminal spark around which everything else gravitates; it is, as
Claudel says somewhere, the true key of the spectacle, and it is a
living being just like every one of us. I love the servants, I love
the whirling boat, the shadows playing on the sail during the
tempest and the décor made of stakes which disappear with ease
and style. I believe in the marriage of the cinema and the theatre,
sharing "the two aspects of the book", the visible and the invisible,
the inside and the outside, the action and its preparation, etc. . . .
but this is a dangerous weapon which must be watched carefully.
. . . What I fear: I fear people might say that this play is not a
play but a poem which comprises one single dramatic scene: the

sailors' rebellion. I fear people might be deceived by the extreme simplicity of Claudel's text and think it thin, when it is simply an extremely purified text. Thanks to the company which has been wonderful, I shall sleep half an hour in that no-man's-land between gestation and birth, chrysalis and butterfly . . . nothing and everything. Within four hours shall we be happy or defeated? Yet if the sixty-eight different lightings, the ten moves of the sail, the countless moves of this great machine are well oiled, everything ought to be all right. I believe that Copeau, Dullin, Artaud and Granval would love this show.'

The public, instead of disgusting me with *Christophe Colomb*, made me love it even more, yet I am still dissatisfied with the end, and Claudel shares my point of view. I have kept on trying to find a solution, and one day I really thought I had discovered one. Unfortunately Claudel was no longer there to tackle it. He had departed, he had left me stuck in the middle of his work. Well, we must respect his work, for we are in need of it and we make use of it. In spite of this little flaw, the show has been liked wherever we have taken it, and it is liked because it is packed with joy and enthusiasm. There are some delicate palates who say that 'the text is thin and is not quite on the same level as the rest of Claudel's work'. In fact *Christophe Colomb* is a fugue, as there are fugues in music. Claudel is here the complete opposite of Wagner, and Wagner impresses easily. *Christophe Colomb* may lack flesh, but it has the transparency of fluid; it is pure marrow. I should not go on talking about *Christophe Colomb*, but I have a weak spot for this theatrical experience. For me every drop contains a grain of humanity, and if the theatre is a celebration, a collective participation, *Christophe Colomb* is a kind of prototype of the theatre. Every object plays its part; as an instance I want to quote the sail. This sail is sometimes the boat, sometimes the screen, sometimes a bird, a rag, or a tempest, and this sail has from the beginning got hold of us and carried us along in its power. It is nine yards long, and it can't be altered. Sometimes when the theatre stage was small, I have tried to reduce it to seven yards; it did not work, it was as worthless as a bad actress. Our sail loses its weight of matter and transforms itself according to the rules of poetic imagination. *Christophe Colomb* carries with it a strange mystery; wherever we gave the play it left behind memories of its own. When we gave it in Buenos Aires at the Grand Théâtre Colon we drew 20,000 spectators in four performances. In New York, on the day when we were about to leave, our impresario received the price of sixty seats for the next visit of the French company which would bring back *Christophe Colomb*. *Christophe Colomb* is the symbol of my faith in life, in art and in man, it is synonymous with enthusiasm, with the universality of all men, and love of the whole earth.

Christophe marked a new step in my intimacy with Claudel. With Louis Laine I had known Claudel wild and anarchical, with Mésa I had struggled with his mind, his flesh and his super reality, with Rodrigue I had assessed his range and size, and with Christophe Colomb I have known his character. Alas, Claudel was getting old; it was not his mind which was growing old but his heart, and he knew it. So he was becoming mellow and more affectionate. When one went to see him he held one back as if he disliked partings, and while before he often left one alone—standing or sitting—in order to follow his great imagination, now on the contrary he looked at you for long moments. His joy and his haughtiness had disappeared and you felt that he was near those whom he loved. It was obvious that such a state might last a year, two years, perhaps five, but that there was no time to lose. From all our schemes which we had begun to discuss twenty years earlier, *Tête d'Or* was the only play I had not produced. I tackled him once more and this time he was more responsive; he reread what he called 'this incomprehensible hotchpotch', and of course he started to work on it. 'How can one understand *Tête d'Or?*' he used to say, 'one would have to recreate the atmosphere of prison in which we lived in the age of Taine and Renan; one would have to rebuild the materialistic lid under which we stifled. I can only see one way out; it is to produce *Tête d'Or* in a concentration camp surrounded by barbed wire, acted by prisoners and with an aerial bombardment in progress. Then we could rediscover the theatre at the moment of its birth. The tubercular prisoner who would play the part of Cébès would really die', etc. He began to rewrite *Tête d'Or*, completed the first part and finally gave up at the beginning of the second act, saying: 'No, it is useless, you can do what you like with it after my death.'

One day in order to test his reaction, I put out a vague statement about it which was taken up by a newspaper. Claudel reacted at once with a telegram containing the single word: 'No.' He too could be stubborn. I could not insist. In order to please me, he wrote a dialogue on Racine which he had thought out when he was in a nursing home waiting to be operated on for cataract; it was a brilliant piece. Once he had recovered from his operation, he decided to give a reading of his composition and he chose as a partner Jean-Pierre Granval, of whom he was very fond. They therefore began to rehearse together. In the course of one of their readings Jean-Pierre, who was rather over-awed by Claudel, was reading in a low voice and he made an error of liaison. Claudel did not like liaisons and he pointed out his mistake to Jean-Pierre who, probably unnerved by shyness and youthful insolence, shouted back: 'I thought that you were deaf.' Claudel blatantly became deaf again and putting his hand to his ear said: 'What?' and Jean-Pierre repeated, 'I thought you were deaf.' Claudel followed quickly with: 'That depends.' On the day of the public reading, Claudel's drawing-room was packed to capacity. Claudel was delighted and enjoyed immensely the reading of this text on Racine which was obviously his last profane writing.

I was still puzzling out how to tackle him. I should have loved to please him and produce *L'Annonce faite à Marie*; but he had given it to the Comédie Française, and his last moments of energy were spent working for this great institution. A few years earlier, Gide had done the same when his play *Les Caves du Vatican* [1] was being produced there. Thus the two men who had given me most died working with this dear, old and implacable institution. Claudel's death was for me a kind of surgical operation. While he was working at the Comédie Française, I did not see much of him for he was saving his energy for his last efforts. Was I a little jealous? Certainly not because of the Comédie Française which I still love, but because of my dear old friend. Some harsh critics hurt him and darkened his last days. The old oak had shaken a bit too much. In spite of my work I tried to visit him regularly and in spite of his great age I did not look upon his departure as imminent. I was due to see him on a Sunday morning, but because of other commitments I had to postpone that appointment until the middle of the week. Two days later he was no longer alive. I never forgave myself for my delay. Maurice Noël brought me the news at 7 a.m. I forgot all conventions, and impelled by a force beyond me I ran to his house, and there in the darkened drawing-room where, a few days before, he had talked about

[1] The cellars of the Vatican.

Racine and Shakespeare, he was laid to rest on a bed, with a
crucifix in his hands. What struck me most was his resemblance
to his bust as a Roman emperor made by his sister. A striking
serenity and nobility emanated from him. I was told that death
had come to him while he was reading Mondor's book on Rimbaud.
The wheel had come full circle. 'Let me die in peace, I am not
afraid.' These were apparently his last words. I returned to see him
again after lunch just before our rehearsals. Madame Claudel and
the children were finishing their meal in the dining-room which
was separated from the drawing-room by a glass door. I remained
alone with him, standing at his feet in the light of the flickering
tapers and here I spoke to him for the last time.

> Nous sommes partis bien des fois déjà
> Mais cette fois-ci est la bonne. . . .[1]
> —*Ballad of Claudel*

From the silence which surrounded me I was becoming more and
more aware of his unchangeable absence, and I could also hear the
vague noises of dishes which came from beyond the glass door;
I thought that they composed a strange background music to the
peace which was certainly his now. Claudel was taken to the crypt
of Notre Dame de Paris and the funeral service took place in front
of this church on a fearfully cold day. It had been snowing and
an icy wind made its cold contribution to a far too severe ceremony. The square was much too large, the catafalque lay much
too far from the tribunes and there were too many barricades.
I should have loved to see youth saying good-bye to Claudel, I
should have loved to see the people of Paris freely milling round
his coffin, I should have loved to see a truly human disorder
mingle with this great official pomp. It was all too cold, and
therefore it was all right for an ambassador or an academician,
but not for a poet. After this frozen official ceremony he was again
put in the crypt of the church where seventy years before he had
felt God's presence for the first time. This filled me with distress.
Happily his work remained to reveal a fully alive Claudel. Shorn
of his gold-braided uniform and his business-man's jacket, the
poet emerged, wearing precisely the young Roman emperor's
mask mentioned before, the mask of a man of great strength and

[1] We have set off for many voyages,
But this time it is the last. . . .

perfect equilibrium. A new life was beginning for him, the immortal life which his genius deserved. We felt like forgetting about the cold and the stiff and official *de profundis* and singing an *Allelujah*. We turned *Connaissance de Claudel* of which he had approved, into *Hommage à Claudel*,[1] and all those who had served him and loved him joined us for an evening which had to be repeated because of the demand from the public. With an audience of young people and of all those who loved him we tried to relive once more the drama of this poet. His faithful admirers decided to take a few steps with him on the road to the new existence which he had just taken on. It was an unforgettable moment in which the emotions were basically those of a religious ceremony, a true celebration.

Claudel remained for seven months in the crypt. His real funeral took place in August when he was buried at Brangues, near Morestel in the Isère. Madame Claudel and her children had asked me to deliver the funerary oration, and although I cry easily and can hardly control my emotions in moments like that, I had accepted without hesitation, I nearly said with joy; I was too full of gratitude to hesitate, it was in a way a kind of reward.

It was the summer and a splendid day 'one of those beautiful days of June, July and August', sung by Péguy. We were all going to meet near Lyons; Charles Gantillon, director of the Théâtre des Célestins, had proposed meeting me there and driving me to Brangues. We slept in Gantillon's country house in Pérouge near Lyons. It was a medieval house which could well have been inhabited by Anne Vercors, the tables were old, rustic and redolent of the simplest life, and Violaine could well have been born in one of the bedrooms where the thick rafters had been gnawed by worms. In spite of my apprehension that I might be overwhelmed by my sorrows, I kept on looking back into my memories. We set off on a bright and glorious morning; the sky was clean swept, and nature dressed in green was resplendent with life, that was really something which resembled Claudel, and I kept on repeating these lines of his to myself:

> Les mailles du filet sont dissoutes et le filet lui-même a
> disparu.
> Le filet ou j'étais retenu s'est ouvert et je n'y suis plus.
> Je n'ai plus pour prison que Dieu et la couleur sublime de la
> terre.

[1] Homage to Claudel.

C'est toujours la même moisson et c'est le même désert.

Bénis soient l'entrave jusqu'ici et les liens qui me tenaient
lié!

Il les fallait forts et sûrs avant que la prison soit arrivée.

Ma prison est la plus grande lumière et la plus grande chaleur,

La vision de la terre au mois d'août, qui exclut toute possi-
bilité d'être ailleurs.

Comment aurais-je du passé souci, du futur aucun désir,

Quand déjà la chose qui m'entoure est telle que je n'y puis
suffire?

Comment penserai-je à moi-même, à ce qui me manque ou
m'attend,

Quand Dieu ici même hors de moi est tellement plus
intéressant?

Ce champ où je suis est de l'or, et là-bas au-dessus des
chaumes,

Cette ineffable couleur rose est la terre même des hommes!

La terre même un instant a pris la couleur de l'éternité,

La couleur de Dieu avec nous et toutes les tribus humaines
y sont campées.

Ineffable couleur de rose et les multitudes humaines y sont
vivantes!

Une mer d'or et de feu entoure nos postes et nos tentes.

Quelle tristesse peut-il y avoir quand chaque année le même
mois d'août est fatal?

La tristesse n'est que d'un moment, la joie est supérieure et
finale.

La lumière a tout gagné peu à peu et la nuit est exterminée.

De grosses compagnies de perdreaux sous mes pas éclatent
sur la terre illuminée.

Je sais et je vois de mes yeux une chose qui n'est pas men-
songère.

Je suis libre et ma prison autour de moi est la lumière!

La terre rit et sait et rit et se cache dans le blé et dans la
lumière!

Pour garder le secret que nous savons, ce n'est pas assez que
de se taire![1]

---

[1] The meshes of the net are dissolved and the net itself has disappeared.
The net which held me has opened and I am no longer in it.
My only prison now is God and the sublime colour of the earth.
It is always the same harvest and the same desert.
Blessed be the fetters and the bonds which until now tied me down
They had to be strong and safe before my prison came.
My prison is the greatest light, the greatest warmth,

Marie Bell was waiting for us at Morestel; on my arrival there I was met by an ambassador, a charming man who had been trained by Claudel. We became engaged in a rather laborious conversation (for on such occasions everyone thinks about the same thing but does not dare to talk about it) in the course of which I said: 'I hope I may manage to deliver my speech', and he replied: 'Oh! why? Have you got a cold or a sore throat?' This shows that in spite of our common sympathy we were anything but attuned. Marie Bell came out of her hotel and we set off on the road from Morestel to Brangues which I had so often trodden with my rucksack on my back and my head ringing with new projects. Soon Brangues's church emerged in front of us, and I could see the long avenue of plane trees and at the end of it, the shuttered windows of Claudel's study, the place where I had so often found my old Master.

We went straight to the church, meeting crowds of people all going in the same direction. These were the official guests, the admirers of Claudel, and there were also curious tourists, journalists, photographers and all sorts of people. As soon as I entered the small church I recognized Claudel's soul; and he was clean and good and just waiting to be stamped. The coffin was covered

---

And the month of August vision of the earth which excludes any
    possibility of being anywhere else.
How could I care about the past, or dream of the future
When what surrounds me is such that I cannot fill it?
How could I think of myself and what is in wait for me
When here, beyond myself, God is so much more interesting?
This field where I am now, is gold, and yonder there, above the
    thatched roofs,
Surge the ineffable pink colours of the earth—the land of men!
The earth has taken for a moment the colour of eternity
The very colour which God has for us, and all human tribes are
    encamped there—
Ineffable pink colour where live the human multitudes!
A sea of fire and gold surrounds our posts and tents.
How can one be sad when every year the same month of August is
    fatal?
Sadness only lasts an instant, joy is superior and final.
Light has conquered everything and darkness is exterminated
Flights of partridges explode at my feet on the illumined earth.
I know and I see with my eyes something which does not lie
I am free and my prison around me is light!
The earth laughs and knows and laughs hiding in corn and light.
It takes more than silence to keep the secret which we know!

with flowers and surrounded by peasants of the village and neigh-
bouring farms dressed up as firemen, and whose plain, naïve
faces produced an atmosphere of truth and also of operetta. People
were rehearsing the hymns in a hubbub of noise, and little flags
placed here and there in the church, together with the firemen,
gave the whole thing the air of a 14 July celebration. Only the
fireworks were missing. The church was too small, people were
jostling one another and the greater part of the attendants were
massed in front of the church, under the trees where stood a
platform draped in black with a microphone on the top of it. I
waited for the arrival of the officials, arms crossed on my chest,
teeth clenched and staring away in the distance. I could feel people
gazing at me in a not unkind way and with sympathy for my
sorrow. On one side of the church there was a little chapel of the
Holy Virgin, where Claudel used to come every morning. The
jostling crowd was sincerely moved, and whatever this ceremony
lacked it would not lack human warmth. The naïve and zealous
firemen stood at attention and suddenly with the first bars of
music and song, I understood that France was present. Catholic
France was represented by Cardinal Gerlier dressed in his sump-
tuous red robes, contrasting with the dark garb of the Bishop of
Belley followed by his canons and priests. Lay France was represented by Edouard Herriot dressed up in his academic robes.
Claudel loved Herriot, who in spite of his age and illness had
insisted on attending the funeral as a friend and as the second
highest citizen of France. This was really a worthy setting for the
friends of Claudel; everyone was there, the firemen, the choruses,
the Government representatives, the friends, the peasants, the
loafers, Claudel's wife, his five children, and his nineteen grandchildren.

Everything went perfectly, the firemen carried out their duties
as required, the choir sang with all their heart, and the audience
listened intently. One could breathe a true atmosphere of religious poetry. The two prelates fought to decide which of them
would read the prayers for the dead; that was part of the ceremony. Cardinal Gerlier lifted a microphone by the side of the
coffin, tapped it two or three times in the most professional
manner, then spoke. The tradition of the Académie Française is
that the newly elected member should be hailed by a witty criticism of his defects, in order probably to temper his pride at his

introduction to this august association. It is a gentle tap on the face of the new academician, a kind of confirmation. Cardinal Gerlier, a great orator full of wit, a true Renaissance prelate, did not forget this tradition and he therefore interspersed his praise of Claudel with sharp condescending criticisms which made it clear that Claudel was now an elect of the celestial academy. At the end of it, we went round the coffin and then regrouped in front of the church. By then the crowd had increased and Brangues was swarming with people who had nothing to do with mourning. The centre of this vast gathering was in mourning, but the widening circles of the periphery were increasingly colourful with their great displays of print dresses, summer shorts and multi-coloured caps. This dappled world blended perfectly with the tiles of the houses, the surrounding greenery and the blue sky. We moved round the black platform, and poor Herriot dragged himself up to say a last good-bye to his friend. The dear old man was completely exhausted, and he had to pause many times because of fits of coughing which broke my heart. I was due to speak in front of the tomb, and I waited for this moment with increasing anxiety. Once Herriot's speech was concluded, the firemen placed their friend Claudel on their shoulders and the procession set off on the road white with dust and shimmering with heat. Standing by the gate, the caretaker's black dog watched his master go by; the procession moved under the shade of the great plane trees along the narrow path towards the end of the park and disappeared; then we had to wait for the gravediggers to do their work, and the firemen to bring the flowers. My heart was throbbing fast, my head burning, I did not know where I was; I only regained consciousness in front of the huge crowd, stiffening myself up against my overwhelming emotions, and delivering my last profession of faith about Claudel. After that the crowd dispersed for lunch. The earth, the sky and men had answered Claudel's call; now, he had had his true funeral, and once more we had obeyed him.

> Obéir! c'est si bon, c'est si fort d'obéir!
> C'est comme la faim qui vous prend aux entrailles.
> On laisse tout en place et va se mettre à table.[1]

---

[1] To obey! It is so good, so strong to obey!
It is like a hunger which wrings one's inside.
One drops everything and rushes for the table.

Madame Claudel, who is an extraordinary woman, a perfect example of tenacity, dignity and selfless devotion, had looked after everything, including a lunch for fifty guests. I have been won over by Claudel's Catholic idea of the family presided over, whatever happens, by the soul of the father. We left the table, and the children began to play on the lawn, in the most natural fashion as if this day was no different from the others. There was not the slightest feeling of artificiality or hypocrisy. A few of us went again to the tomb where the gravediggers were rolling the flat stones over the grave. The architect was supervising the work which was done with care, for everyone knew that Claudel loved work well done. The children cast a last glance over the hole where lay the coffin covered with flowers and one of them, pointing to an empty space, said: 'Look, that is where grandmother will be put.' Side by side with Claudel's grave there was a small grave where lay one of his grandchildren. Claudel very often came to pray at this grave. Soon everything was over and we were left with the words carved on the stone:

> Here lie the remains and the
> substance of Paul Claudel.

And all around this, the fields, the comings and goings of the agricultural labourers, the centuries-old lime trees, the castle full of children and grandchildren, and the quiet willows where the poet had hung his lyre at the end of his long journey through the world:

> et ce peuplier mince comme un cierge,
> comme un acte de foi, comme un acte d'amour. [1]

'And high above, in the sky this shining star (is it not Mary in the sky?) which triumphs over death', which we shall not cease to contemplate, thinking about what Claudel has given us. From that day, I have known a kind of solitude which will never disappear.

---

[1] And this poplar slender as a taper,
Something like an act of faith, or an act of love.

TEXT OF MY LAST FAREWELL
TO PAUL CLAUDEL
SPOKEN BY HIS TOMB
AT BRANGUES

Master:

You might be surprised to see me walking towards you to pay you my last tribute. Madame Claudel and your children must have hoped to make this sad ceremony more intimate when they conferred this harrowing honour upon me; they knew that I loved you as a son loves his father, and that is probably why they thought of me. If I falter or make mistakes, I hope I may be forgiven. This place now full of silence reminds me of my first visit to Brangues twenty years ago. We did not know each other well; only a few brief meetings had enabled us to recognize each other across the years which separated us. I was very moved, and shy, and I spoke very little. You looked at me attentively, probably weighing me up; we were waiting for each other; and we walked about by these old willow trees where you had come after your long journey through the world. Our walk took us near the foot of this poplar by the grave of your little grandson and you said: 'This is the place where I have chosen to rest.' I did not believe you. The words sounded hollow, and without meaning. Every time one thought about your possible departure, imagination froze; could Claudel die? We could not reconcile such a thought with reality. Today we are at the foot of this poplar which you had chosen, and what you had decided has been carried out once more, and I am struck by this cruel sad reality, I am struck by its resemblance to you. 'What do I care about the past, I only live in the present which God urges me to decipher.' In front of you what strikes me most is the impressive force of your reality, as real as these sheaves of corn. If there ever was a realist poet, it was Claudel; beyond realism we find intellectualism and we know what you thought about it. Reality is not thin, reality is profound, it reaches towards the depth and contains inexhaustible wealth. Plunging deep down in this mysterious reality you have been able to explore each one of its various layers. First, one finds the life of the flesh, then the life of the spirit and beyond flesh and spirit a kind of supra-spiritual life which you called super-reality, and which enabled you to come into communion with God. The seat of this super-reality was the heart, and all these various layers were connected. The star which twinkles in the sky is as real as the rose which lies in my hand. The Holy Virgin, seated between the ox and the donkey, and feeding her child, is as real as any peasant woman doing the same thing. Both have the same calm appearance, the very serenity of a good cow when she has just given birth to a young calf which she protects with her body and warms with her warm breath. All that is true life and nothing else. God and the small grain of sand are in solidarity and hold each other's hands. For over seventy years you have moved about in that life and you have drawn from it the inexhaustible wealth of your work; this work which I shall compare to a kind of nest where three generations have found shelter and have been fed by you. That is why you are a man, a complete man who creates and feeds.

Recently a friend of mine, a monk, was talking to me about the vocation of the priest. The priest, he told me, knows the pangs of labour, that is to say, he is the father and the mother of people present and of those to come but he is also the father of his own father and mother and of all his ancestors, or of the Past, for he engenders in eternal life. I believe that the vocation of the poet is like that of the priest. He not only fecundates the present and engenders the future generations, he retraces his steps into the past and gives life, force and lustre to the history of his country; now I understand why, having detected the poet in you, God and his priests have not allowed you to become one of them. The 'little priest', Mésa, could best fulfil his mission by making use of what in him was obscure, complicated and laborious, by being in fact the Poet Claudel. This was a mission which, by the suffering, the fecundation and the nourishment which it produced, was worth a priesthood. Nothing less resembles literature than your poetic adventure which is the sublime and powerful transformation of a whole life, a life which you have grasped in all its physical aspects. If the 'word' is for you an intelligible mouthful, God's word is your food, your wine and your bread, and the blood which you draw from it; you pour it over our heads as *Tête d'Or* does for Cébès. You teach us how to bleed. You begin by freeing the internal light which inhabits us. You free from the weight of materialism the force which derives its strength from the depth of the earth and shoots up like a flame in the sky. You remember that it is not only with stones that one builds, but also with a flame which Rimbaud has transmitted to you and which helps to illumine the world. With *L'Annonce faite à Marie* you have given a new life to the France of the Middle Ages with her cathedrals and her mysteries. You burnt your life for us; you have relived for us in the middle of your life the eternal struggle of flesh and spirit, and you have put us back in communication and communion with God. Conquistador who has been all over the earth, you encouraged us to persist in our vocation and in making the gift of ourselves to others. You have taught us never to expect rewards, only ingratitude, you have taught us that respect is nothing and that love is all; for how can one respect what one does not love? No aspect of a truly great love is useless, 'even sin serves', says the guardian angel to Prouhèze. Above all, one must live fully, and offer everything to God; one must be as open as a book, and know everything in order to be known.

You have shown us that a poet must not be separated from life; you have felt with Louis Laine the danger of what you call 'a poet without pockets', that is to say a poet separated and divorced from society. Your aim was to do and to act, and you participated fully in life; you were a full man, who kept on doing. You founded a family and it is a large and beautiful family, you have a solid big house built on rock and your trees are these centuries-old lime trees with their bark-like skins and their refined perfume. You were a poet and also a business man, for without that, how could you have known Turelure? You were a father and a family man, and you never stopped feeling Life as a lover, while as a diplomat you never lost your peasant wisdom. In your life you never ceased to fight for your country, your family, your faith and your art. Your life was a victory and a victory all the more exceptional that, right up to the end of your life, you never ceased being the poet of youth. Your work is that of a young man, and that is due to the fact that throughout your concrete poetic activity you have kept alive in you the holy virginity of revolt and indignation. You have fought in the army of your Church, but your soul has never lost its revolutionary desire for renewal. Your solidly based spiritual situation has enabled your individualistic traits to maintain their lucidity throughout your life. 'We anarchists', you said to me one day, and I understood by these words that an artist must endeavour to maintain alive a continuous internal revolt against himself; the aim is to have a revolutionary plan always within reach. I shall only quote as an instance of that what you used to call 'your love of tinkering'. You were always ready to rewrite your works, and it was not because you were dissatisfied by what the genius of inspiration had given you, although you were as proud as a child about it, and without hypocrisy, for you did not know the meaning of such a word; but you knew above all the importance of true reality, and you knew that God's wealth was inexhaustible. You were not a man of letters attached to your commas or your images. What interested you was reality, and whenever necessary you invented words as Homer or Dante had done before. You brought us joy; 'let us laugh', you used to say, 'for that is good'. You loved humour, you lived with humour, you have given us the love of the transient and you have filled us with enthusiasm. All your life you have been criticized and you will be so again, at least I hope so, for it is a sign of vitality. If some people have not understood you in spite of their intelligence, it is because in your procession from earth to heaven you were operating at a level which is not normal. Seen from your vantage point, life had another appearance. That is precisely your originality, something which places you among the first geniuses of mankind, among the poets of first magnitude. Your ceaseless peregrinations round the earth had communicated to you the sense of movement and of cosmic activity; you have helped us to understand that life is connected with the happenings of the universe and is never at a standstill. You never stopped and death itself caught you in the middle of a flight. You worked till the last minute.

I can picture you in your last moments installed in your armchair, working; the sun slowly sets and you lift your head to the sound of these words: 'Good-bye, my beautiful sun, we loved each other well.' Don't you remember these words of Ysé? Suddenly your piercing eyes have recognized the lady who makes signs to you. You welcome her with quite a whimsical smile, knowing that this time she will not leave without you, and you speak to her in the friendly way in which you spoke to God. . . . 'Do you hear me, friend?' you used to say. Then you begin to think, your gaze lost in the distance, and you say, 'All right, this is the end, voyager, let us put down our book; strange, that it should be a study of Rimbaud! So the wheel has come full circle. A moment please, dear lady, I want to put my temporal and spiritual affairs in order, then you can do what you like.' And so we discovered you with the youthful, noble ivory mask which is the last memory we have of you. As for the rest we had once more to follow you as you had written: 'There at the bottom of the park in the most remote corner, there is the poplar, slender, tall like a taper, like an act of faith or an act of love; I have marked my place by the side of a moss-covered wall; I want to rest there, close to the country and to its life which goes on, and by the side of the innocent little child whom I have lost and with whom I have so often unfolded my rosary. The Rhône also unfolds its rosary, its glorious rosary interrupted every now and then by the lyrical exclamation of a jumping fish. Is the star, victorious over death, and which I have contemplated for so long, Mary in Heaven?'

Now you are near Mary, happily lying for eternity like a little star at her feet. Your captive soul is free at last. But here on earth your work continues and with it you will begin a new life. I promise you that we shall devote all our energies to spreading the understanding and the love of your work. Just as I never came to see you without taking away with me some nourishment supplied by your mind, I hope that the generations to come may turn this poplar, this Shakespearian place into a centre of pilgrimage where they will come in order to draw from you enthusiasm, vigour, courage, pertinacity, passion, pride, modesty, stubbornness and humility, in short all that goes into the making of the greater love of God's reality. In the name of your wife, your children and grandchildren, in the name of all those to whom you have given life and food, in the name of our country, and of all men on earth, lastly in my name, and like a very unhappy child, I thank you with all my being for the true life you have given us.

ABOUT TOTAL DRAMA AND
CHRISTOPHE COLOMB [1]

In 1949, when I wrote my first book *Reflections on the Theatre*, I was perhaps unwise to use repeatedly the expression 'total drama' without ascertaining whether or no this expression had already been used before. Today, this expression which seems to have travelled a long way, worries me; it worries me because it looks like a formula, and I hate formulae, particularly in the theatre. Formulae entail a certain rigidity and fixity, and anything that freezes is anti-theatre; in fact a made-up expression or a dramatic formula does not introduce a style but a fashion. I believe, as I said previously, that the art of the theatre is the art of life, and life is the contrary of rigidity and fixity; it is on the contrary something moving, complex and varied, and it can't be enclosed in any formula. In brief, what was perhaps acceptable in a written text today seems to me dangerous if taken literally. The expression 'total drama' or 'complete drama' belongs purely and simply to the theatre, that is to say to the theatre of Shakespeare, of Corneille, Racine, Molière, Marivaux and in our time that of Claudel. It is probably as a reaction to the formula 'psychological drama' used in the nineteenth, and in the beginning of the twentieth century, that we wish to return to 'total drama'. In fact we invent nothing, we only want to return to the true tradition of the theatre. Yet this notion of total drama considered as the true drama requires some explanation. First of all we must revert to a definition which is always the same: drama is an art which re-creates life in its complexity, simultaneousness and presentness, that is to say, in its most fragile aspects through the medium of the human being involved in conflict, in space. Space is the painter's canvas, the human being is the brush, the colours and the charcoal, the author is the artist; the human being is the necessary instrument put at the disposal of the artist of the theatre: the author. We have total drama when the resources of this human being are used to the full. Total drama must use all the colours of the human easel. Compared with fragmentary drama which is like a monochrome painting, total drama is coloured painting and has every chance of being

[1] *Christopher Columbus.*

more alive, more human and warmer. In total drama all parts of man's anatomy: feet, hands, chest, spine, eyes, voice, etc., are used to the full. The miming resources of man know no bounds. Man sighs, articulates, cries, sings in harmony with the beats of his heart, with his glances, the suppleness of his back and the skill of his legs. He vibrates and moves with increasing rhythm so as to become fire and flame. One man alone standing on floor boards and using all his means, can produce total drama. Real drama can have no other attitude. Greek, Elizabethan, classical and every other theatre in the world, particularly eastern theatre, all insist on the full use of all means of expression of the human being. It could be objected that psychological or bourgeois drama, which we call fragmentary drama by comparison with total drama, also uses man in his totality. After all, the actor is fully present on the stage, and there are the famous silences, the dumb acting of certain actresses who can wring tears from crowds, by merely inhaling the perfume of a bunch of flowers. There are in fact any amount of other examples which show that psychological drama makes use of the full man. Yet I am not convinced by this argument. In this case man seems to me an orchestra with which the conductor uses always the same instrument: words. Sometimes, it is true, the performer uses a few different bars; he opens a door with eloquence or locks another, and these are precisely the moments which will impress the spectator and remain in his memory. Paul Mounet used to describe psychological or bourgeois drama as drama with one's hands in one's pockets. Drama is also a spectacle, and around this 'man—drama' who moves, burns and dies and who is the whole drama, the other arts are grouped as if to pay homage to it or to frame it, in the same way as one frames a painting. Just as a good spectacle has never spoiled a good dramatic action, it does sometimes happen that too big a frame kills a painting, or that too elaborate a production kills a play, but although the problem of harmonizing the text with its production is difficult to resolve, it is something which cannot be avoided. One does not solve the problem by entirely suppressing the spectacle. The public like a spectacle which prepares their receptivity for the drama, therefore why deprive them of it? The spectacle according to Baudelaire is 'the coincidence of the arts', it is up to producers not to reduce it to the level of an accomplice of the arts in order to offer the public bad drama.

The art of the theatre rests on two elements of varying importance. The first element is the painting itself or the material which
must bring into use all the aspects of an actor's possibilities: this
element pertains to the author. The second element is the frame,
that is to say the spectacle with its mixture of all the arts of decoration, music, costumes, lighting, etc; this second element is always
entrusted to a man in charge of production who could be the author
himself or someone who is described nowadays as the producer.
Whatever the contribution of the producer may be, it is never
more than that of choreographer, who brings all things together.
Anybody who tries to give him a greater importance than that
makes a big mistake. As Copeau used to say: 'Those who get lost
in the facile byways of decoration and refinements of lighting with
the pretence of "total art" are on the wrong road.' The rôle of
'choreographer' does not therefore contribute greatly to the
realization of total drama. But there are times when the spectacle
goes beyond the fact of being a framework to drama, and when it
raises itself to the level of the very essence of drama. Then it
becomes a kind of character taking part in the action, and together
with the actors, it contributes to its meaning. A décor which only
seems to be on the stage in order to please the eye, suddenly
becomes alive and begins to move. I remember an instance like
that in Cocteau's *La Machine infernale* [1] with settings by Christian
Bérard, who was one of our greatest men of the theatre. Bérard's
settings were designed in such a way that at the moment of the
revelation of Oedipus's crime, the bedroom exploded and turned
itself into the public square of Thebes, where men and things
were all bursting with despair. I should place in the same category
certain transformations in *Le Soulier de Satin* and *Antony and
Cleopatra*. There are moments when accessories like an armchair,
a spear, a bunch of flowers, or costumes become absolutely real,
and this is all the more so with music in which there are things
which appear like a magic emanation of human nature. As long as
the spectacle is simply a frame, it does not contribute much to
drama, but the moment it participates in a live way in the action,
it participates in pure drama and becomes an integral part of
total drama. The vital point in the production of a play consists in
finding the means to raise the spectacle as part of a play which
comprises décor, music, lighting, etc., to the level where it is no

[1] *The Infernal Machine.*

longer a frame but becomes an integral part of the action and contributes to drama as if it were a true character. Once one reaches such a stage, total drama has found its unity. *Christophe Colomb* was an attempt at total drama. This is the way I conceived it: a group of men and women called actors and actresses come on to the stage singing and decide to retrace for their pleasure or for their spiritual nourishment the life of Columbus. From then on, whether by acting or singing, they endeavour to relive Columbus's life which is imprinted with universality. Columbus made the world round, round as an orange. There are so many things required to make a world, that sometimes all one needs is a human being—oneself. For instance, we needed an inn, and whoever thinks of an inn, thinks of the inside of a house; a house suggests a door, and a door can be represented by two men facing each other each stretching out an arm; anyone who has to enter could pass under the arch made by these two men. We needed a mule; a mule is something with four legs, that is to say a rear which follows a front part in a melancholy, affectionate way as befits Columbus's mule. Spinning wool, playing the guitar, walking, running, pretending to be dead, becoming waves or shadows, playing at being Indian gods, howling as if they were a tempest, gossiping like old wives, singing with joy, showing enthusiasm, standing still like painted characters, dancing like possessed people, going in and out of the action, spectator, commentator, these performers endeavour to produce an idea of the total drama of which we are dreaming. Let us pretend that this dream is realized. This company of men makes use of all the human means at its disposal, the objects become human, the chairs creak as required, the sail behaves like a human being. Do we need a court dress? Two folds of the one we are wearing make one. Do we need a peasant dress? The back of the dress is folded up on the head, and there is the peasant's dress. Do we need sailors? We tuck up our trousers, take off our shirts and there are the sailors. Let us continue our dream. The lighting comes into play, the projectors move, the objects cast strange shadows which come and go. As for music, it plays the same part as the actors; sometimes it acts, sometimes it comments; it intervenes in the action, it lingers with joy, stampedes with impatience or vitality and shows throughout that it has a human soul. Men and objects play together. Men play at being objects, and objects play at being men. And there is the crux of the problem. While the humanized objects contribute to the action, the actor in his turn, without slipping out of his character, becomes every now and then one of them. For instance, the waves (human beings) cast a half-dead sailor on the shore. Columbus enters the water to help the half-dead sailor. The two actors who play these parts must convey the idea of their respective characters, together with the swaying elements of the waves. Thus the actor represents not only the human aspect but also the elements and objects of nature; he is at the same time human being and object; he is at the centre of life and bathes in it; he sticks to life in its wholeness. The theatre makes use of the specialized human being in order to recreate life in its fullness, human element and things. It is because of that that *Christophe Colomb* seems to me an attempt at total drama, and it is so because of the points I have just mentioned and not because filming has been added to music, setting and lighting.

The idea of filming certain scenes belonged to Claudel and therefore it could not be resisted. On the surface, this idea of film in a play seems to be in opposition to total drama which is all the more pure that it only makes use of man and nothing else. The cinema is a mechanical medium; therefore, how could one bring it into the middle of such rigour and nakedness? It seems to me that this first experiment was only made possible by the fact that the sail which was used as a screen is a truly human element, a symbol of the whole work and not a lifeless object. It is possible to wonder whether *Christophe Colomb* was not a unique case; yet, I don't think so; I don't think that *Christophe Colomb* was a unique case, and I believe that the marriage between theatre and cinema is possible. What can the cinema contribute to the theatre? If the cinema were to contribute only what cannot be put on the stage there is no doubt that such a contribution would constitute, on the plane of art, an impurity, a means of offering something which the theatre itself cannot offer. If the film was only used for enlargements, in order to enable the spectators to see details which they could not see otherwise, it would merely replace opera glasses and would have a very limited use. But the film has other advantages which can truly combine with a scenic action, and therefore it has a necessary part to play. It can show actions which are simultaneous. Every action, like a coin, has two faces—one visible, the other invisible. Life also has two faces—the apparent and the secret one, the external and the internal, the physical and the metaphysical, the natural and the supernatural, etc. In life we comprehend these two aspects simultaneously. Filming joined with drama can enable us to see these two aspects at the same time. Man's behaviour only shows what it wants to show, but if it were possible to see inside him or through him, we could see what he is trying to hide. There are times when some of his gestures contradict his words and show the true man under the appearances. A trembling knee shows the fear which a given person is trying to dissimulate under angry replies. The film can reveal these secret states. If we imagine a dramatic scene expressed in two different and complementary ways, one on the screen and one on the stage, we shall have what we might call 'drama in relief'. In ordinary drama, that is to say in the *théâtre de boulevard*, only the visible is expressed; it is therefore 'flat' drama. In *Partage de Midi* the characters pass from the visible to the invisible: 'Mésa, I am Ysé, it's me'. This mixture of the two behaviours—the visible and the invisible, played by the same character, on a screen and on the stage, could produce results of impressive vitality and relief. In *Christophe Colomb*, our attempt to blend film and theatre was a very shy attempt; yet it is something well worth exploring, for with it one could do what music does, express many things at the same time. But I must add that in *Christophe Colomb* the producer only obeyed the author, and it ought always to be so. In this case the author having had the vision of this kind of theatre, the producer could only follow. Whatever we do in the future, we shall never forget that drama is man, and that if there were only one man alone on four boards, and making up all of his means of expression, this would be 'complete drama'. As for the tricks of lighting, settings and other things which pertain to the art of putting together and not to the creator, they are only useful if they are not given a prominent and essential rôle, and they can only cause confusion if they are mistaken for what we call, provisionally, 'total drama'.

SUPPLEMENTARY NOTE

It seems that this central position of the actor in the middle of life, entrusted with the task of representing not only human nature (which of course remains the chief task) but the whole of nature from the animal to the elements, could be examined a little more thoroughly. If the actor only interprets the human element, the rest being represented by décor, settings, etc., it means that he is separated from nature and looked upon as more important than the rest of nature. If, on the contrary, man is considered as an integral part of nature, the actor represents nature as well as man. Man encompasses the whole animal, vegetable and mineral world; he is the quintessence of nature. Besides that, the whole of nature reflects the human soul; every element of nature is intent on becoming humanized, and all the notions such as justice, faith, charity, are emanations from man inspired by nature. Nature is all around man, and any actor interpreting man, interprets also the bits of nature which hang about him. In our age, when there are some attempts to ban décor altogether, this remark is important. First of all, we must realize that décor can't be suppressed entirely, for the spectator's eye must somehow be given some kind of boundary. The only way in which the décor is suppressed is when the spectator closes his eyes. If he keeps his eyes open, he requires some boundaries on his horizon, and that is the beginning of the décor—whether it is cyclorama or curtains. Neither of these things can avoid having a personality. Curtains, like masks, are not impersonal. Even black has a meaning, and expresses something. Every colour is symbolic of something and every curtain says something; everything in nature speaks. The second point to remember is that if one suppresses the décor completely one puts the actor and the play in a vacuum. The actor then moves in a sterilized atmosphere as if he were under glass, and this may be all right for a laboratory but it is not a re-creation of life. In order to re-create life in the theatre, man must be placed in the atmosphere and nature to which he belongs, then a re-creation of life takes place in a world of colours and not in a black box. The third point is that if one wishes to reduce the material décor to the minimum, something which has always been our aim, one must replace it by something else, something alive and which can be supplied by the actor who can represent both man and the space pertaining to him. The actor can create both his character and his décor; that is exactly what children do, and the theatre has the duty of preserving the youth of man. Lastly, if one wishes to suppress the material décor, one must produce works which lend themselves to that. In order to do so one must choose the few ancient or classical plays which fit the bill and try to find modern plays. If one tries to apply this personal vision of the theatre to plays whose face has been thoroughly moulded by time, one runs the risk of applying ready-made formulae, and of distorting these works. A dramatic work has its own requirements and imposes its own style. One must either accept it or try to rewrite the whole work. Molière's style does not conform to that of Plautus, any more than Racine's conforms to that of Euripides, or Corneille's to that of Tirso de Molina. These modern writers used the same subjects as their ancient models but they wrote new plays. Therefore whenever we produce a classical work our only duty is to be modest. On the other hand when we work with a modern play we always fall short of the boldness which could be applied to it. Yet in both cases we must always follow Racine's advice: 'Never put anything in drama which is not absolutely necessary.' [1] The day when there will no longer be an urge to talk about total drama by contrast with a form of drama which falls short of it, on that day the real traditional drama will at last have been rediscovered.

[1] Preface to *Mithridate*.

Note: The music of *Christophe Colomb* was composed by Darius Milhaud, the dress and costumes were by Max Ingrand with the help of Marie-Hélène Dasté.

LIST OF PLAYS PRODUCED BY THE RENAUD-BARRAULT COMPANY

FRENCH PLAYS

CLASSICS

Note: If an English language version of a play has been published or produced the English title is given in italics, where no translation is known, a literal translation is given in brackets.

24 October 1946
Les Fausses Confidences
(The false confessions)
by Marivaux

5 December 1947
Amphitryon
by Molière

18 February 1949
La Seconde Surprise de l'Amour
(The second surprise of love)
by Marivaux

18 February 1949
Les Fourberies de Scapin
(Scapin's tricks)
by Molière

7 June 1951
L'Épreuve
by Marivaux

14 December 1951
On ne badine pas avec l'Amour
(One does not trifle with love)
by Alfred de Musset

14 May 1954
Le Misanthrope
by Molière

21 July 1954
Il faut qu'une porte soit ouverte ou fermée
(A door must either be open or shut)
by Alfred de Musset

8 January 1955
Bérénice
by Racine

MODERN REVIVALS

4 March 1948
Occupe-toi d'Amélie
Look after Lulu
by Georges Feydeau

16 December 1949
Le Bossu
(The hunchback)
by Paul Féval and Anicet Bourgeois

1 March 1950
On purge bébé
by Georges Feydeau

25 March 1950
Marlborough s'en va-t-en guerre
(Marlborough goes to war)
by Marcel Achard
from the Académie Française

231

29 May 1950
Les Mains sales
Crime passionnel
  by Jean-Paul Sartre

14 December 1951
L'Échange
(The exchange)
  by Paul Claudel

18 May 1954
Le Cocu magnifique
(The magnificent cuckold)
  by Fernand Crommelynck

27 January 1955
Volpone
  by Jules Romains
  from the Académie Française
  (in collaboration with Stefan
  Zweig)
  from Ben Jonson

18 March 1955
Intermezzo
  by Jean Giraudoux

17 December 1957
Madame Sans Gêne
  by Victorien Sardou
  (in collaboration with Émile
  Moreau)

12 November 1958
La Vie Parisienne
  by Meilhac and Halévy
  Music by Offenbach

18 December 1958
Le Soulier de Satin
The Satin Slipper
  by Paul Claudel

NEW PRODUCTIONS

12 December 1946
Les Nuits de la Colère
(The nights of wrath)
  by Armand Salacrou

11 October 1947
Le Procès
The Trial
  from Kafka's novel translated
  by Alexandre Vialatte,
  adapted by André Gide and
  Jean-Louis Barrault

11 October 1947
Le Pays des Cerisiers
(The cherry trees country)
  by André Dhotel

28 October 1948
L'État de Siège
(The state of siege)
  by Albert Camus

17 December 1948
Partage de Midi
(The division of noon)
  by Paul Claudel

1 March 1950
L'Impromptu

27 October 1950
La Répétition ou l'Amour puni
(The rehearsal or love punished)
  by Jean Anouilh

21 December 1950
Malatesta
  by Henry de Montherlant

5 April 1951
Oedipe
Oedipus
  by André Gide

5 April 1951
Maguelone
  a dramatic poem by Maurice
  Clavel

22 November 1951
Lazare
Lazarus
  by André Obey

21 December 1951
Bacchus
  by Jean Cocteau

2 April 1952
Connaissance de Paul Claudel
(Introduction to Claudel)
by J.-L. Barrault

21 May 1953
Christophe Colomb
(Christopher Columbus)
by Paul Claudel

6 November 1953
Pour Lucrèce
Duel of Angels
by Jean Giraudoux

31 January 1954
La Soirée des Proverbes
(The evening of proverbs)
by Georges Schehadé

8 December 1955
Le Chien du Jardinier
(The gardener's dog)
from Lope de Vega
adapted by Georges Neveux

1 February 1956
Le Personnage combattant
(The fighting character)
by Jean Vauthier

15 October 1956
Histoire de Vasco
(The story of Vasco)
by Georges Schehadé

23 October 1957
Le Château de Kafka
The Castle by Kafka
four acts by Pol Quentin
translated by Max Brod

2 April 1959
Le Tir Clara
(Clara's rifle-range)
by Jean-Louis Roncoroni

PANTOMIMES

24 October 1946
Baptiste
Pantomime-ballet by Jacques
Prévert
Music by Kosma

5 December 1947
La Fontaine de Jouvence
Pantomime by Boris Kochno
Music by Georges Auric

13 January 1954
Renard
Pantomime by Strawinsky
French text by Ramuz

8 December 1955
Les Suites d'une Course
(The aftermath of a race)
Pantomime-farce by Jules Sup-
ervielle
Music by Henri Sauguet

FOREIGN PLAYS

CLASSICS

17 October 1946
Hamlet
by Shakespeare
translated by André Gide

26 May 1955
L'Orestie
The *Oresteia*
The *Agamemnon*, The *Choephori*,
The *Eumenides* of Aeschylus,
adapted by André Obey

MODERN REVIVALS

19 October 1947
  L'Ours
  (The bear)
    by Chekhov

20 May 1954
  La Cerisaie
  The Cherry Orchard
    by Chekhov
    French text by Georges
    Neveux

NEW PRODUCTIONS

11 November 1949
  Elisabeth d'Angleterre
  (Elizabeth of England)
    by Ferdinand Bruckner,
    translated by Renée Cave

17 November 1954
  Irène Innocente
  (Innocent Irene)
    by Ugo Betti,
    adapted by Maurice Clavel

13 January 1955
  Le Songe des Prisonniers
  A Sleep of Prisoners
    by Christopher Fry
    French text by Morvan-
    Lebesque

Index

235

01